Inequality in America

Inequality in America

What Role for Human Capital Policies?

James J. Heckman and
Alan B. Krueger

The Alvin Hansen Symposium on Public Policy
Harvard University

edited and with an introduction by
Benjamin M. Friedman

The MIT Press
Cambridge, Massachusetts
London, England

This book was set in Palatino on QuarkXPress by Asco Typesetters, Hong Kong, and was printed and bound in the United States of America.

Library of Congress Cataloging-in-Publication Data

Alvin Hansen Symposium on Public Policy (3rd : 2002 : Harvard University)
Inequality in America : what role for human capital policies? / James J. Heckman and Alan B. Krueger ; The Alvin Hansen Symposium on Public Policy, Harvard Unviersity ; edited and with an introduction by Benjamin M. Friedman.
p. cm.
"Papers and discussions ... presented at the third Alvin Hansen Symposium on Public Policy, held at Harvard University on April 25, 2002"—P..
Includes bibliographical references and index.
Contents: Introduction / Benjamin M. Friedman — Inequality, too much of a good thing / Alan B. Krueger — Human capital policy / Pedro Carneiro and James J. Heckman — Comments / George Borjas, Eric Hanushek, Lawrence Katz, Lisa Lynch, Lawrence H. Summers — Responses / Alan B. Krueger, Pedro Carneiro and James J. Heckman — Rejoinders / Alan B. Krueger, Pedro Carneiro and James J. Heckman.
ISBN 0-262-08328-0 (hc : alk. paper)
1. Income distribution—United States—Congresses. 2. Human capital—Government policy—United States—Congresses. 3. Manpower policy—United States—Congresses. 4. United States—Social policy—Congresses. 5. Equality—United States—Congresses. I. Heckman, James J. (James Joseph) II. Krueger, Alan B. III. Friedman, Benjamin M. IV. Title.

HC110.I5A66 2002
339.2′2—dc22 2003059277

10 9 8 7 6 5 4 3 2 1

In memoriam

Marian Hansen Merrifield

Contents

Introduction

Benjamin M. Friedman

The increasing inequality of income and wealth that has attracted so much attention in the United States during the last quarter century at first took most economists, as well as most of the American public, by surprise. Throughout most of the twentieth century, incomes in America had been growing more equal over time as the strong gains accruing to those at the top of the scale came alongside even stronger gains in the middle and at the bottom. The widening inequality that had marked much of the nineteenth century was increasingly seen as a historical episode, attributable to the nation's initial transformation into an industrial economy. Moreover, according to economic historians, Britain had earlier followed a similar path: widening inequality during the early surge of industrialization, followed in time by narrowing inequality as the industrial economy matured. Indeed, not long after World War II, economists like Simon Kuznets hypothesized, on the basis of this experience, that this pattern was characteristic of economic development more generally. Hence although the newly developing countries of our own day might well see their income distributions become more unequal, in time this phenomenon would reverse itself, as long as their average income levels continued to rise. In any case, with America's industrial revolution now a distant memory, the trend toward greater equality here would presumably continue.

Matters have not worked out that way. Since 1974 the share of pretax cash income in the United States that goes to families in the top fifth of the income distribution has risen from 40.6 percent to 47.7 percent, whereas the share going to those in the bottom fifth has fallen from 5.7 percent to 4.2 percent. Although prewar data on the distribution of incomes are not necessarily reliable, what is clear at a minimum is that this surge of inequality since the mid-1970s has more than reversed all of the movement toward equality that took place in the first few decades of the postwar period. In 1947 the shares of pretax cash income going to the top and bottom fifths were 43.0 percent and 5.0 percent, respectively.

Moreover, during the last quarter century, inequality has widened within narrower slices of the society and the economy as well. It is not just that the share of income going to the top fifth has risen, but that even within the top fifth's growing share, what goes to the top fifth of the top fifth has risen too. (Of the additional 7.1 percent of the nation's pretax income that now goes to the top fifth of families compared to the mid-1970s, 6.2 percent—in other words, roughly seven-eighths of the aggregate increase—goes to those in just the top 5 percent of families.) The widening of skill- and education-based pay differentials, which has accounted for much of the overall increase in inequality during this period, has exhibited a similar pattern. Not only have more highly skilled and educated workers moved ahead faster than those with less skills and education, but even within the upper groups, those with the most skills, and the best education, have moved ahead faster still.

Such a surprising development in so important and sensitive an area of social concern has, as would be expected, spurred an energetic search in the scholarly community for explanations. Among the general public as well as scholarly researchers, it has also spurred a vigorous debate about how to regard widening inequality and what, if anything, to do about it. These two lines of discussion are, of course, related.

The papers offered here by James Heckman and Pedro Carneiro and by Alan Krueger focus on a specific nexus of this overall discussion around which there is sufficient conceptual agreement to warrant a detailed scientific debate about which policies are likely to work and which aren't, and why. Although there has been (and continues to be) much debate over whether the proper object for public-policy concern is inequality per se or simply the low incomes of those at the bottom of the distribution (in other words, is the real problem inequality or is it poverty?), either view leads to the conclusion that it would be good to raise the earning power of the lowest-income workers. And although there remains widespread disagreement about the relative importance of different explanations for the recent increase in inequality and the stubborn persistence of poverty, the role of labor market skills and workers' education (in the broadest sense) figures high on nearly everyone's list. Hence providing potentially low-income workers with more of the kind of "human capital" that matters for labor market outcomes is an avenue for public policy that can command support from a broad array of opinion on both the economics and the politics of this subject—*if*, that is, such human capital programs actually work, and if they do so at a cost that the American body politic is prepared to bear.

Further, for practical policy purposes the question at issue is not simply *whether* human capital policies on the whole are an effective policy approach to this end, but *which* specific policy approaches offer the prospect of effectively serving the intended purpose and which do not: Is the best way to provide more and better education to children of low-income families to increase the amount of general resources devoted to the nation's public-school systems and to restructure the incentives that public-school teachers and administrators face? Or is a better answer to rely on more narrowly targeted programs like Head Start? How important is it to relax credit constraints that keep some able students from attending college? Are vocational training programs for adults actually effective? What is the best balance of roles for the public and the private sector? And (to repeat) for those programs that do "work," how much benefit can the public reasonably expect, and at what cost?

The papers and discussions published here were presented at the third Alvin Hansen Symposium on Public Policy, held at Harvard University on April 25, 2002.[1] In introducing the proceedings of this symposium, I want to express my very sincere personal thanks, as well as the gratitude of the Harvard Economics Department, to Leroy Sorenson Merrifield and the late Marian Hansen Merrifield, together with numerous former students of Alvin Hansen, whose generosity made possible this series of public-policy symposia that the Economics Department now sponsors at Harvard in Alvin Hansen's name. Their eager participation in this effort stands as testimony to the profound and positive effect that Professor Hansen had on so many younger economists. It was with great sadness that my colleagues and I learned of Marian's death only days before this third symposium (which she was eagerly looking forward to attending, as she had attended the first two). She was a valued friend and a loyal supporter of this department and its mission. This volume is dedicated to her memory.

I am also grateful to James Duesenberry and Richard Musgrave, who served with me on the organizing committee that first established the Alvin Hansen Symposium series and then arranged the content of all three of these symposia; to Helen Deas, who did her usual outstanding job in managing the symposium's logistics; to John Covell, for his support in bringing these proceedings to publication; and especially to James Heckman, Pedro Carneiro, and Alan Krueger, as well as our five discussants, for contributing their papers and comments.

In 1967, in his 80th year, Alvin Hansen received the American Economic Association's Francis E. Walker medal. James Tobin, in presenting this award, described him as follows:

> Alvin H. Hansen, a gentle revolutionary who has lived to see his cause triumphant and his heresies orthodox, an untiring scholar whose example and influence have fruitfully changed the directions of his science, a political economist who has reformed policies and institutions in his own country and elsewhere without any power save the force of his ideas. From his boyhood on the South Dakota prairie, Alvin Hansen has believed that knowledge can improve the condition of man. In the integrity of that faith he has had the courage never to close his mind and to seek and speak the truth wherever it might lead. But Professor Hansen is to be honored with as much affection as respect. Generation after generation, students have left his seminar and his study not only enlightened but also inspired—inspired with some of his enthusiastic conviction that economics is a science for the service of mankind.

Note

1. The first Alvin Hansen Symposium, in 1995, was entitled "Inflation, Unemployment, and Monetary Policy," with principal papers by Robert Solow and John Taylor. The second, in 1998, addressed the question "Should the United States Privatize Social Security?" and featured principal papers by Henry Aaron and John Shoven. The papers and discussions from each of these prior symposia have also been published by The MIT Press.

1 Inequality, Too Much of a Good Thing

Alan B. Krueger

As the title of this essay suggests, I believe inequality has both positive and negative effects. On the positive side, differential rewards provide incentives for individuals to work hard, invest, and innovate. On the negative side, differences in rewards that are unrelated to productivity—those that result from racial discrimination, for example—are corrosive to civil society and cause resources to be misallocated. Even if discrimination did not exist, however, income inequality is problematic in a democratic society if those who are privileged use their economic muscle to curry favor in the political arena and thereby secure monopoly rents or other advantages. Moreover, for several reasons discussed in the next section, poverty and income inequality create negative externalities. Consequently, it can be in the interest of the wealthy as well as the poor to raise the incomes of the poor, especially by using education and training as a means for redistribution.

The term *inequality* is often used rather loosely and can be a lightning rod.[1] Some have argued that only extreme poverty is a concern. Others have argued that the gap in income or wealth between the well off and the poor is a concern. Yet others have argued that the rapid growth in income disparity between the richest of the rich and everyone else is an issue. I will argue that, for various reasons elaborated below, all of these forms of inequality are of concern to contemporary American society, and that America has reached a point at which, on the margin, efficiently redistributing income from rich to poor is in the nation's interest.

A theme of my contribution to this debate is that societies must strike a *balance* between the beneficial incentive effects of inequality and the harmful welfare-decreasing effects of inequality. The optimal balance will differ across societies and time, but too much inequality can be harmful in any society, just as too much equality can suppress innovation and drive. Evidence presented below suggests that expanding education and training programs for less-skilled workers could be an effective component of a strategy to restore a better balance.

Trends in Inequality

To put income disparities in the United States in perspective, Figure 1.1 reports the average hourly wage at the 10th percentile, 30th percentile, 50th percentile, 70th percentile, and 90th percentile of the wage distribution. In the figure, wages have been converted to constant 2000 dollars using the new "research series" Consumer Price Index (CPI-RS). Real wages for workers at the 10th percentile of the distribution grew by 8.6 percent from 1973 to 1979, declined by 14 percent from 1979 to 1989, held steady from 1989 to 1995, and grew an impressive 14 percent when the economy heated up and the minimum wage increased in the second half of the 1990s. Despite that increase, however, the worker at the 10th percentile of the wage distribution in 2001 earned

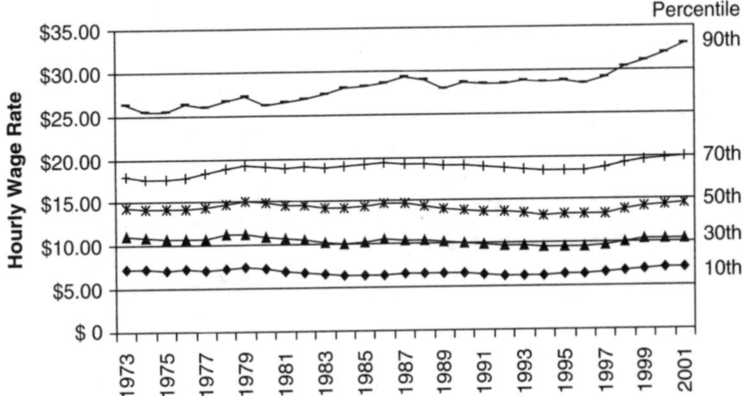

Figure 1.1
Real hourly wage rates, by decile, 2000 dollars
Source: Economic Policy Institute analysis of *Current Population Survey* data. The Consumer Price Index research series is used to deflate wages.

four cents *less* per hour than a similarly situated worker in 1979.

Workers in the middle of the wage distribution did not experience much wage growth either in the 1980s but at least avoided the sharp decline in earnings endured by the lowest wage earners in that period. From 1979 to 2001, the median worker's wage increased by 7 percent, with all of the increase coming after the mid-1990s.

By contrast, workers at the top of the distribution have experienced near-continuous wage growth since the early 1970s. The wage at the 90th percentile of the distribution was 23 percent higher in 2001 than it was in 1979.

Measured differences in education and experience account for around a third of wage variability across members of the workforce. Figure 1.2 shows average male hourly earnings by education level. Those with a college degree or

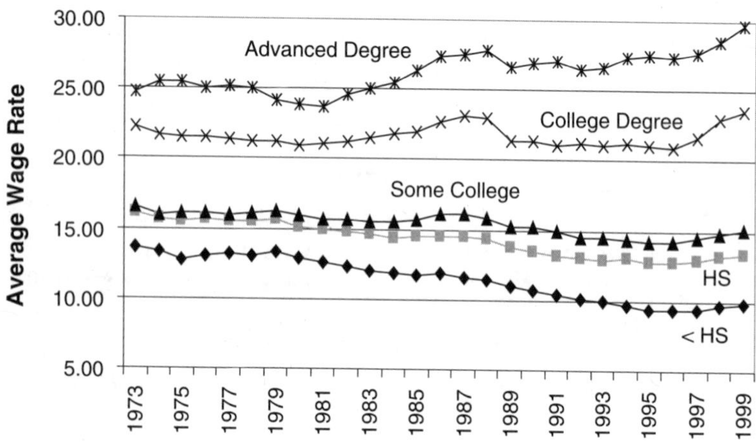

Figure 1.2
Average hourly earnings by level of education, men (1999 dollars)
Source: Economic Policy Institute analysis of *Current Population Survey* data.

higher fared well in the 1980s, whereas those with a high school degree or less fared badly. Indeed, workers with a high school diploma or less have seen a near-continuous decline in their earning power since the early 1970s. The average male high school dropout earned $13.61 per hour in 1973 and $9.78 in 1999, a drop of 28 percent. The hourly pay of the average high school graduate fell from $16.14 in 1973 to $13.61 in 1999, a drop of 16 percent. By contrast, workers with an advanced degree earned 20 percent more per hour in 1999 than in 1973.

Wages for women display a similar pattern, though the declines for poorly educated workers are not as steep, probably because increases in work experience partly offset the erosion in their earning power. Figure 1.3 shows the ratio of average hourly earnings of workers with a college degree to that of workers with a high school degree and the ratio of

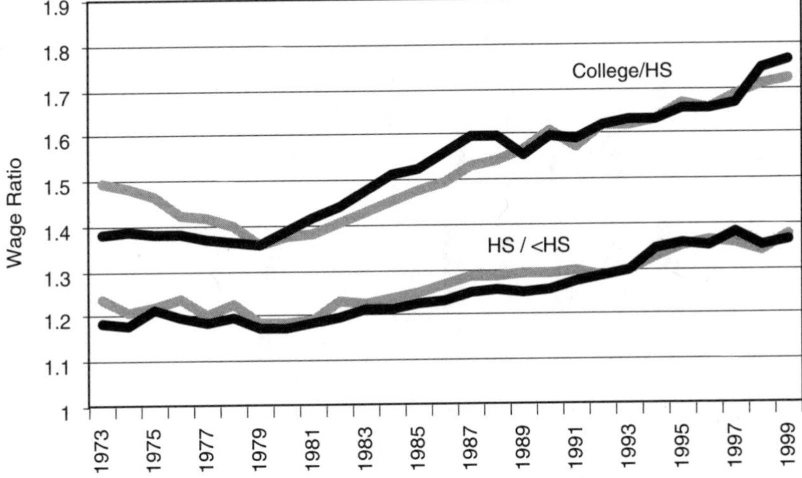

Figure 1.3
College–high school wage ratio and high school–high school dropout wage ratio, by sex, 1973–1999. Ratios for women are shown in gray, those for men in black.
Source: Economic Policy Institute analysis of *Current Population Survey* data.

average hourly wages of high school graduates to those with less than a high school education. As is well documented, the earnings-education gradient fell in the 1970s and rose sharply in the 1980s. What is less well known is that the relative earnings advantage for more highly educated workers continued to rise in the 1990s, even as the bottom decile regained much ground. This finding, coupled with evidence summarized in the paper's third section, suggests that the payoff to increasing the skills of the workforce is at a historically high level.

An examination of wages alone, of course, misses large disparities in nonlabor income, and an individual's well-being depends in large part on his or her family's economic

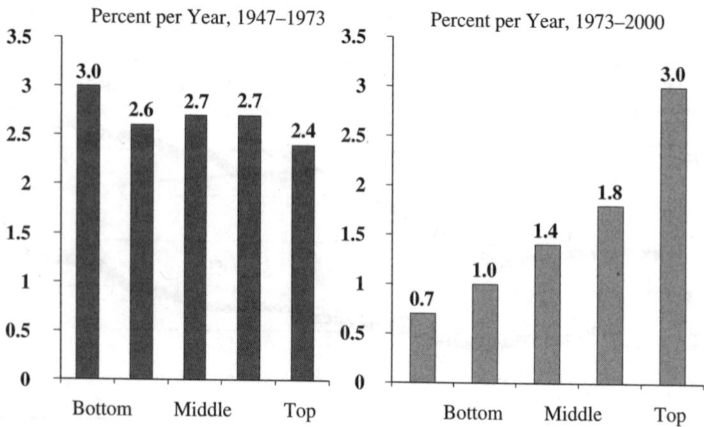

Figure 1.4
Real family annualized income growth by quintile, postwar period
Source: Census Bureau.

situation.[2] Figure 1.4 shows growth in real annualized family income by quintile for the first and second halves of the post–World War II period. In the first half of the postwar period, real family income growth was more evenly distributed and more rapid. In the second half of the period, real income growth slowed for all but the highest quintile of families. In terms of family living standards, the nation has been growing apart since the 1970s.

The top 20 percent of families amassed 62 percent of total income growth between 1973 and 2000, with more than half of that growth going to the top 5 percent, whereas the bottom 20 percent accrued only 2 percent of total income growth; the second-lowest quintile accrued only 5 percent. The income pie grew larger, but hardly any of the increase went to those at the bottom.

What is more, these household survey data probably grossly understate the share of income accruing to the

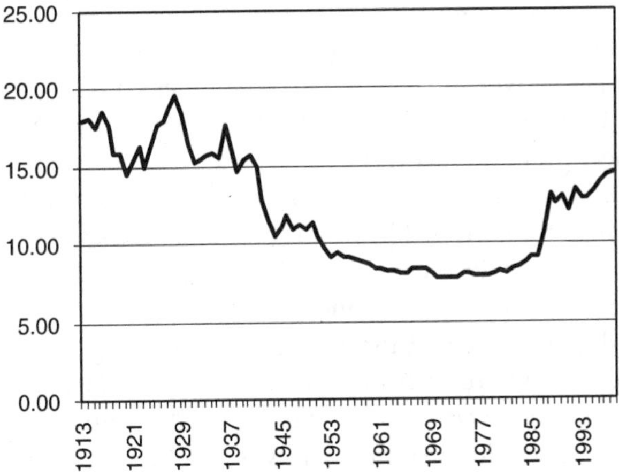

Figure 1.5
Top percentile's share of income in the United States, 1913–1998
Source: Piketty and Saez 2001, figure 3.

wealthiest households. Piketty and Saez (2003) use income tax data to measure the share of income going to the top fractiles from 1913 to 1998. Their analysis replicates, updates, and extends the well-known work of Kuznets (1955). Their data imply that from 1973 to 1998, the growth in income of the top 5 percent of tax filers exceeded the overall growth in income (holding the number of tax units constant) by 33 percent; that is, although overall average income grew, during the period average income fell for everyone below the top 5 percent. Fully 94 percent of the growth in average income went to the top 1 percent of the population. These figures suggest that there is substantial underreporting in the incomes of the top families in the household survey data cited earlier.

Figure 1.5 reproduces Piketty and Saez's graph of the fraction of income reported by the top 1 percent of tax units over the twentieth century. Contrary to Kuznets's hypothesis that income inequality would follow an inverted-U-shaped pattern over the course of development, the figure reveals a U-shaped pattern. Piketty and Saez's results turn the Kuznets curve on its head.

Many other authors have also observed that inequality fell sharply in the early 1940s, when wage and price controls were imposed during World War II (see, e.g., Thurow 1975, Williamson and Lindert 1980, and Goldin and Margo 1992). But how does one account for the fact that high-wage earners did not begin to recover until some thirty years after the controls were removed? Piketty and Saez (1998) argue that "this pattern of evolution of inequality is additional indirect evidence that non-market mechanisms such as labor market institutions and social norms regarding inequality may play a role in the setting of compensation at the top" (p. 34). Revelations about executive compensation at companies like Enron, WorldCom, and Adelphia, as well as academic studies of executive compensation such as Bertrand and Mullainathan 2001, would not contradict that conclusion.

Evidence on the extreme low end of the distribution also suffers from reporting problems but points to little progress or a deteriorating situation over the last thirty years, especially for children. Despite declining for six consecutive years, the poverty rate, for example, was no lower in 2000 than in the early 1970s. Throughout the 1990s, the poverty rate averaged 20 percent for all children; it averaged 42 percent for black children in the 1990s. It is true that the poverty rate for black children exceeded 50 percent in the mid-1960s, so progress has been made, but hardly anyone would argue that there is not room for much more progress. It is certainly possible that many low-income families have unreported income that would make their situation look less dire. On the other hand, Ehrenreich (2001) provides much anecdotal evidence of hidden costs borne by the poor. Ehrenreich's examples include low-wage workers who live in their cars or rundown hotels because they cannot afford the deposit for an apartment, which would be cheaper by the month, and who have higher food costs because they lack a kitchen in which to prepare or store their own meals.

Using the United States's poverty line as the standard in all countries (in purchasing-power parity dollars), Smeeding, Rainwater, and Burtless (2001) find that 15.7 percent of the population in the United States was in poverty in 1994 and 1995, compared with only 9.9 percent in France, 7.4 percent in Canada, 7.3 percent in Germany, 6.3 percent in Sweden, and 4.3 percent in Norway. All of these countries had GDP per capita ranging from 68 to 82 percent as large as that of the United States. Going even further than I would in criticizing inequality, Smeeding and his colleagues conclude that "[t]he supposed efficiency advantages of high inequality have not accrued to low-income residents of the United States, at least so far" (p. 170).

Jan Pen (1971) famously described the income distribution as a parade in which each person in the economy passes by in the span of an hour in order of increasing height, with the heights of the marchers corresponding to their incomes. The average income in the economy is set equal to the average height of the marchers. Those at the end of the line will be so tall that "their heads disappear into the clouds," Pen explained. The heads of those at the end of the procession today would be reaching even further up into the stratosphere than when Pen applied his analogy.

Figure 1.6, reproduced from Wolff 2002, shows the even greater imbalances in wealth than in income. According to the figure, as of the early 1990s, the top 1 percent of wealth

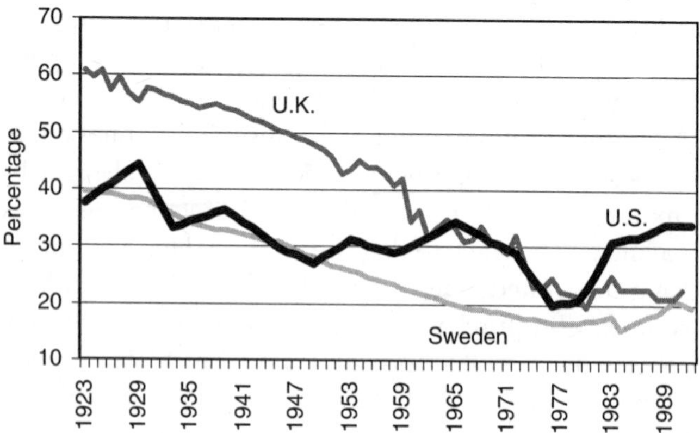

Figure 1.6
Share of marketable net worth held by top 1 percent of wealth holders: Sweden, United Kingdom, and United States, 1923–1992
Source: Wolff 2002, table 5-1.

holders owned 34 percent of the nation's wealth in the United States, but only 20 percent in Sweden and the United Kingdom. Moreover, as the figure shows, the United States had a more equal wealth distribution than Sweden and the United Kingdom until the 1940s.

Intergenerational correlations in income also reveal that the United States has less mobility in income across generations than most other countries. Solon (2002), for example, reviews evidence indicating that the correlation between fathers' and sons' earnings is 0.40 or higher in the United States, 0.23 in Canada, 0.34 in Germany, and 0.28 in Sweden. Only South Africa, still scarred by apartheid, and the United Kingdom have close to as much immobility across generations as the United States.

Probably because of greater disparities in both income and school quality, the United States has wider disparities in cognitive performance than other high-income countries. According to the International Adult Literacy Survey, the U.S. score at the 10th percentile on the prose literacy test ranked nineteenth among twenty-one high-income countries. Its median score ranked eighth among the twenty-one countries, and its score at the 85th and 90th percentiles ranked third (see Educational Testing Service 2002). The same pattern holds on other tests.

These statistics paint a picture in which the United States has become a more polarized and static society, one in which children have become comparatively more disadvantaged. For the main, these facts are not in dispute. As James Heckman is quoted (in Stille 2001, A17) as saying, "Never has the accident of birth mattered more. If I am born to educated, supportive parents, my chances of doing well are totally different than if I were born to a single parent or abusive parents." The question is whether U.S. society collectively feels something should be done about such inequality, and whether education and training should be part of the solution. These are the questions addressed in the next sections.

Why Care about Rising Inequality?

Philosophers have argued about income inequality and social justice for centuries. I will sidestep most of that debate. What follows is a thumbnail sketch of reasons why I think it is in our interest for U.S. public policy to try to restore a more balanced distribution of income in the country. Because such a conclusion fundamentally rests on one's values as well as an empirical view of the world, I will touch lightly on these reasons.[3] Suffice it to say that I hope there are enough arguments here to persuade the reader that it is worth considering using education and training as part of an overall strategy to reduce income inequality in America.

Philosophy

As Atkinson (1983) observes, "different principles of justice lead to quite different views about inequality" (p. 5). Principles of justice provide guidelines for society's welfare function, and with a welfare function for a particular society, economists could judge the distribution of inequality in that society against the optimal level. The rub, of course, is that the welfare function in a society is *not* observable and depends on philosophical arguments that are not testable. In addition, one has the Arrow impossibility theorem with which to contend. Consequently, appealing to philosophical arguments can never be universally dispositive.

Principles of social justice can be divided into those that focus on fair exchange starting from a just distribution of endowments, and those that focus on the equality of outcomes.[4] Rawls invites readers to arrive at a theory of justice by selecting the principles they would desire if they were choosing such principles in an original position behind a veil of ignorance, unaware of their standing in society or initial endowment of talents. He argues that in this case the social justice that would be desired would involve two principles: one protecting liberties and the other providing for an egalitarian distribution of opportunities and material goods. This leads him to a maximin welfare function in which the well-being of the worst off in society should be as high as possible.[5] Interestingly, Adam Smith arrived at a somewhat similar conclusion nearly two hundred years earlier, positing that "[n]o society can surely be flourishing and happy, of which the far greater part of the members are poor and miserable. It is but equity, besides, that they who feed, clothe and lodge the whole body of the people, should have such a share of the produce of their own labour as to be themselves tolerably well fed, clothed and lodged" (Smith 1776, 110–111).

Nozick (1974) questions whether a theory of justice can be based on the distribution of outcomes. Using the analogy of fans who are willing to pay a fee to watch Wilt Chamberlain play basketball—an updated analogy might substitute Shaquille O'Neal—Nozick argues that "no end-state principle or distributional patterned principle of justice can be continuously realized without continuous interference with people's lives" (p. 163). Who could complain about Wilt Chamberlain's exorbitant salary if it results from rational choices?[6] Nozick also raises the issue of the adverse incentive effects Rawls's theory of justice would have on the acquisition of talent.

Religion

I would argue that religious beliefs provide as strong (or weak) a justification for views toward society's implicit welfare function as do philosophical reflections behind a veil of ignorance. Indeed, I would go further and say that religious tenets reflect the demand for equality among the public. If people did not adhere to the basic tenets of their religion, they would not practice or would eventually change faiths. Thus, long-standing religious views toward inequality provide something of a revealed-preference argument. And with regard to wealth inequality, the world's major religions are united in favoring redistribution of wealth toward the poor. Robert Nelson (1991), for example, observes that "Roman Catholicism has traditionally instilled a strong concern for the poor; in the Middle Ages the church itself provided much of the care for the indigent. The welfare state today similarly accomplishes substantial internal redistribution with the approval of many of the wealthier contributing members of the community" (p. 326). The Jewish *Siddur* advises followers to "Be just to the poor and the orphan; Deal righteously with the afflicted and the destitute" and comments, "Happy are they who are thoughtful of the needy; In time of trouble may the Lord Keep them from harm." And the Koran criticizes the egoism of the rich inhabitants of Mecca and urges believers in Islam to support poor people, orphans, and captives. Islam requires five major obligations of its followers, including *zakat*, an obligatory contribution to the needy (which today is implemented in the form of a tax).

Enlightened Self-Interest

Another line of argument for achieving and maintaining a minimum level of equality rests on self-interest. If wide disparities in income or education create negative externalities for a majority of people, then it clearly is in the self-interest of members of society to reduce those disparities. Individuals acting on their individual preferences (e.g., paying to see Shaquille O'Neal play basketball) will not internalize these externalities. What might such externalities be? An incomplete list would involve the following.

• More-educated voters make the democratic process work better. First, people with more education are more likely to be informed and more likely to participate in democracy. Second, more-informed citizens are likely (though not guaranteed) to make better decisions. For the latter reason, even a devout defender of free markets like Milton Friedman

(1982) can be found supporting a minimum compulsory level of education.

• Available evidence suggests a link between crime and inequality (e.g., Ehrlich 1973; Freeman 1983, 1995; and Imrohoroglu, Merlo, and Rupert 2001). Other things being equal, the incentive for those with limited market opportunities to commit property crimes rises as inequality increases. From the criminal's perspective, the potential gain from crime is higher if inequality is higher, and the opportunity cost is lower. Society can devote more resources to crime prevention and incarceration, or to reducing inequality.

• Society is not willing to allow citizens to be totally destitute, to fall below some minimum level of basic consumption when it comes to food or health care (see, e.g., Pauly 1971). By providing those likely to have low incomes with skills, therefore, and thereby raising their future earnings, society can reduce the cost of providing transfer payments later on. Bruce and Waldman (1991) show that in the case of the "Samaritan's dilemma," it may be in society's interest to make wealth transfers in kind (e.g., through education) rather than in cash to avoid a moral-hazard problem on the part of the recipient.

• Nelson and Phelps (1966) and Romer (1990) model the level of education in a society as generating positive externalities for economic growth, although empirical support for this model is mixed (see Krueger and Lindahl 2001).

Low Wages, Imperfect Monitoring, and Public Safety

In an advanced economy, people are connected via markets in a myriad of ways. Employee performance can be monitored only imperfectly. If an employee performs poorly because he or she feels poorly compensated, others may suffer as a result of his or her poor performance. The tragic events of September 11th, for example, highlighted the importance of paying baggage screeners better wages.

Market Failure

More generally, market failures could lead the distribution of income in a society to be suboptimal. Credit constraints, for example, might prevent children from poor families from investing adequately in education.[7] Monopsony power on the part of employers might enable firms to pay workers less than the value of their marginal products. Statistical discrimination might lead to lower-than-optimal investment in education for discriminated-against groups (e.g., Lundberg and Startz 1983).

Efficient Policy Changes

Another type of externality could arise in the political arena in a society if income inequality in that society is viewed as excessive. Treaties to reduce international trade barriers offer an example. A policy that reduces trade barriers undoubtedly will increase national income in the society that enacts it. However, there will be winners and losers from such a policy. If some segments of society feel that they have not benefited from developments in the economy, then they are unlikely to support efforts to reduce trade barriers. I am not talking here just about the losers from the trade barrier reduction policy specifically, who are usually few in number and concentrated in a handful of industries. Instead, views toward free trade seem to be class related. For example, Blendon et al. (1997) find that 72 percent of those with less than a college education say one reason the U.S. economy is not doing better is that "companies are sending jobs overseas," whereas only 53 percent of college graduates agree with the same statement, and just 6 percent of American Economic Association members. Less-educated people are also less likely than those with more education to respond in the survey that trade agreements are good for the economy. I suspect that one reason Presidents (George W.) Bush and Clinton had difficulty securing fast-track authority for the passage of trade agreement is that large segments of the public perceived that they would lose from free trade, an inference that they drew because they had seen their real incomes stagnate or decline over the previous twenty years while trade expanded. Although I suspect trade has had little to do with rising wage inequality in the United States, it is understandable why so many people would draw such an inference.

Unless the public perceives that it will benefit from more efficient policies, there is little reason to suspect it will support such policies, and with 94 percent of income growth accruing to the top 1 percent of the U.S. population since 1973, it is understandable why the American public might be a little skeptical that it gained from past changes such as expanded trade.

Money Buys Influence

Economists at least since Adam Smith have fretted that wealthy merchants and manufacturers would be led by self-interest to seek government regulation and privilege to protect their monopoly position, thereby preventing the invisible hand from working its magic. One need look no further than the formation of the (George W.) Bush administration's energy bill to see the relevance of this concern. Money buys access and influence in politics. It also buys influence through think tanks. A negative consequence of the skewed distribution of income in the United States is that some individuals have much more political influence than others.

Benabou (2000) develops a formal model in which the progressivity of educational funding and taxation is endogenous. He shows that the political influence of the wealthy interacts with income inequality to block efficient progressive policies or impose inefficient regressive ones. When income inequality is high, he finds, the wealthy are more likely to block *efficiency-enhancing* programs that would improve educational opportunities for the less well off.

Growth and Income Inequality

Persson and Tabellini (1994) develop a model of economic growth in which income inequality negatively influences growth through the political process. In their model, income inequality leads to policies that do not protect property rights and therefore do not allow full private appropriation of the returns from investment. A growing body of cross-country and cross-state studies have estimated the relationship between initial income inequality and subsequent GDP growth.[8] Although attributing causality is difficult in these studies, the correlation between income inequality and growth is negative, conditional on variables like initial GDP per capita and average education. Two-stage least-squares estimates that use variables such as initial literacy and infant mortality as instruments for income inequality also show an inverse relationship between GDP growth and such inequality.

Health and Income Inequality

One common argument I will *not* make concerns health and income inequality. Wilkenson (1996), for example, argues that average health is negatively affected by the societal level of income inequality. The evidence in support of this view, however, is far from compelling (see, e.g., Smith 1999 and Deaton 2001), although Eibner and Evans (2002) provide evidence that relative deprivation affects health, and a large body of evidence finds that a person's own income level is related to his or her health.

Winner-Take-All Inefficiency in Superstar Markets

Frank and Cook (1996) argue that technological changes have facilitated a shift to superstar markets in many top-paying professions. The reward received by the one who finishes first is much greater than the reward received by the also-rans. They lament that this shift is inefficient and inequitable, causing too many students to pursue careers in law, finance, and consulting at the expense of more socially beneficial fields such as engineering, manufacturing, civil service, and teaching. The winner-take-all society engendered by this shift may create the same type of misallocation of talent that Murphy, Shleifer, and Vishny (1991) attribute to rent seeking. To some extent, income inequality probably leads to legions of tax lawyers and lobbyists who look for ways to help wealthy clients avoid taxation. Frank and Cook believe that superstar markets have led to inefficient investment and wasteful competition. Although I think we are at little risk of becoming a nation of Tonya Hardings, there may be something to the argument that superstar salaries provide perverse incentives and unnecessary competition in some sectors and divert some workers from pursuing more socially rewarding careers.

Public Preference

Last but not least, I would surmise that a majority of the public demands a certain amount of equality and is particularly supportive of using education and training to achieve more equality of outcomes. A survey of 1,001 adults by

Lake, Snell, Perry & Associates in July 2000 posed the following request to respondents: "I am going to read some different ways the government can help poor Americans find and keep good jobs. For each, please tell me if you strongly support, somewhat support, somewhat oppose, or strongly oppose this idea." Fully 90 percent supported "helping to pay for education and job training for people leaving welfare." Similarly, a Gallup poll sponsored by General Motors in May 1998 asked the following free-form question: "Just your opinion, in what ways do you think the government should help the poor?" By far, the top two responses were providing better/more affordable education (38 percent) and providing job training/skills training (29 percent). The next-highest response was providing more jobs/job opportunities, at 16 percent. Only 5 percent of those surveyed cited lowering taxes as a way the government might assist poor people.

Even when given an explicit choice of lower taxes, the public prefers education and training. A CBS News poll in September 1999, for example, asked 1,376 respondents, "Which comes closer to your view? Government should provide tools to help families better their lives, such as education and job training programs. The best thing that government can do for families is to cut taxes and allow individual families to decide for themselves how to allocate their money." Fifty-five percent of respondents said the first statement more closely reflected their views, whereas only 42 percent replied that the second statement came closer to what they believed.

Wrapping Up

In supporting minimum schooling, Milton Friedman (1982) argued that "[a] stable and democratic society is impossible without a minimum degree of literacy and knowledge on the part of most citizens and without widespread acceptance of some common set of values" (p. 86). I would argue that inequality could grow so extreme that it eventually jeopardizes any type of "widespread acceptance" of a democratic capitalist society that might be established. This leads me to agree with Victor Fuchs (1979): "For me the key word is *balance*, both in the goals that we set and in the institutions that we nourish in order to pursue these goals. I value freedom *and* justice *and* efficiency, and economics tells me that I may have to give up a little of one goal to insure the partial achievement of others" (p. 180).

Targeted Education and Training: Part of the Solution

In a perfect world, children from all families would invest in educational resources up to the point that their marginal return equaled their discount rate, and all families would have equal access to credit and discount investments at the same prevailing rate. The evidence suggests, however, that education decisions are not made in a perfect world. Children from poor families *behave* as if they have higher discount rates. The most plausible explanations for this phenomenon are that poor families are credit constrained (i.e., cannot borrow at the same rate as everyone else), or that they discount future benefits of human capital investments at a higher than market rate because they are impatient, have a greater disutility of schooling, or fail to appreciate the benefits of education. Of these possible explanations, credit constraints have received the most attention in the literature, because students cannot easily use the return on their future human capital as collateral to borrow for human capital investments. This may be a reason for discount rates to vary. Poor families face different borrowing costs than rich ones.

The following five observations are consistent with the view that low-income families face credit constraints when it comes to education. First, Ellwood and Kane (2000) find that when the return to college education increased in the 1980s (see figure 1.2), four-year college enrollment increased for children from all quartiles of the income distribution except the bottom one. Second, Behrman and Taubman (1990) find that the timing of parental income matters for children's educational attainment. Using data from the Panel Study of Income Dynamics (PSID), they find that father's income earned when children are teenagers has a stronger effect on children's educational attainment than income earned later on. Third, Shea (2000) looks at the effect on children's human capital of differences in parental income emanating from noncompetitive factors, such as employment in a high-paying union job or industry. Wage differences for reasons such as these arguably are independent of parents' ability. Shea finds that family income matters for children's human capital investment in a sample of low-income families, but not for the broader population. He concludes that this finding is consistent with the idea that the accumulation of observable skills by poverty sample fathers may have been suboptimal due to liquidity constraints. Fourth, Björklund and Jantti (1997) find stronger family income effects on children's outcomes in the United States than in Sweden, which provides much more generous educational subsidies than the United States. Fifth, the reaction of college enrollment to changes in tuition, especially at the two-year-college level, is substantially larger than the reaction of college enrollment to equivalent, present-value changes in the payoff to education (see Kane 1999).[9]

Although it is possible to construct complicated explanations of the above findings that are consistent with all families' having equal access to credit—and I suspect part of the association between education and parental income reflects intergenerational transmission of ability and motivation for schooling, as Cameron and Heckman (2001) argue —Occam's razor and common sense suggest that families have different access to credit. For example, some families borrow for college costs by accumulating debt on their credit cards at exorbitant rates, whereas others tap into their family finances or take out home equity loans that are given tax-preferred treatment.

One does not have to resort to theoretical assumptions or indirect tests of credit constraints, however, to support the view that redistribution of wealth via targeted education and training is desirable. *It is clear that returns to education and training are at least as big at the bottom of the income distribution as at the top.* I will present evidence below indicating that the *social return* from investment in education and training for poor children, from infancy through early adulthood, is at least as great as the social return from investments in education and training in the general public.

A theme that emerges from my survey of the evidence is that the real rate of return from investment in various education and training programs for the disadvantaged is 6 to 11 percent. This range applies to a diverse set of programs, ranging from preschool to Job Corps to conventional K–12 public schools. To put this figure in perspective, note that the historical real rate of return on the stock market has been calculated at 6.3 percent (Burtless 1999).[10] So investment in human capital for the disadvantaged seems to yield at least as great a return as investment in the equity market. Also, because there is not currently universal access to most of the educational and training programs considered here, and many willing participants in these programs are thus turned away, I would argue that the returns estimated from various evaluations reviewed below would approximately apply if the programs were greatly expanded to accommodate more participants.

The remainder of this section reviews the most compelling evidence available on the payoff from a variety of education and training programs targeted for the disadvantaged, organized in order of the age of the program participants. I have tried to focus on evidence from randomized experiments or natural experiments, so that one can be reasonably confident that differences between participants and nonparticipants are, on average, due to the programs under study, rather than to preexisting, uncontrolled differences between the participants and nonparticipants.[11]

Preschool

Economists and other social scientists have studied the effects of early education programs on children's life outcomes extensively. Barnett 1992 and Currie 2001 contain thorough surveys of the literature.

The federally funded Perry Preschool program in Ypsilanti, Michigan, has provided the most influential results in the literature, although I suspect many proponents of the program exaggerate the strength of the results. The goal of the Perry program was to improve the educational outcomes of children in the low-income black community defined by the Perry School area. The "treatment" consisted of the children's attending a half-day preschool program for five days a week plus a ninety-minute home visit once a week, both for eight months a year. The student-teacher ratio was six to one, and all the teachers in the program had master's degrees in child development. The population of students eligible to participate in the program consisted of three- or four-year-olds whose IQ was one standard deviation or more below the mean and who showed no signs of mental retardation or physical handicap. Perry was evaluated with a randomized design: fifty-eight students were assigned to a treatment group that entered Perry Preschool, and sixty-five were assigned to a control group that was denied entry.[12] Five waves of participants are included in the evaluation, having entered Perry from 1962 to 1965. In addition to its randomized design, a great advantage of the Perry analysis is that the sample has been followed for a long time, and attrition among the participants was low.[13]

Table 1.1, reproduced from Barnett 1992, summarizes the main findings from evaluations of Perry Preschool. Although the program had only transitory effects on participants' IQ scores, it had lasting effects on their achievement test scores (at least through age 19), educational attainment, employment, and social outcomes like arrests and teen pregnancies. For example, 67 percent of members of the treatment group had graduated from high school, whereas only 49 percent of the control group had. Thirty-one percent of the treatment group had been arrested, compared to 52 percent of the controls.

Barnett (1992) provides a cost-benefit analysis of the Perry Preschool. He estimates that the real social internal rate of return was 8 percent: that is, the present value of the social costs of the program would equal the present value of the social benefits if the discount rate were as high as 8 percent. His estimate uses the results in table 1.1 and forecasts benefits after age 19. Barnett (1996) extends this cost-benefit analysis, using data on outcomes through age 27 and forecasting benefits thereafter. The estimated benefit due to a

Table 1.1
Summary of Perry Preschool findings

Outcome	Treatment group	Control group	p^{a}
Intelligence test scores			
At study entry	79.6	78.5	—
After one year	95.5	83.3	.001
Age 6	91.3	86.3	.024
Age 7	91.7	87.1	.040
Age 8	88.1	86.9	—
Age 9	87.7	86.8	—
Age 10	85.0	84.6	—
Age 14	81.0	80.7	—
Achievement test scores			
Age 7	97.1	84.4	.216
Age 8	142.6	126.5	.079
Age 9	172.8	145.5	.042
Age 10	225.5	199.3	.040
Age 14	122.2	94.5	.003
Age 19	24.6	21.8	.059
School success (to age 19)			
Years spent in special education	16%	28%	.004
Classified mentally retarded	15%	35%	<.05
Graduated from high school	67%	49%	<.05
Received postsecondary education	38%	21%	<.05
Economic success (at age 19)			
Employed	50%	32%	<.05
Median earnings[b]	$3,860	$1,490	.061
Self-supporting	45%	25%	<.05
Receives welfare	18%	32%	<.05
Social adjustment (to age 19)			
Arrested	31%	51%	.021
Average number of arrests	1.3	2.3	.001
Average number of teen pregnancies	0.7	1.2	.076

Table 1.1
(continued)

Source: Barnett 1992, table 8.
Note: Sample size is 123 or fewer, depending on outcome.
a. Statistical analyses for IQ test scores, achievement test scores, and years in special education were analyses of covariance, with gender, family background variables (including mother's employment), and initial IQ as covariates. Comparable probit analyses were performed for dichotomous variables. Differences in number of arrests and pregnancies per group were tested for significance using a chi-square test. The median test was applied to median earnings.
b. Expressed in 1988 dollars. The earnings difference appears to be primarily the result of differences in employment rather than wages.

reduction in crime and associated costs is much larger in the subsequent analysis, owing primarily to different assumptions about the cost of crime and the number of crimes committed per arrest. Barnett estimates that the social benefits exceed the costs of the Perry program even if an interest rate of 11 percent is used to discount benefits and costs. At a 5 percent interest rate, social benefits are five and a half times as great as the costs, although the private benefits to participants are slightly less than the costs. A remarkable two-thirds of the social benefit derived from Perry, according to Barnett, is due to a reduction in crime and associated costs, but discounted social net benefits are still positive if savings from crime are set to zero.

Although the findings from the Perry program suggest a very high rate of return that has persuaded some that preschool is the most (or only?) effective educational intervention for the disadvantaged, the limitations of the cost-benefit analysis are important to bear in mind. Most important, many of the posited benefits were estimated over future years, and these estimates are thus subject to substantial uncertainty.[14]

The Perry program was more time intensive and more expensive than most preschool programs for poor children. Moreover, evaluations of the program are based on a small, geographically limited sample, and the data on which the evaluations are based have not been made publicly available to outside researchers. There is also the possibility that the very fact that Perry was found to be so successful contributed to its having been studied for so long. That is, one needs to be concerned about selection bias: Had the initial results found Perry to be a bust, the program probably would have slipped into obscurity.

So it is reassuring to note that the weight of the rest of the evidence on preschool programs points in the same direction as that concerning the Perry program, if not always as strongly.[15] Consider the Carolina Abecedarian Program.[16] Like Perry, Abecedarian used a random-assignment design. The Abecedarian program, however, was even more intensive than Perry. At birth, fifty-seven infants were randomly selected to receive center-based child care services emphasizing language development for eight hours a day, five days a week, fifty weeks a year for five years. Another fifty-four infants were randomly assigned to a control group. The student-teacher ratio in the preschool ranged from three to one to six to one, depending on the age of the children assigned to the teacher. This phase of the program lasted from age 0 to age 5. The cost per year was $11,000 in 1999 dollars. The pool of eligible participants was restricted to healthy infants free of conditions associated with mental retardation who were born to low-income families and were likely to remain in the area for several years. Four cohorts of infants born between 1972 and 1977 were included in the study. Only a quarter of the infants lived with both parents at birth; average maternal education was 10 years, and average maternal age at birth was 20. Ninety-eight percent of participants were black.

The children were studied from infancy until age 21. A follow-up survey at age 15 found that students in the preschool group performed significantly higher on math and reading tests and had lower rates of in-grade retention and lower rates of placement in special education classes than control students. The latest follow-up was conducted from 1993 to 1999. One hundred four of the original 111 subjects participated in the age 21 follow-up. The outcomes were similar to those in Perry: 40 percent of the preschool group were attending school at age 21, compared to 20 percent of the controls, and 35 percent of the preschool group had attended a four-year college at some point, compared to 14 percent of the controls. For those with a child, the age at first birth was also significantly higher for the preschool group. Unfortunately, a cost-benefit analysis of Abecedarian has not (so far) been performed.

Head Start is the government's largest preschool program. Head Start has not been evaluated with random assignment, but Mathematica Policy Research is in the midst of conducting a random-assignment evaluation of Early Head Start, a program begun in 1995 that extends the Head Start concept to low-income pregnant women and families with infants and toddlers. Early Head Start targets children from ages 0 to 3 and their families. Mathematica's interim findings, based on 3,000 families in seventeen communities, are promising.[17] Children participating in Early Head Start performed significantly better on cognitive, language, and social-emotional development assessments than their peers who did not participate. Effect sizes on the Bayley Mental Development Index and MacArthur Communicative Development Index were 0.10–0.15 standard deviations for two-year-olds. The program, as intended, also had impacts on aspects of the home environment, including parenting behavior, parents' knowledge of infant-toddler development, and parents' school attendance and job training.

Currie (2001) performs a cost-benefit analysis of Head Start, using estimates of the short- and medium-term benefits and costs of the program. She concludes that "Head Start would pay for itself if it yielded long-term benefits that were even a quarter as large as those of Perry Preschool" (p. 234).

The evaluations of preschool programs that have been conducted in the past have been restricted to specialized, poor populations. These evaluations may show heterogeneous effects of the programs. However, there is probably little risk from extrapolating to a wider population from the effects discussed in respect to Currie's evaluation, because just under half of eligible children currently participate in Head Start. Doubling Head Start's budget to provide universal access to the program is unlikely to materially alter the mix of children who participate.

Elementary and Secondary School

Summertime Fadeout Studies of over-the-year and over-the-summer learning suggest that public elementary schools serve low-income students better than is commonly appreciated. Table 1.2 summarizes the findings of Entwisle, Alexander, and Olson (1997). These three sociologists have been studying a random sample of 800 students since they entered first grade in one of twenty Baltimore public schools in 1982. At the beginning and end of each school year in the study, students have taken the California Achievement Test. The researchers have examined gains and losses in test scores over the school year and summer break. Students

Table 1.2
School year and summer gains on California Achievement Test in reading and math over elementary school years, by family socioeconomic status level

	Reading socioeconomic status		Math socioeconomic status	
	Low	High	Low	High
School year gains				
Year 1	56.7	60.8	49.0	45.0
Year 2	48.0	40.1	42.9	42.2
Year 3	31.2	33.7	36.0	35.6
Year 4	33.1	31.7	33.2	35.7
Year 5	24.3	24.6	24.7	27.8
Total gain	193.3	190.9	185.8	186.3
Summer gains				
Year 1	−3.7	15.0	−4.8	8.8
Year 2	−3.5	8.5	−5.2	3.3
Year 3	1.6	14.9	−1.9	1.3
Year 4	4.5	10.4	4.8	5.6
Year 5	1.9	−2.2	−0.9	5.9
Total gain	0.8	46.6	−8.0	24.9

Source: Entwisle, Alexander, and Olson 1997.
Note: Sample consists of Baltimore public school students who entered first grade in 1982. Test "scale scores" are calibrated to measure growth over a student's twelve-year school career.

were classified into groups based on their parents' socioeconomic status, which depended on their education, occupation, and income. As found in other studies, the gap in achievement scores between high- and low-SES children grows over time.

Remarkably, children from high- and low-socioeconomic-status families made equivalent gains on math and reading exams during their elementary school years. But the achievement level of children from low-income families either fell or stagnated during the summer, whereas that of children from higher income families continued to improve.

Children from poor families enter school with a gap in achievement compared to that of those from well-off families. But the entire subsequent increase in that gap results from periods when school is out of session. This pattern, which also holds in studies of other data sets (see Cooper et al. 1996 for a literature review), suggests that public schools are doing more to help poor children overcome the obstacles they face in their homes and neighborhoods than is commonly appreciated.

These findings come as no surprise to teachers, who regularly review material in the beginning of the school year that students learned in the previous year. Students from poor families receive less academic enrichment over the summer than do students from more advantaged families. Indeed, a Gallup poll taken in July 2000 even found (by my calculation from data Gallup provided) that children in low-income families were much less likely to have read *Harry Potter* over the summer months than were their counterparts in middle- and upper-income families. The problem is that children from low-income families are unlikely to read *Harry Potter* or much else during the summer, which causes their skills to atrophy when school is out of session.

I suspect that students from poor families are particularly poorly served by America's comparatively short 180-day school year; they receive little academic enrichment when school is not in session. As a solution to this problem, I have previously proposed giving low-income parents a scholarship, or voucher, to send their children to some type of a summer learning program. Only 9 percent of students in the United States attend summer school. Unlike other voucher programs, summer school vouchers would supplement, rather than substitute for, the public-school system.

The 180-day U.S. school year is, as noted, short by international standards. Japan's school year, for example, runs about 240 days a year. By the end of high school, children in Japan have had the equivalent of four more years of schooling than American children. Although it would be desirable to use the 180-day school year more constructively, one thing is clear: More time on task helps students learn. Almost everyone agrees that obtaining more years of schooling would raise most individuals' earnings and productivity. It seems plausible to me that adding thirty days of schooling each year would raise students' earnings by about the equivalent return to two years of schooling for a high school graduate ($30 \times 12/180 = 2$).

Though not all summer school programs have been found to be successful, a meta-analysis of ninety-three evaluations of separate summer school programs by Cooper et al. (2000) concludes that summer school has an average positive effect on student achievement, when performance is compared either to participants' presummer scores or to that of a randomly selected control group of nonparticipants.

School Resources Matter, and They Matter Most at the Bottom Hanushek (1997) argues that "[t]he close to 400 studies of student achievement demonstrate that there is not a strong or consistent relationship between student performance and school resources, at least after variations in family inputs are taken into account" (p. 141). This inference has led some to doubt whether investing more in education is a useful strategy for helping low-income children. Elsewhere I have criticized the evidence on which this view is based. Here I highlight my critique.[18]

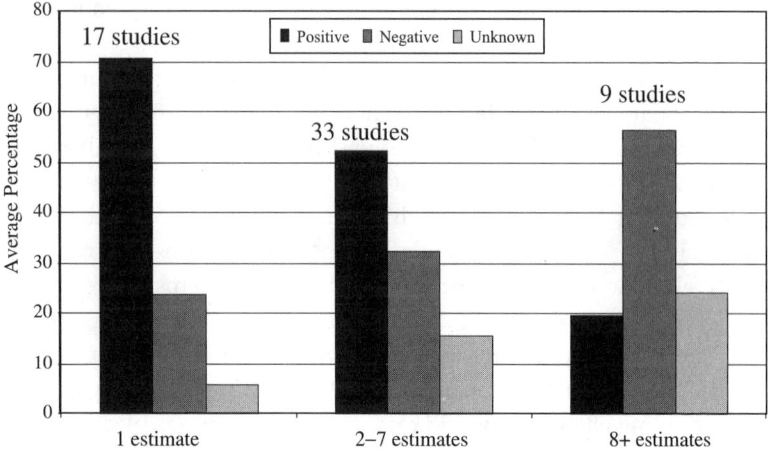

Figure 1.7
Percentage of estimates of the effect of smaller classes that are positive, negative, or of unknown sign, by number of estimates Hanushek extracted from each study. Arithmetic averages of percentage positive, negative, and unknown sign are taken over the studies in each category. See Krueger 2003 for details.
Source: Based on data from Hanushek 1997.

Hanushek's latest tabulation of the results in the literature is based on fifty-nine articles on class size and forty-one on expenditures per student; twenty-two of these articles were included in both groups. Hanushek extracted information on the sign and significance of 277 estimates of the effect of class size drawn from fifty-nine studies. (Each estimate is referred to as a study in Hanushek 1997.) The number of estimates extracted from each of the studies varied widely: As many as twenty-four estimates were extracted from each of two papers, and only one apiece from seventeen studies.

Figure 1.7 divides the fifty-nine studies Hanushek examined into three groups based on the number of estimates Hanushek extracted from each study and shows the fraction of estimates in each of the three groups that are positive, negative or of unknown sign in regard to the effect of class size. For the vast majority of studies, from which Hanushek took only a small number of estimates, there is a clear and consistent association between smaller class sizes and student achievement. For the seventeen studies from which Hanushek took only one estimate each, for example, over 70 percent of the estimates indicate that students tend to perform better in smaller classes, and only 23 percent indicate a negative effect of class size on student performance. By contrast, for the nine studies from which he took a total of 123 estimates (eight or more per study), the opposite pattern holds: Small classes are associated with lower student performance. These nine studies are closely scrutinized in Krueger 2002; many are found to have statistical problems that cast doubt on their findings vis-à-vis class size. For example, three of the studies (i.e., one-third of those in this group) control for both expenditures per student and class size in the same regression, rendering the results difficult to interpret.

By using estimates as the unit of observation, Hanushek implicitly weights studies by the number of estimates he has extracted from them. It is difficult to argue that the studies that receive the most weight in Hanushek's approach deserve more weight than the average study. For example, Summers and Wolfe's (1977) *American Economic Review* article received a weight of one in Hanushek's analysis, while Link and Mulligan's (1986) *Economics of Education Review* article received a weight of twenty-four.

When all of the studies in Hanushek's survey are given equal weight, however, the literature exhibits systematic evidence of a positive relationship between class size and achievement, and between expenditures and achievement. Using Hanushek's coding of the studies, the number of studies that find positive effects of expenditures per student outnumber those that find negative effects by almost four to one. The number of studies that find a positive effect of smaller classes exceeds the number that find a negative effect by 57 percent. Differences of these magnitudes are unlikely to have occurred by chance.

One could also question the logic of the coding of many of Hanushek's estimates. For example, if a study provided two results, one for a sample of black students and one for a sample of white students, Hanushek would count each result separately, for a total of two estimates. But if the same study interacted a dummy variable indicating whether the student was black with school resources and included a school resources "main effect" in the regression to allow for a differential impact of resources by race, Hanushek would take only one estimate from the study: the main effect, which pertains just to white students. This is quite unfortunate, because Hanushek's surveys often have been used to draw inferences for poor and minority students.

A consensus is emerging that smaller classes raise student achievement, both on average and in particular for children from low-income families and for minorities. This conclusion emerges both from meta-analyses (e.g., Hedges, Laine, and Greenwald 1994) and from the only experimental evaluation of class size, the Tennessee Student-Teacher Achievement Ratio (STAR) experiment.

The Tennessee STAR experiment has been described by Mosteller (1995) as "one of the most important educational investigations ever carried out," and Mosteller notes that it "illustrates the kind and magnitude of research needed in the field of education to strengthen schools" (p. 113). Project STAR was an experiment involving the wave of students who entered kindergarten in participating Tennessee schools in 1986. Students who moved into this wave at participating schools were added to the experiment. A total of 11,600 students in kindergarten through third grade within seventy-nine Tennessee schools were randomly assigned to a small class (target of thirteen to seventeen students), a regular-sized class (target of twenty-two to twenty-five students), or a regular-sized class with a full-time teacher's aide.[19] The initial design called for students to remain in the same class type from grade K through grade 3, although students were randomly reassigned between regular and regular/aide classes in first grade. Students who left the school in which they started the study or repeated a grade were dropped from the sample being tracked during the experiment, although data on their subsequent performance in many cases was added back into the sample after third grade, as other data sources were used. In fourth grade, all students were returned to regular classes.

Data are available for about 6,200 students per year in grades K through 3 and about 7,700 students per year in grades 4 through 8, after the experiment ended. The average student who was assigned to a small class in the experiment spent 2.3 years in a small class. An important feature of the experiment is that teachers were also randomly assigned to class types. Krueger (1999) evaluates some of the problems in the implementation and design of the STAR experiment, including high rates of attrition and possible nonrandom transitions between grade levels, and concludes that they did not materially alter the main results of the experiment.

It is important to emphasize that the small-class effects are measured by comparing students from different class assignments in the same schools. Because students were randomly assigned to a class type within schools, student characteristics—both measurable, such as free-lunch status, and unmeasurable, such as parental involvement in students' education—should be the same across class types, on

Table 1.3
Summary of findings from Tennessee STAR class size reduction intervention: Estimated intent-to-treat effects

	All	Black	Free lunch
Achievement test scores (standard deviations)			
K	0.200**	0.272**	0.229**
1	0.229**	0.378**	0.255**
2	0.209**	0.390**	0.272**
3	0.200**	0.369**	0.251**
4	0.092**	0.181**	0.102**
5	0.085**	0.207**	0.105**
6	0.098**	0.187**	0.133**
7	0.091**	0.170**	0.119**
8	0.089**	0.168**	0.133**
Took ACT or SAT	0.070*	0.204**	0.113*
College exam score (ACT or SAT)	0.109**	0.238**	0.203**

Note: Table shows difference in average outcome between students initially assigned to a small class and those initially assigned to a regular-sized class or regular-sized class with aide, conditional on school attended. For grades K through 3, the Stanford Achievement Test was used to assess performance; for grades 4 through 8 the Comprehensive Test of Basic Skills was used. ACT and SAT scores are adjusted for participation differences using the two-step normal-selection correction described in Krueger and Whitmore 2001. In all cases, test scores are expressed relative to the standard deviation. The difference in the probability of having taken the ACT or SAT is expressed as a proportion of the fraction of students in regular-sized classes who took the ACT or SAT.
*Statistically significant at .05 level
**Statistically significant at .01 level

average. On observed characteristics, the treatment and control groups did not exhibit significant differences (see Krueger 1999).

Table 1.3 summarizes key findings from Project STAR. Results are presented separately for all students, for black students, and for students who participated in free lunch. The reported coefficients are the differences between those who were assigned to a small class and those who were assigned to a regular-sized class (with or without an aide).[20] Because about 10 percent of the students did not attend the size class they were assigned to, the reported coefficients understate the impact of attending a small class. Nevertheless, assignment to a small class appears to have raised test scores by about 0.2 standard deviations while students were in small classes in grades K–3, and by about 0.10 standard deviations from grades 4 through 8. Moreover, attending a small class appears to have raised the likelihood that students would take a college entrance exam, either the SAT or ACT exam. As is commonly found in the class-size literature, the effect sizes are substantially larger for Black students and those on free lunch. Krueger and Whitmore (2001) also find that those who were randomly assigned to small classes were less likely to have been arrested and to have become teenage parents.

In Krueger 2002 I conducted a cost-benefit analysis in respect to reducing class size by seven students, using the effect size for test scores found for the full sample in the STAR experiment. The only benefit considered in the analysis is future earnings, which were predicted from differences in test scores and the assumption that real wages will grow by 1 percent per year in the future. I concluded that the internal real rate of return is 6 percent for all students combined.[21] The analogous calculation yields an internal rate of return for black students of 8 percent.[22]

Evidence on the Returns to Schooling A large literature surveyed in Card 1999 and elsewhere estimates the payoff from additional years of schooling in terms of higher earnings, using variability in schooling resulting from factors such as compulsory schooling or geographic proximity to a college. The findings in this literature are consistent with the interpretation that credit constraints induce some students to leave school earlier than others.

For example, Angrist and Krueger (1991) estimate the effect of compulsory schooling on earnings by exploiting the fact that it was common in the 1930s and 1940s for schools to require students to turn age 6 by January of the school year to start school in that school year or else wait another year before starting school. Because most states require students to attend school until they reach their sixteenth or seventeenth birthday, this combination of rules sets up a natural experiment in which the day of the year on which students are born determines their age upon entering school and the compulsory-schooling law enables students born early in the year to drop out of school at a lower grade level. Assuming that date of birth is uncorrelated with other attributes of individuals (an assumption that is not too difficult to accept unless one believes in astrology), then date of birth can be used to generate exogenous variability in educational attainment.

Instrumental-variables (IV) estimates identified by differences in date of birth suggest that an additional year of education obtained because of compulsory-schooling laws leads to about 6 to 8 percent higher earnings among workers in 1970 and 1980. These estimates are slightly higher than the estimates one obtains from estimating a Mincerian earnings function in these years. Presumably, the return to compulsory schooling would be substantially higher in 2002 because of the large increase in the payoff to schooling since 1980.

Other studies point in the same direction. Honoré and Hu (2001) provide IV versions of quantile estimates using the Angrist and Krueger (1991) identification strategy and a sample of 302,596 white men. They find that the return to years of compulsory schooling is higher for the *lower* quantiles and conclude that "[t]his suggests that the impact of education is larger at the lower end of the income distribution" (p. 19). Harmon and Walker (1995) more directly examine the effect of compulsory schooling by studying the effect of changes in the compulsory-schooling age in the United Kingdom. They find that the payoff to compulsory schooling is considerably higher than the Mincerian estimate. Card (1995) exploits variations in schooling attainment owing to families' proximity to a college in the United States and finds that the return to education is higher using this source than using all sources of variability. And Kane and Rouse (1999) find that the return per year of attending a community college is at least as great as the return per year of attending a four-year college.

Ashenfelter, Harmon, and Oosterbeek (1999) compiled estimates from twenty-seven studies representing nine different countries. They find that the conventional Mincerian return to schooling is .066, on average, whereas from a natural experiment like those just described, the average IV estimate using variability in schooling is .093.

This literature on returns to schooling suggests that those who are most likely to drop out of school early—and either are compelled to complete more schooling or are induced to do so only because they live near a college—receive the greatest return from education, on the margin. Such a finding is consistent with the notion that credit constraints or impatience causes low-achieving students to invest less in their education. Regardless of the reason for the finding, if the cost of school attendance is primarily one's foregone earnings, then this literature suggests that the private return to completing additional schooling is 6 to 9 percent for the disadvantaged.

The social return to education is likely to be even higher, because studies have found that incarceration rates decline with educational attainment. For example, Lochner (1999, 25) finds that "[h]igh school graduation reduces the probability that a young man earns an income from crime by .09 on average—about a 30% reduction from the average probability of non-graduates," holding constant the effect of Armed Forces Qualification Test (AFQT) score, parental education, race, and many other variables.

Second-Chance Education and Training

By second-chance education and training I mean programs intended for youth who drop out of school before completing high school or who fall into trouble in their early twenties. This population inflicts the greatest social costs on society. If one thinks about it, however, one realizes that this population also receives the least support from society. If such youth drop out of school early, they do not receive publicly subsidized high school education. If they fail to attend college, they do not receive government and private tuition subsidies. Both efficiency and fairness suggest that effective training should be available for second-chance opportunities.

Federally subsidized job training has been greatly curtailed in the last two decades. Because of budget cuts at the federal level, the total number of participants in federal job training (Job Training Partnership Act (JTPA), Comprehensive Employment and Training Act (CETA), and Job Corps combined) fell from around 1.3 million per year in 1979 to around 450,000 in 1998 (Ways and Means Committee 2000).[23] The Bush administration proposes further cuts of about $0.5 billion in fiscal 2003.

The Job Corps Program The Job Corps is the most intensive and expensive of the government programs for disadvantaged youth. The $1.4 billion cost in 2001 amounts to about $20,000 for each participant. Although critics mistakenly argue that a year in the Job Corps is as expensive as a year at Harvard—ignoring the public subsidy and endowment spending that raise Harvard's true costs for each student well above $50,000 a year—the costs are nevertheless high compared to those for most second-chance programs.

Because the intervention conducted by the program is so intensive, and because there are few substitutes for Job Corps, the program provides a better ground for testing the effect of federal training on adolescents than do less intensive programs, such as those provided under the Job Training Partnership Act (JTPA).

The Job Corps program annually serves more than 60,000 disadvantaged high school dropouts ages 16 to 24. A third of the male participants have been arrested at least once before joining the program; two-thirds of all participants have never held a full-time job. The average participant reads at the eighth-grade level. The primary reason the Job Corps program is expensive is that 90 percent of participants are sent from their neighborhoods to one of 116 residential campuses in forty-six states, where they stay for about eight months of academic education, vocational training, counseling, health education, and job placement assistance.

Burghardt et al. (2001) summarize final results of Mathematica's four-year National Job Corps Study. These researchers followed 9,409 eligible applicants to the Job Corps between November 1994 and December 1995 who were randomly selected for the program and another 5,977 eligible applicants in the same time period who were randomly assigned to a control group that was excluded from Job Corps services for three years. In addition to the baseline survey, applicants were surveyed twelve, thirty, and forty-eight months after they applied; 80 percent responded in the last survey.[24] This is a much larger sample than the ones previously used in randomized evaluations of youth training programs.

Burghardt et al.'s report compares the self-reported employment, earnings, and criminal activity of the participant and control groups in the forty-eight months after they applied to the program. By the last survey, participants had typically lived on their own or with their family, away from the Job Corps, for about three years. The findings complement—and in many ways mirror—those of Mallar et al.'s (1982) nonrandomized evaluation of the Job Corps.

Table 1.4 summarizes the key findings from the final Job Corps summary report (Burghardt et al. 2001). The first column of the table reports means for youth assigned to the program group, and the second column reports means for those assigned to the control group. Because participants were randomly assigned to one of the two groups when they were determined to be eligible for Job Corps, but before they enrolled, only 73 percent of those assigned to the program group actually enrolled in the Job Corps program. Consequently, the difference between the program group and the control group shown in the third column *understates* the impact of participation in the program on the

Table 1.4
Estimated impacts of Job Corps program, 1996–1999

Outcome	Program group	Control group	Estimated impact per eligible applicant	Estimated impact per participant
1. Average amount of public assistance	$3,696	$4,156	−$460*	−$639*
2. Percentage arrested or charged	28.8	32.6	−3.7*	−5.2*
3. Percentage served time in jail	15.8	17.9	−2.1*	−2.9*
4. Percentage received GED	42	27	15*	21*
5. Percentage high school diploma	5	8	−3*	−4*
6. Percentage vocational certificate	38	15	23*	32*
7. Average weekly earnings	$217.5	$199.4	$18.1*	$25.2*
8. Percentage employed	71.1	68.7	2.4*	3.3*

Source: Based on Burghardt et al. 2001.
Note: Rows 1–6 pertain to outcomes during the forty-eight months after random assignment. Rows 7–8 pertain to the sixteenth quarter after random assignment, the latest quarter for which data were available.
*Statistically significant at .05 level, two-tailed test.

participants' outcomes. The effect of participation reported in the fourth column was derived by inflating the program group–control group difference by the difference in the participation rates between the program group and control group.

Job Corps appears to have had a substantial impact on the participants' outcomes relative to controls'. Welfare payments to program participants were reduced by 16 percent

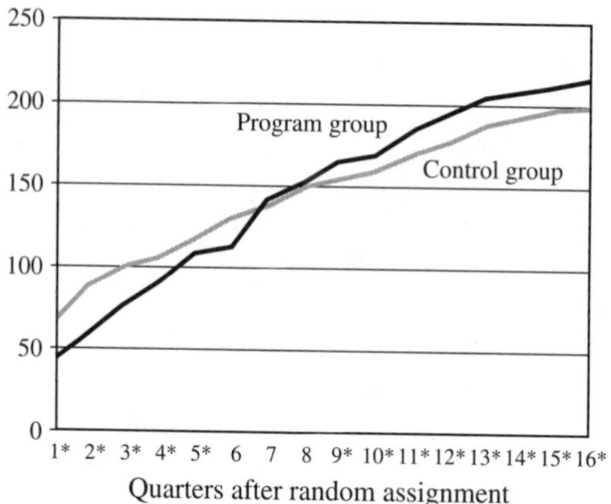

Figure 1.8
Average weekly earnings, program group and control group, National Job Corps Study (1995 dollars). Asterisks indicate quarters in which the difference was statistically significant.
Source: Burghardt et al. 2001.

in the first forty-eight months after they applied to Job Corps. Arrests were down by 16 percent, and the fraction of participants who served time in jail was also down by 17 percent.

Figure 1.8 reports average weekly earnings by assignment status for each quarter after random assignment. Mathematica estimates that participation in the Job Corps raised participants' average weekly earnings in the fourth year after random assignment by 12 percent ($p<.01$).[25] About one-third of the earnings gain came from a higher hourly wage rate and about two-thirds from more hours of work per week. If the sample is broken down by age, statistically significant earnings gains are also found for sixteen- to seventeen-year-olds. For this group, the average weekly earnings gain for participants was 9.8 percent in the fourth year after random assignment, suggesting that job training interventions can be successful for this young age group.[26]

The large earnings gains for the Job Corps participants are all the more impressive in light of the fact that the job market was extremely strong in the late 1990s. One would have expected a tight labor market to provide relatively more help for those with lower skills, which would have benefited the control group.

Note that figure 1.8 shows that earnings were lower for the program group than for the control group in the first year and a half after random assignment. Average earnings do not become significantly greater statistically for the program group compared to the control group until more than two years *after* random assignment. The reason for the initially lower but steeper earnings profile for the program group is that Job Corps participants spend much of their time in the program acquiring skills instead of in the labor market. Consequently, the program group has spent less time searching for a job and less time acquiring work experience. Age-earnings profiles are particularly steep for young workers. As emphasized below, the finding that Job Corps participants initially had lower earnings than their control group counterparts suggests that one should be cautious about drawing inferences from other youth training programs that have a short follow-up period.

About 10 percent of Job Corps participants attend a nonresidential program. On intake into the experiment, evaluators make an assessment as to whether a particular applicant will likely attend a residential or nonresidential program. Mathematica found that except for men and women with children, students slotted for a *nonresidential* Job Corps program had a statistically insignificant improvement relative to comparable control group members. This result suggests that sending youth without children to residential campuses, where they can study away from the distractions of gangs, drugs, and poverty that plague their normal neighborhoods, is a critical component of the success of the Job Corps program.[27] This feature, however, should be fairly straightforward to replicate if the program is expanded to include more participants.

Heckman (1996 and elsewhere) relies heavily on the Perry Preschool evaluation to make the provocative argument that "skill begets skill." On the basis of presumed high returns from preschool programs and low returns from second-chance programs targeted toward young adults, Heckman (1996, 340) argues, "The available evidence clearly suggests that adults past a certain age, and below a certain skill level make poor investments." The results of the Job Corps evaluation necessitate a reassessment of that view.[28] Mathematica estimates that the social internal rate of return of the Job Corps program is 10.5 percent—in the same ballpark as the most successful preschool programs.

Moreover, I would argue that there are grounds for being more confident in the estimated rate of return from the Job Corps evaluation than in that for the Perry Preschool program. The Job Corps sample was 125 times the size of the Perry sample, and the Job Corps sample was drawn from a national set of communities, rather than just one grammar school catchment area in one city.

The number of available Job Corps slots per year has been stable for decades, even though the number of disadvantaged youth in the United States has exploded. If the Job Corps program is expanded, it is quite likely that the additional youth who are served by the program will benefit in ways similar to those who participated in the National Job Corps Study.

Why JTPA Does Not Make the Case against Youth Job Training A common view is that job training for out-of-school youth is ineffective. I used to be sympathetic to this view. However, the accumulation of results from the Job Corps program has led me to change my mind.

The most compelling evidence on the effectiveness of youth job training prior to the National Job Corps study was probably from the National Job Training Partnership Act Study. Bloom et al. (1997) provide an analysis of the key findings from the JTPA study, a randomized evaluation of JTPA funded by the U.S. Department of Labor. They conclude that "[i]t appears that employment and training programs for adults can be cost-effective from a societal perspective" (p. 574). The youth results, however, are generally considered much less encouraging. For example, the authors write, "For out of school youths, we are at a more primitive stage in our understanding of how to increase labor market success; we have not found *any* way to do so." This conclusion appears to be widely accepted. Heckman, LaLonde, and Smith (1999), for example, also conclude that "the cost-benefit analyses indicate that JTPA services generated a substantial net social benefit when targeted toward adults, but none when targeted toward youths" (p. 2050).

Insofar as this debate is concerned, the adult results are encouraging.[29] Indeed, the findings of the JTPA study led the Department of Labor to shift substantial JTPA funds away from youth training and toward adult training. But for the following five reasons, I think Bloom et al. are much too pessimistic on the efficacy of training programs for out-of-school youth.

First, as discussed above, Job Corps appears to be highly cost effective for a population that is similar to that served by JTPA. Second, Heckman, Hohmann, and Smith (2000) document that there was substantial substitution between JTPA classroom training and other training for those youth in the JTPA study who were randomly denied access to the program. Many of those in the control sample managed to obtain training that was probably not too different from JTPA. Heckman, Hohmann, and Smith report that 56 percent of male youth in the JTPA study's treatment group received classroom training services, compared with 35 percent of those in the control group: The difference was only 21 percentage points, so the treatment-control difference should arguably be inflated by a factor of five to gauge the impact of training.

Third, JTPA is not very intensive to begin with; the program typically lasts three to five months and costs only about one-fifth as much as the Job Corps per participant. Consequently, the treatment effect might have been small because the treatment was *small*. In the Job Corps study, the participants received 1,000 more hours of training than the control group, approximately equivalent to a year of high school. For JTPA, the treatment was much more modest, so it is not very surprising that a return to the training is much harder to detect. But this does not mean that the training was not worth the investment. Indeed, Heckman, Hohmann, and Smith find that, after taking into account the effect of substitution on their estimates, "Under different assumptions about the persistence of benefits (thirty-three months, five and ten years), the estimated rates of return are quite large, ranging from 21 percent to 263 percent annually" (p. 669).[30]

Fourth, participants in the Job Corps without children who were sent to residential campuses seemed to benefit more than those who received nonresidential training. JTPA is a nonresidential program. Fifth, the JTPA follow-up period in Heckman and Smith 1998 and Bloom et al. 1997 is short, only six or ten quarters after random assignment.[31] Recall that figure 1.8 indicated that the earnings gain from Job Corps did not turn positive until two years after random assignment. If the JTPA program lasted for five months (and started immediately after random assignment), then the control group would have had about half a year's head start in terms of labor market experience and job search effort compared to the treatment group. Given how steep the age-earnings profile is at the beginning of the working career, one probably would not expect the earnings of the treatment group to overtake those of the controls until at least one and a half years after random assignment, even if the program is highly cost effective. If this is the case, the short follow-up window in the JTPA study would have caused researchers to miss any gain in earnings due to the program.

This is not just idle speculation. The U.S. General Accounting Office (GAO) (1996) linked Social Security earnings records to observations in the JTPA study for three years before random assignment and five years after. The GAO reported the difference in average earnings between the treatment and control groups separately for male youth and female youth, as well as for adults. Separating the sample by gender reduces the precision of the estimates, and the GAO found insignificant effects for male youths and female youths each year. But if the goal of the exercise is to estimate the average payoff from training for all young workers, there is no need to disaggregate the estimates by sex. Therefore, to increase the precision of the estimates, I calculated the unweighted average treatment-control differences for men and women.[32] (Youths are defined as those ages 16 to

21 who were not attending school when they applied for the program.) Figure 1.9 shows the resulting average "intent-to-treat" effect for the youth.

Interestingly, by the fourth year after random assignment, the average earnings of the male and female youths in the treatment group overtook those of the control group. And in the fifth year after random assignment, the difference is both statistically significant ($t = 2.1$) and substantial: In year 5, earnings are 11 percent higher for males in the treatment group than males in the control group and 4 percent higher for females in the treatment group than females in the control group; for males and females pooled together, the gain is 8 percent of earnings.[33] Given the low cost of JTPA train-

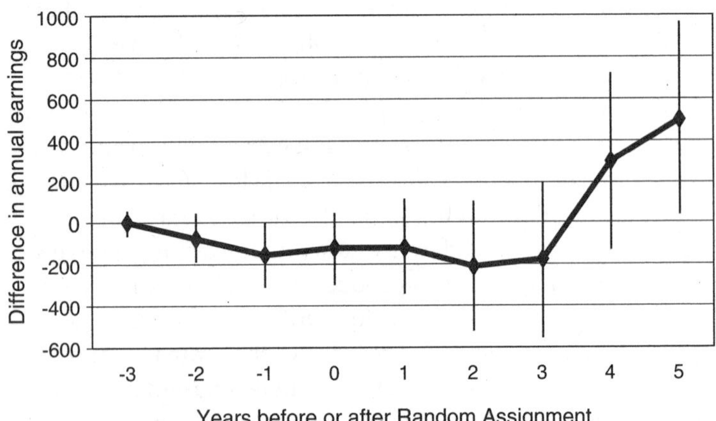

Figure 1.9
Five-year follow-up of JTPA study treatment-control differences in mean earnings, by year, average for male and female youths. Diamonds indicate average control-treatment difference for men and women. Vertical lines indicate width of 95 percent confidence interval.
Source: Author's calculations from U.S. Government Accounting Office 1996.

ing, the low take-up rate of JTPA, and the substantial amount of training by members of the control group, these earnings gains are noteworthy.

I should emphasize that I do not interpret the results in figure 1.9 as suggesting that analyses of administrative earnings data yield markedly different results of the effectiveness of JTPA than do analyses of self-reported earnings data (e.g., Bloom et al. 1997). The administrative Social Security earnings data assembled by GAO show the *same* pattern of results as previous analyses of self-reported earnings in the first three years after random assignment (that is, in the period when they overlap), but the self-reported data are not available for a longer follow-up period. The GAO data suggest that treatment-control earnings differences for youth do not arise until the fifth year after random assignment to the program. In addition, as of this writing, analyses of administrative earnings records from the unemployment insurance system, such as Kornfeld and Bloom 1999, have not examined earnings data beyond 2.25 years after random assignment, so they are not inconsistent with the results in figure 1.9 either. Indeed, the unemployment insurance data are consistent with the finding of noneffects in the Social Security data in the period when the two bodies of data overlap.

Nevertheless, I am reluctant to interpret the results in figure 1.9 as indicating that JTPA was a wild success for youth. I am not sure that it was. Longer-term follow-up with administrative unemployment insurance records may overturn the results in figure 1.9. I have a less ambitious conclusion, however. The results in figure 1.9 and the four other considerations noted here should give pause to those who believe, based on the JTPA program, that training programs for young adults are necessarily a failure.

College

Research suggests that the payoff, in terms of subsequent earnings, associated with attending a highly selective college is greater for students from poor families than for those from wealthy families. Figure 1.10 illustrates results found in Dale and Krueger 2002. Dale and Krueger used data from the College and Beyond Survey of individuals who were freshmen in 1976. Their earnings were surveyed as of 1995. College selectivity in Dale and Krueger's study is based on the average SAT score of each college's freshman class. Although the data came from only thirty moderate to highly selective colleges, similar results are obtained if a nationally representative sample, the National Longitudinal Study of the High School Class of 1972, is used.

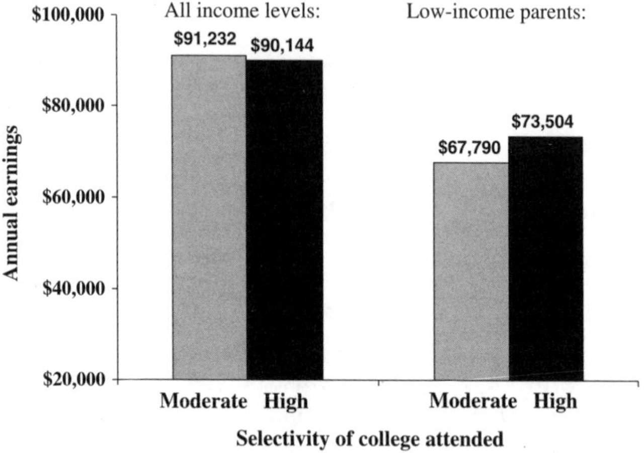

Figure 1.10
Average earnings in 1995, by selectivity of college attended, for students who applied to and were accepted by both highly and moderately selective colleges

The average earnings for the 519 students in Dale and Krueger's study who had been accepted by both moderately selective (average SAT scores of 1,000 to 1,099) and highly selective (average SAT scores greater than 1,275) schools varied little, no matter which type of college they attended. Students from lower-income families (defined approximately as the bottom quarter of families who send children to college), however, had higher annual earnings fifteen years after finishing college if, from their menu of choices, they chose to attend a highly selective college. Their annual earnings in 1995 were nearly $6,000 (8 percent) higher if they had chosen to attend one of the elite schools over one of the moderately selective schools. Even for those in their late teens and early twenties, the payoff to quality schooling seems to be higher for those from lower-income families.

Theoretical Interpretations

Figure 1.11a provides a simple theoretical explanation of many of the findings in the human capital literature. The concave (from below) curves in the figure represents the structural log earnings functions facing poor and nonpoor children. The y-intercept is lower for the poor children because of the intergenerational transmission of ability. As in the Becker–Rosen–Ben-Porath model, individuals choose their schooling level by finding the tangency between their supply of funds and the structural earnings function. The supply-of-funds curves are convex, however, because families first use lower-cost sources, and then higher-cost ones. Children from poor families have less access to credit, and hence more-convex (from below) supply-of-funds schedules. (Alternatively, the convex supply-of-funds curves could be interpreted as reflecting an increasing marginal distaste for

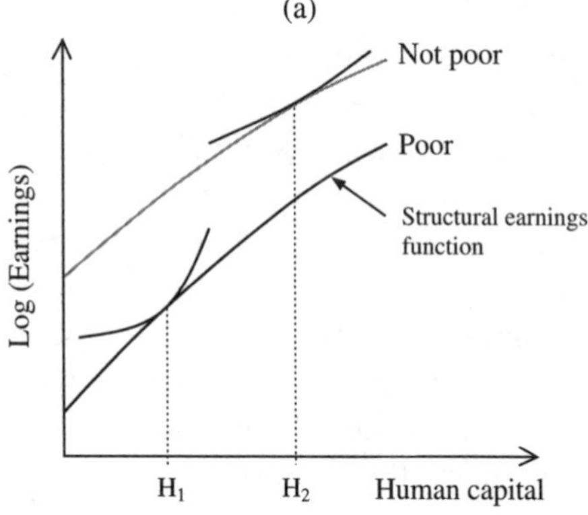

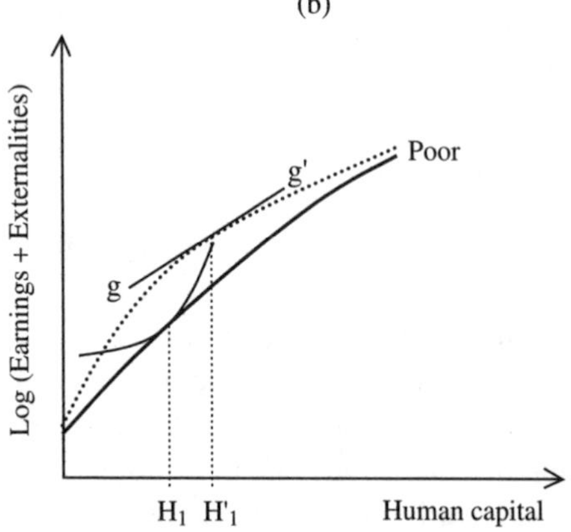

Figure 1.11
Illustrative human capital earnings functions: (a) with credit constraints; (b) with credit constraints and social externalities

school that varies with family income.) This constrained-income maximization problem would lead children of poor families to have H_1 invested in their education and children of nonpoor families to have H_2 invested in theirs. Note also that the marginal payoff to additional money invested in human capital is greater for children from poor families than it is for children from nonpoor families.

The model portrayed in figure 1.11a ignores the possibility that credit-constrained children could temporarily leave school to work for a while to accumulate funds to pay for tuition and living costs and return to school later on. In a model without credit constraints, children would never leave school to work and then return to school again (unless the payoff to education unexpectedly changed). With credit constraints, human capital investment decisions are more complicated than in the optimal stopping rule of the Becker–Rosen–Ben-Porath model. Nevertheless, I suspect the model captures an important aspect of behavior. Moreover, many public-school districts prohibit students from attending public schools after they exceed a certain age.

Figure 1.11b extends the model to allow for social externalities from human capital accumulation.[34] The line labeled gg' represents the government's discount rate, reflecting among other things the Treasury's borrowing rate and deadweight loss from raising tax revenue, under the assumption that the government is not constrained in terms of how much it can raise for human capital investments at the prevailing rate. From society's perspective, the optimal level of human capital investment in children from poor families is H_1', which exceeds the prevailing level, H_1.

Notice also that improving the quality of schooling (for example, by increasing the length of the school year, reducing class sizes, or recruiting more-effective teachers) would make the structural earnings functions steeper. This would lead to an increase in educational attainment and higher earnings. (See Card and Krueger 1996b for a formal model.)

It should also be noted that even without credit constraints, risk aversion would cause children from low-income families to underinvest in human capital and have a higher average return, assuming preferences exhibit decreasing absolute risk aversion. As with other investments, the return to investment in education is uncertain, and the variance in returns to education probably increased, along with the mean, in the 1980s and 1990s. Unlike the risk in other investments, however, the risk inherent in investing in education is not easily diversifiable by individuals (e.g., because of moral-hazard problems or inability to use human capital as collateral). The government, however, can diversify this risk by investing across many individuals. In a situation with undiversified risk, the expected return from additional investment in education and training of low-income students would be higher than that from investments in high-income students, because a premium would be required to induce low-income students to take on the additional risk.

Conclusion

The evidence reviewed in this paper suggests to me that allocating more resources to education and training of the disadvantaged could reduce inequality. These educational and training programs could be paid for by rejecting budgetary proposals that would exacerbate income disparities, including the elimination of the estate tax and cuts in the capital income tax and top income tax rate. Moreover, as noted earlier, education and training are popular ways to transfer income, probably because of the Good Samaritan's dilemma. Economists should not ignore practical political-economy constraints on which specific proposals for redistributing income can be included in the feasible set.

My priority list of education and training initiatives would include

- fully funding Head Start and Early Head Start so every eligible child can participate
- fully funding Job Corps so every eligible youth can participate
- increasing the length of the school year by thirty to forty days, especially in inner-city areas, either by extending the school year or offering summer school vouchers
- targeting reductions in class size to low-income areas
- increasing the compulsory schooling age to eighteen
- improving the quality of teachers, especially in low-income areas, by raising merit-related pay for teachers and pursuing other initiatives
- expanding funding for adult training programs in the current structure of the Workforce Investment Act
- providing income maintenance allowances for up to two years (as is done in trade adjustment assistance) to individuals who are undergoing training.

Note that this is a comprehensive list, not focused on any particular age group. Given the evidence that the Job Corps program generates large gains for participants and society, there seems little reason to me to disregard older youth when it comes to government-supported training. Old dogs can learn new tricks. Even if JTPA had been demonstrated ineffective for youth (which, as noted above, is not the case), a workable, replicable model for youth training exists: the Job Corps program. Furthermore, since the delay between when human capital investments are made and when participants enter the labor force is shorter for out-of-school teenagers than it is for preschool children, there is much less discounting of future benefits for programs involving teenagers than for those aimed at preschoolers.

But more important than the specifics of my wish list, I would recommend the general principle that wise investment in education and training pays off. The optimal set of programs is likely to vary across areas with different needs. But as a general rule, on the margin, the payoff from public human capital investments seems to be higher from investments in lower-income areas than from those in higher-income areas. Money invested wisely matters. This leads me to recommend a policy of giving ample resources to local governments in low-income areas to invest in the initiatives that they think best meet their needs—and holding the local governments accountable for the results.

Heckman (1994) makes the provocative calculation that to restore educational earnings ratios to their 1979 level would require an investment of $1.66 trillion. This calculation assumes a 10 percent return on educational investments, which strikes me as reasonable based on the evidence presented here.[35] Heckman (2000) writes, "Given the magnitude of the required investment to restore real earnings levels, and the stringency of current government budgets, it is necessary to use funds wisely" (p. 12). I have three reactions to this argument.

First, it is not clear why restoring the wage structure to its 1979 form should be a zero-sum goal for public policy. If programs to improve human capital, especially that of children in low-income families, have higher returns than other competing uses of government funds, then it seems to me a wise use of funds to expand the programs on the margin. Just because expanding the Job Corps would not revive the 1979 wage structure does not mean that expanding the program is an unwise use of government funds.[36] Second, if skilled and unskilled workers are complementary inputs in production, as is likely, then reducing the number of unskilled workers and increasing the number of skilled workers in the country's economy would have an added effect of reducing inequality (see, e.g., Bishop 1979). Third, $1.66 trillion for a major national initiative sounds like a lot less money in 2002 than it did in 1994. The estimated cost of the Bush tax cut from 2001 to 2011 is $1.8 trillion, with *another* $4.1 trillion in expected cost from 2012 to 2021.[37] The illustrative target of $1.66 trillion does not seem so far beyond reach if there is the collective will to reduce inequality.

Nonetheless, Heckman's exercise of putting the magnitude of the returns and costs of the investment in perspective is important. The benefits of investment in education and training should not be oversold. How much additional equity is possible through a greater emphasis on government training and education? I have not costed out the components on the wish list I presented above, but the expenditure required is sure to be an order of magnitude below $1.66 trillion. For the sake of argument, suppose it is $100 billion per year. (The most expensive component would be expanding the length of the school year by around one-sixth.) Cumulatively over five years this would result in a $500 billion increase in investment in human capital for children of lower-income families. A 10 percent return on this investment would lead to a $50 billion per year increase in income, ignoring general-equilibrium effects, which would likely increase that amount.

Is this small potatoes? A good basis for comparison is the expansion of the Earned Income Tax Credit (EITC) in 1993, one of the most progressive changes in government policy in the last decade. The expansion of the EITC transferred an additional $6–7 billion per year, so the proposal that I have in mind would have a substantially larger effect. Indeed, the entire EITC transferred $31 billion in 2000, less than the return that could be garnered from a major step up in investment in education and training for the disadvantaged. And the net redistributive effect of the EITC is smaller than $31 billion once incidence is taken into account, because of wage adjustments in response to the subsidy.

I would acknowledge, however, that $50 billion per year is small compared with the magnitude of the problems caused by extreme inequality. But I would emphasize that I do not envision investment in human capital development as the sole component of a program to address the adverse consequences of income inequality. It is part of the solution, not the whole solution. In principle, the optimal government policy regarding income inequality would employ multiple instruments, up to the point at which the social benefit per additional dollar of cost of each instrument is equal across the instruments. To restore more balance to the distribution of income across society, I would also recommend seriously considering the following policy changes:

- another increase in the EITC
- another increase in the minimum wage, which is 22 percent below its real level from 1979
- a reconsideration of immigration policy, which currently places little weight on the human capital of immigrants and labor force needs of the economy
- universal national health insurance.

These proposals strike me as more desirable than eliminating the estate tax and cutting the highest income tax bracket. I'll leave these topics, however, for another Alvin Hansen Symposium on Public Policy.

Notes

I have benefited from helpful discussions with Roland Benabou, Anders Björklund, David Card, B. J. Casey, John Donohue, Ken Fortson, Victor Fuchs, Tom Kane, Jeff Kling, Mike Rothschild, Peter Schochet, and Jeffrey Smith. Ken Fortson and Diane Whitmore provided valuable research assistance. All errors in fact or judgment are my own. This paper was prepared for the third Alvin Hansen Symposium on Public Policy at Harvard University, April 25, 2002.

1. Indeed, I am on record in the *Wall Street Journal* (January 24, 1995) as preferring the term *dispersion* over *inequality*. But in the spirit of this debate, I will use the term *inequality*. See Atkinson 1983 for a thoughtful discussion of alternative meanings of *inequality*.

2. Hamermesh (1999) and Pierce (2001) find that accounting for nonmonetary fringe benefits and working conditions, such as health insurance, exacerbates the real declines in wages workers at the bottom have experienced.

3. Jencks 2002, of which I was unaware when I wrote the first draft of this paper, reviews empirical evidence on the effects of inequality. Jencks concludes "that the social consequences of economic inequality are sometimes negative, sometimes neutral, but seldom positive. The case for inequality seems to rest entirely on the claim that it promotes efficiency, and the evidence for that claim is thin."

4. Sen (1973) draws a useful distinction between assessing the actual income distribution relative to the distribution according to needs and assessing it according to some concept of desert.

5. Others have reached an expected utility maximization welfare function as a result of the same reflection.

6. A problem arises with this view if Wilt is highly paid in large part because basketball team owners lobby for public subsidies to build lavish stadiums, which raises Wilt's marginal product. But this was less common in 1974 than today.

7. Benabou (2002) analyzes a model in which credit constraints prevent optimal investment. Not surprisingly, subsidized education improves efficiency and enhances growth in these models. Benabou's calibrated

simulations suggest that the beneficial effects of relaxing credit constraints exceed the corresponding tax-induced distortions. Evidence on credit constraints is discussed below.

8. Early papers are Persson and Tabellini 1994 and Alesina and Rodrik 1994. See Benabou 1996 for a survey of the empirical and theoretical literatures.

9. It is true that tuition subsidies and government loans are available to many individuals, but the amount of such assistance is small compared to the opportunity cost of attending college and probably insufficient to overcome credit constraints. Moreover, such subsidies do not help with credit constraints at the precollege level.

10. Burtless based his calculation of this rate of return on the average real rate of return over every fifteen-year period ending in 1885 through 1998. The rate of return was calculated by assuming that $1,000 was invested in the composite stock index defined by Standard and Poor's, with quarterly dividends reinvested in the composite index. From a survey of ninety-five chief financial officers at Fortune 500 companies, Summers (1987) estimates that the median firm applies a very high discount rate (15 percent) to depreciation allowances, and most firms do not discount different cash flow components at different rates. The high discount rate that chief financial officers say that they use may, however, reflect inflated expectations of future cash flows.

11. See Heckman and Smith 1995 for an accessible discussion of limitations of social experiments.

12. There were two exceptions to randomization. First, siblings of children already participating in the study were assigned to the same group as their older sibling. Second, and more important, Barnett (1992) notes that "a few working mothers could not participate in the afternoon home visits and their children were shifted to the control group" (p. 295). This might explain why 33 percent of control group mothers were working at baseline, whereas only 13 percent of treatment group mothers were working at that time. This was the only reported baseline characteristic on which the control and treatment groups had a statistically significant difference.

13. Note, however, that five students who were assigned to the treatment group did not complete Perry Preschool because they died or moved away. They appear to have been dropped from the sample.

14. See figure 3.5 in Karoly et al. 1998 for estimated confidence intervals.

15. See Karoly et al. 1998 for an overview of preschool programs.

16. The information on Carolina Abecedarian in this section is drawn from ⟨http://www.fpg.unc.edu/~abc/index.htm⟩.

17. The material on Early Head Start is drawn from Love et al. 2001.

18. The debate over this point is played out in Krueger 2002 and Hanushek 2002.

19. See Word et al. 1990, Nye et al. 1994, or Krueger 1999 for more detail on the experiment.

20. In most cases, the differential between the regular-sized classes with or without an aide was small and statistically insignificant. Having an aide in a regular-sized class raised the likelihood that black students took one of the college entrance exams, however.

21. On the other hand, using parameter estimates from Card and Krueger 1996a, Peltzman (1997) presents back-of-the-envelope calculations that he argues imply that "reducing class size would be a bad investment" (p. 225). Peltzman's calculations assume, however, that real wages will not grow at all over the next fifty years; see Card and Krueger 1997.

22. This calculation assumes that annual earnings of black workers will be 80 percent of overall average earnings.

23. These figures probably understate the decline, because the 1979 figure is for new enrollees and the 1998 figure is for total participants.

24. The response rate was 81.5 percent for the program group and 77.8 percent for the control group.

25. These figures are different from those in table 1.4 because they pertain to the entire twelve-month period beginning three years after random assignment. Table 1.4 reports earnings and employment data for the latest quarter available, sixteen quarters after random assignment. Earnings were 13 percent higher as a result of participation in the Job Corps in that quarter.

26. For black sixteen- to seventeen-year-olds, the earnings gain was 6.7 percent but was not statistically significant.

27. For participants with children, however, the nonresidential program appears to be effective.

28. Others challenge the scientific basis for the importance of early learning. See, for example, Bruer's (1999) review of the neurological evidence.

Apparently, the frontal cortex, a part of the brain critical to higher cognitive functions, is the region that takes longest to develop and continues to develop well into adolescence. Furthermore, functional magnetic-resonance imaging (MRI) studies demonstrate that adults can learn, and cortical reorganization can take place, after a stroke impairs reading ability (see Small, Flores, and Noll 1998).

29. Abadie, Angrist, and Imbens (2002) find that the proportionate effect of JTPA participation on earnings was largest in the middle quantiles for adult men and largest in the lower quantiles for adult women.

30. In view of such high returns, the fact that control group received significantly less training than the treatment group suggests that credit constraints were binding.

31. Orr et al. (1994) and Heckman, Hohmann, and Smith (2000) present results spanning two and a half years after random assignment. Figure 1.9 suggests that this period might also be too short to capture any effects of JTPA training on youths' earnings. Heckman, Hohmann, and Smith's figures suggest that earnings of the treatment group were rising relative to those of the controls (especially for females) between eighteen and thirty-two months after random assignment, although the difference was not statistically significant at thirty-two months.

32. The sample had approximately equal numbers of men and women, so weighting by sample size would cause little difference in the calculations.

33. The GAO emphasized that the effects were statistically insignificant when male and female youth were considered separately. But the effect for all youth (i.e., males and females combined) is of interest for policy evaluation and is more precisely estimated.

34. For a related model, see Pauly 1967. Pauly models education as a normal good that generates positive externalities, although the marginal value of the externalities declines with educational attainment. He shows that without credit constraints, economic efficiency is enhanced if education is more highly subsidized for children from lower-income families.

35. The calculation seems to exclude from the cost of investment the opportunity cost of individuals' time, which reduces the cost of the government's investment.

36. My point also seems in the spirit of Heckman's (1995, 1103) critique that *The Bell Curve* failed because "the authors do not perform the cost-benefit analyses needed to evaluate alternative social policies for raising labor market and social skills."

37. See Friedman, Kogan, and Greenstein 2001. These figures ignore the extra costs associated with higher interest payments due to deficit spending.

References

Abadie, Alberto, Joshua Angrist, and Guido Imbens. 2002. "Instrumental Variables Estimates of the Effect of Subsidized Training on the Quantiles of Trainee Earnings." *Econometrica* 70, no. 1 (January): 91–117.

Alesina, Alberto, and Dani Rodrik. 1994. "Distributive Policies and Economic Growth." *Quarterly Journal of Economics* 109 no. 2 (May): 465–490.

Angrist, Joshua, and Alan Krueger. 1991. "Does Compulsory School Attendance Affect Schooling and Earnings?" *Quarterly Journal of Economics* 106, no. 4 (November): 979–1014.

Ashenfelter, Orley, Colm Harmon, and Hessel Oosterbeek. 1999. "A Review of Estimates of the Schooling/Earnings Relationship, with Tests for Publication Bias." *Labour Economics* 6, no. 4 (November): 453–470.

Atkinson, Anthony. 1983. *The Economics of Inequality*, 2d ed. Oxford: Oxford University Press.

Barnett, W. Steven. 1992. "Benefits of Compensatory Preschool Education." *Journal of Human Resources* 27, no. 2 (spring): 279–312.

Barnett, W. Steven. 1996. *Lives in the Balance: Age-27 Benefit-Cost Analysis of the High/Scope Perry Preschool Program*. High/Scope Educational Research Foundation Monograph no. 11. Ypsilanti, Mich.: High Scope Press.

Behrman, Jere, and Paul Taubman. 1990. "The Intergenerational Correlation between Children's Adult Earnings and Their Parents' Income: Results from the Michigan Panel Survey of Income Dynamics." *Review of Income and Wealth* 36, no. 2: 115–127.

Benabou, Roland. 1996. "Inequality and Growth." In *NBER Macroeconomics Annual 1996*, Ben S. Bernanke and Julie Rotenberg, eds. Cambridge: MIT Press.

Benabou, Roland. 2000. "Unequal Societies: Income Distribution and the Social Contract." *American Economic Review* 90, no. 1 (March): 96–129.

Benabou, Roland. 2002. "Tax and Education Policy in a Heterogeneous Agent Economy: What Levels of Redistribution Maximize Growth and Efficiency?" *Econometrica* 70, no. 2 (March): 481–517.

Bertrand, Marianne, and Sendhil Mullainathan. 2001. "Are CEO's Rewarded for Luck? The Ones without Principals Are." *Quarterly Journal of Economics* 116, no. 3 (August): 901–932.

Bishop, John. 1979. "The General Equilibrium Impact of Alternative Antipoverty Strategies." *Industrial and Labor Relations Review* 32, no. 2 (January): 205–223.

Björklund, Anders, and Markus Jantti. 1997. "Intergenerational Income Mobility in Sweden Compared to the United States." *American Economic Review* 87, no. 5 (December): 1009–1018.

Blendon, Robert, John Benson, Mollyann Brodie, Richard Morin, Drew Altman, Daniel Gitterman, Mario Brossard, and Matt James. 1997. "Bridging the Gap between the Public's and Economists' Views of the Economy." *Journal of Economic Perspectives* 11, no. 3 (summer): 105–118.

Bloom, Howard, Larry Orr, Stephen Bell, George Cave, Fred Doolittle, Winston Lin, and Johannes Bos. 1997. "The Benefits and Costs of JTPA Title II-A Programs: Key Findings from the National Job Training Partnership Act Study." *Journal of Human Resources* 32, no. 3 (summer): 549–576.

Bruce, Neil, and Michael Waldman. 1991. "Transfers in Kind: Why They Can Be Efficient and Nonpaternalistic." *American Economic Review* 81, no. 5 (December): 1345–1351.

Bruer, John. 1999. *The Myth of the First Three Years.* New York: Free Press.

Burghardt, John, Peter Schochet, Sneena McConnell, Terry Johnson, R. Mark Gritz, Steven Glazerman, John Homrighanser, Robert Jackson. 2001. *Does Job Corps Work? Summary of the National Job Corps Study.* Princeton: Mathematica Policy Research. Available online at ⟨wdr.doleta.gov/opr/⟩.

Burtless, Gary. 1999. "Risk and Returns of Stock Market Investments Held in Individual Retirement Accounts." Testimony before the House Budget Committee Task Force on Social Security Reform, May 11.

Cameron, Stephen, and James Heckman. 2001. "The Dynamics of Educational Attainment for Black, Hispanic, and White Males." *Journal of Political Economy* 109, no. 3 (June): 455–499.

Card, David. 1995. "Earnings, Schooling, and Ability Revisited." In *Research in Labor Economics*, vol. 14, Solomon Polachek, ed. Greenwich, Conn.: JAI.

Card, David. 1999. "The Causal Effect of Education on Earnings." In *Handbook of Labor Economics*, vol. 3, Orley Ashenfelter and David Card, eds. Amsterdam: Elsevier.

Card, David, and Alan Krueger. 1996a. "School Resources and Student Outcomes: An Overview of the Literature and New Evidence from North and South Carolina." *Journal of Economic Perspectives* 10, no. 4 (fall): 31–50.

Card, David, and Alan Krueger. 1996b. "Labor Market Effects of School Quality: Theory and Evidence." In *Does Money Matter? The Link between Schools, Student Achievement and Adult Success*, Gary Burtless, ed. Washington, D.C.: Brookings Institution Press.

Card, David, and Alan Krueger. 1997. "Class Size and Earnings: Response to Sam Peltzman. *Journal of Economic Perspectives* 11, no. 4 (fall): 226–227.

Cooper, Harris, Kelly Charlton, Jeff Valentine, and Laura Muhlenbruck. 2000. "Making the Most of Summer School: A Meta-analytic and Narrative Review." *Monographs of the Society for Research in Child Development* 65, no. 1 (serial no. 260): 1–118.

Cooper, Harris, Barbara Nye, Kelly Charlton, James Lindsay, and Scott Greathouse. 1996. "The Effects of Summer Vacation on Achievement Test Scores: A Narrative and Meta-analytic Review." *Review of Educational Research* 66, no. 3 (fall): 227–268.

Currie, Janet. 2001. "Early Childhood Intervention Programs: What Do We Know?" *Journal of Economic Perspectives* 15, no. 2 (spring): 213–238.

Dale, Stacy, and Alan Krueger. 2002. "Estimating the Payoff to Attending a More Selective College: An Application of Selection on Observables and Unobservables." *Quarterly Journal of Economics* 117, no. 4 (November): 1491–1527.

Deaton, Angus. 2001. "Health, Inequality, and Economic Development." Research Program in Development Studies working paper, Princeton University.

Educational Testing Service. 2002. "The Twin Challenges of Mediocrity and Inequality: Literacy in the U.S. from an International Perspective." Policy Information Report, Princeton, N.J.

Ehrenreich, Barbara. 2001. *Nickel and Dimed: On (Not) Getting By in America*. New York: Metropolitan.

Ehrlich, Isaac. 1973. "Participation in Illegitimate Activities: A Theoretical and Empirical Investigation." *Journal of Political Economy* 81, no. 3 (May): 521–565.

Eibner, Christine, and William Evans. 2002. "Relative Deprivation, Poor Health Habits and Mortality." University of Maryland, College Park, mimeo.

Ellwood, David, and Thomas Kane. 2000. "Who Is Getting a College Education? Family Background and the Growing Gaps in Enrollment." In *Securing the Future: Investing in Children from Birth to College*, Sheldon Danziger and Jane Waldfogel, eds. New York: Russell Sage.

Entwisle, Doris, Karl Alexander, and Linda Olson. 1997. *Children, Schools, and Inequality*. Boulder, Colo.: Westview.

Frank, Robert H., and Philip J. Cook. 1996. *The Winner Take All Society*. New York: Free Press.

Freeman, Richard. 1983. "Crime and the Labor Market." In *Crime and Public Policy*, James Wilson, ed. San Francisco: Institute for Contemporary Studies.

Freeman, Richard. 1995. "The Labor Market." In *Crime*, James Wilson and Joan Petersilia, eds. San Francisco: Institute for Contemporary Studies.

Friedman, Joel, Richard Kogan, and Robert Greenstein. 2001. "New Tax-Cut Law Ultimately Costs as Much as Bush Plan." Washington, D.C.: Center on Budget and Policy Priorities.

Friedman, Milton. 1982. *Capitalism and Freedom*. Chicago: University of Chicago Press.

Fuchs, Victor. 1979. "Economics, Health, and Post-Industrial Society." *Health and Society* 57, no. 2 (Spring): 153–182.

Goldin, Claudia, and Robert Margo. 1992. "The Great Compression: The U.S. Wage Structure at Mid-century." *Quarterly Journal of Economics* 107, no. 1 (February): 1–34.

Hamermesh, Daniel. 1999. "Changing Inequality in Markets for Workplace Amenities." *Quarterly Journal of Economics* 114, no. 4 (November): 1085–1123.

Hanushek, Eric. 1997. "Assessing the Effects of School Resources on Student Performance: An Update." *Educational Evaluation and Policy Analysis* 19, no. 2 (summer): 141–164.

Hanushek, Eric. 2002. "Evidence, Politics, and the Class Size Debate." In *The Class Size Debate*, Lawrence Mighel and Richard Rothstein, eds. Washington, D.C.: Economic Policy Institute.

Harmon, Colm, and Ian Walker. 1995. "Estimates of the Economic Return to Schooling for the UK." *American Economic Review* 85, no. 5 (December): 1278–1286.

Heckman, James. 1994. "Is Job Training Oversold?" *Public Interest* 115 (spring): 91–115.

Heckman, James. 1995. "Lessons from the Bell Curve." *Journal of Political Economy* 103, no. 5 (October): 1091–1120.

Heckman, James. 1996. "What Should Be Our Human Capital Investment Policy?" In *Of Heart and Mind: Social Policy Essays in Honor of Sar A. Levitan*, Garth Mangum and Stephen Mangum, eds. Kalamazoo, Mich.: Upjohn.

Heckman, James. 2000. "Policies to Foster Human Capital." *Research in Economics* 54: 3–56.

Heckman, James, Neil Hohmann, and Jeffrey Smith. 2000. "Substitution and Dropout Bias in Social Experiments: A Study of an Influential Social Experiment." *Quarterly Journal of Economics* 115, no. 2 (May): 651–694.

Heckman, James, Robert LaLonde, and Jeffrey Smith. 1999. "The Economics and Econometrics of Active Labor Market Policies." In *Handbook of Labor Economics*, vol. 3, O. Ashenfelter and D. Card, eds. Amsterdam: North-Holland.

Heckman, James, and Jeffrey Smith. 1995. "Assessing the Case for Social Experiments." *Journal of Economic Perspectives* 9, no. 2 (Spring): 85–110.

Heckman, James, and Jeffrey Smith. 1998. "Evaluating the Welfare State." In *Econometrics and Economic Theory in the 20th Century: The Ragnar Frisch Centennial*, S. Strom, ed. Cambridge: Cambridge University Press.

Hedges, Larry V., Richard Laine, and Rob Greenwald. 1994. "Does Money Matter? A Meta-analysis of Studies of the Effects of Differential School Inputs on Student Outcomes." *Education Researcher* 23, no. 3: 5–14.

Honoré, Bo and Luojia Hu. 2001. "On the Performance of Some Robust Instrumental Variables." Princeton University, mimeo.

Imrohoroglu, Ayse, Antonio Merlo, and Peter Rupert. 2001. "What Accounts for the Decline in Crime?" Penn Institute for Economic Research working paper no. 01-012.

Jencks, Christopher. 2002. "Does Inequality Matter?" *Daedalus* 131 (winter): 49–65.

Kane, Thomas. 1999. *The Price of Admission Rethinking How Americans Pay for College*. Washington, D.C.: Brookings Institution Press.

Kane, Thomas, and Cecilia Rouse. 1999. "The Community College: Educating Students at the Margin between College and Work." *Journal of Economic Perspectives* 13, no. 1 (winter): 63–84.

Karoly, Lynn, Peter Greenwood, Susan Everingham, Jill Houbé, M. Rebecca Kilburn, C. Peter Rydell, Matthew Sanders, and James Chiesa. 1998. *Investing in Our Children*. Santa Monica, Calif.: Rand Institute.

Kornfeld, Robert, and Howard S. Bloom. 1999. "Measuring Program Impacts on Earnings and Employment: Do Unemployment Insurance Wage Reports from Employers Agree with Surveys of Individuals?" *Journal of Labor Economics* 17, no. 1: 168–197.

Krueger, Alan. 1999. "Experimental Estimates of Educational Production Functions." *Quarterly Journal of Economics* 114, no. 2 (May): 497–532.

Krueger, Alan. 2003. "Economic Considerations and Class Size." *Economic Journal*, forthcoming.

Krueger, Alan, and Mikael Lindahl. 2001. "Education and Growth: Why and for Whom?" *Journal of Economic Literature* 39, no. 4 (December): 1101–1136.

Krueger, Alan, and Diane Whitmore. 2001. "Would Smaller Classes Help Close the Black-White Achievement Gap?" Industrial Relations Section working paper no. 451, Princeton University.

Kuznets, Simon. 1955. "Economic Growth and Income Inequality." *American Economic Review* 45, no. 1 (March): 1–28.

Link, Charles, and James Mulligan. 1986. "The Merits of a Longer School Day." *Economics of Education Review* 5, no. 4 (1986): 373–381.

Lochner, Lance. 1999. "Education, Work, and Crime: Theory and Evidence." Rochester Center for Economic Research working paper no. 465.

Love, John, Ellen Kisker, Christine Ross, Peter Schochet, Jeanne Brooks-Gunn, Kimberly Boller, Diane Paulsell, Allison Fuligni, and Lisa Berlin. 2001. *Building Their Futures: How Early Head Start Programs Are Enhancing the Lives of Infants and Toddlers in Low-Income Families*. Vol. 1, *Technical Report*. Princeton: Mathematica Policy Research. Available online at ⟨http://www.mathematica-mpr.com/PDFs/buildingvol1.pdf⟩.

Lundberg, Shelly, and Richard Startz. 1983. "Private Discrimination and Social Intervention in Competitive Labor Markets." *American Economic Review* 73, no. 3 (June): 340–347.

Mallar, Charles, Stuart Kerachsky, Craig Thornton, and David Long. 1982. *Evaluation of the Economic Impact of the Job Corps Program: Third Follow-Up Report.* Princeton: Mathematica Policy Research.

Mosteller, Frederick. 1995. "The Tennessee Study of Class Size in the Early School Grades." *The Future of Children: Critical Issues for Children and Youths* 5 (summer/fall): 113–127.

Murphy, Kevin M., Andrei Shleifer, and Robert Vishny. 1991. "The Allocation of Talent: Implications for Growth." *Quarterly Journal of Economics* 106, no. 2 (May): 503–530.

Nelson, Richard, and Edmund Phelps. 1966. "Investment in Humans, Technological Diffusion, and Economic Growth." *American Economic Review* 56, no. 2 (March): 69–75.

Nelson, Robert. 1991. *Reaching for Heaven on Earth.* Savage, Md.: Rowman & Littlefield.

Nozick, Robert. 1974. *Anarchy, State, and Utopia.* New York: Basic.

Nye, Barbara, Jayne Zaharias, B. Dewayne Fulton, C. M. Achilles, Van Cain, and Dana Tollett. 1994. *The Lasting Benefits Study: A Continuing Analysis of the Effect of Small Class Size in Kindergarten through Third Grade on Student Achievement Test Scores in Subsequent Grade Levels.* Seventh Grade Technical Report. Nashville: Center of Excellence for Research in Basic Skills, Tennessee State University.

Orr, Larry, Howard Bloom, Stephen Bell, Winston Lin, George Cave, and Fred Doolittle. 1994. *The National JTPA Study: Impacts, Benefits, and Costs of Title II-A.* Bethesda, Md.: Abt Associates.

Pauly, Mark V. 1967. "Mixed Public and Private Financing of Education: Efficiency and Feasibility." *American Economic Review* 57, no. 1 (March): 120–130.

Pauly, Mark V. 1971. *Medical Care at Public Expense: A Study in Applied Welfare Economics.* New York: Praeger.

Peltzman, Sam. 1997. "Class Size and Earnings." *Journal of Economic Perspectives* 11, no. 4 (fall): 225–226.

Pen, Jan. 1971. *Income Distribution: Facts, Theories, Policies.* New York: Praeger.

Persson, Torsten, and Guido Tabellini. 1994. "Is Inequality Harmful for Growth?" *American Economic Review* 84, no. 3 (June): 600–621.

Pierce, Brooks. 2001. "Compensation Inequality." *Quarterly Journal of Economics* 116, no. 4 (November): 1493–1525.

Piketty, Thomas, and Emmanuel Saez. 1998. "Income Inequality in the United States, 1913–1998." *The Quarterly Journal of Economics* 118, no. 1 (February): 1–40.

Rawls, John. 1971. *A Theory of Justice*. Cambridge: Belknap Press of Harvard University Press.

Romer, Paul. 1990. "Endogenous Technological Change." *Journal of Political Economy* 98, no. 5 (October): 71–102.

Sen, Amartya. 1973. *On Economic Inequality*. Oxford: Clarendon.

Shea, John. 2000. "Does Parents' Money Matter?" *Journal of Public Economics* 77, no. 2 (August): 155–184.

Small, Steven L., Diane K. Flores, and Douglas C. Noll. 1998. "Different Neural Circuits Subserve Reading before and after Therapy for Acquired Dyslexia." *Brain and Language* 62, no. 2: 298–308.

Smeeding, Timothy, Lee Rainwater, and Gary Burtless. 2001. "United States Poverty in a Cross-National Context." In *Understanding Poverty*, Sheldon Danziger and Robert Maveman, eds. New York: Russell Sage Foundation.

Smith, Adam. [1776]. *The Wealth of Nations*. New York: Random House.

Smith, James P. 1999. "Healthy Bodies and Thick Wallets: The Dual Relation between Health and Economic Status." *Journal of Economic Perspectives* 13, no. 2 (spring): 145–166.

Solon, Gary. 2002. "Cross-Country Differences in Intergenerational Earnings Mobility." *Journal of Economic Perspectives* 16, no. 3: 59–66.

Stille, Alexander. 2001. "Grounded by an Income Gap." *New York Times*, 15 December.

Summers, Anita, and Barbara Wolfe. 1977. "Do Schools Make a Difference?" *American Economic Review* 67, no. 4 (September): 639–652.

Summers, Lawrence. 1987. "Investment Incentives and the Discounting of Depreciation Allowances." In *The Effects of Taxation on Capital Accumulation*, Martin Feldstein, ed. Chicago: University of Chicago Press.

Thurow, Lester. 1975. *Generating Inequality: The Distributional Mechanisms of the Economy*. New York: Basic Books.

United States General Accounting Office. 1996. *Job Training Partnership Act: Long-Term Earnings and Employment Outcomes*. GAO/HEHS-96-40. Washington, D.C.

Ways and Means Committee, U.S. House of Representatives. 2000. *Green Book 2000*. Washington, D.C.

Wilkenson, Richard. 1996. *Unhealthy Societies: The Afflictions of Inequality*. London: Routledge.

Williamson, Jeffrey, and Peter Lindert. 1980. *American Inequality: A Macroeconomic History*. New York: Academic.

Wolff, Edward. 2002. *Top Heavy: The Increasing Inequality of Wealth in America and What Can Be Done about It*. New York: New Press.

Word, Elizabeth, John Johnston, Helen Bain, B. Dewayne Fulton, Jayne Zaharias, Charles M. Achilles, Martha Lintz, John Folger, and Carolyn Breda. 1990. *The State of Tennessee's Student/Teacher Achievement Ratio (STAR) Project: Technical Report 1985–1990*. Nashville: Tennessee State Department of Education.

2 Human Capital Policy

Pedro Carneiro and
James J. Heckman

1. Introduction and Motivation

Introduction

The aphorism that the source of a nation's wealth is the skill of its people has special meaning for contemporary American society. Growth in the quality of the U.S. workforce has been a major source of productivity growth and economic mobility over the past century. By many measures, since 1980, the quality of the U.S. workforce has stagnated, or its growth has slowed down dramatically (see Ellwood 2001; Jorgenson and Ho 1999; DeLong, Goldin, and Katz 2003).[1] Figure 2.1 shows that after a half century of progress, cohorts born after 1950 did not improve much, or at all, on the educational attainment of their predecessors. This is true for Americans of all racial and ethnic backgrounds. Moreover, the stagnation in educational attainment in the aggregate is not due solely to migration. Although immigrants in general are more unskilled than the remainder of the workforce and contribute to growth in the pool of unskilled labor, stagnation in aggregate college participation is also found among native-born Americans, although immigrants do contribute to the growing pool of high school dropouts (figure 2.2).

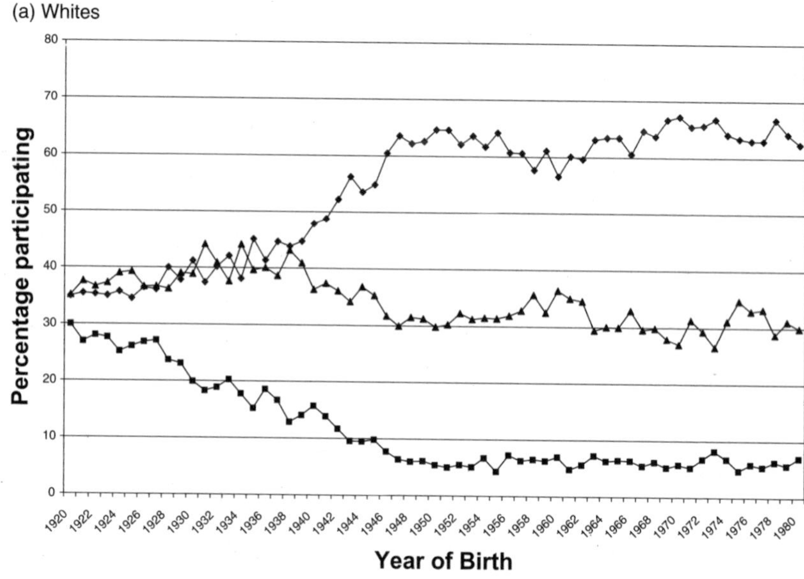
(a) Whites
Percentage participating
Year of Birth
0
10
20
30
40
50
60
70
80
1920
1922
1924
1926
1928
1930
1932
1934
1936
1938
1940
1942
1944
1946
1948
1950
1952
1954
1956
1958
1960
1962
1964
1966
1968
1970
1972
1974
1976
1978
1980

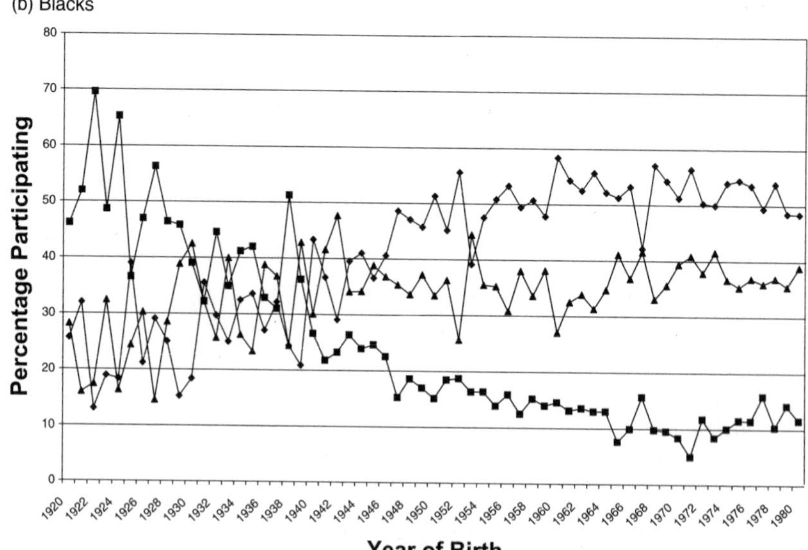
(b) Blacks
Percentage Participating
Year of Birth
0
10
20
30
40
50
60
70
80
1920
1922
1924
1926
1928
1930
1932
1934
1936
1938
1940
1942
1944
1946
1948
1950
1952
1954
1956
1958
1960
1962
1964
1966
1968
1970
1972
1974
1976
1978
1980

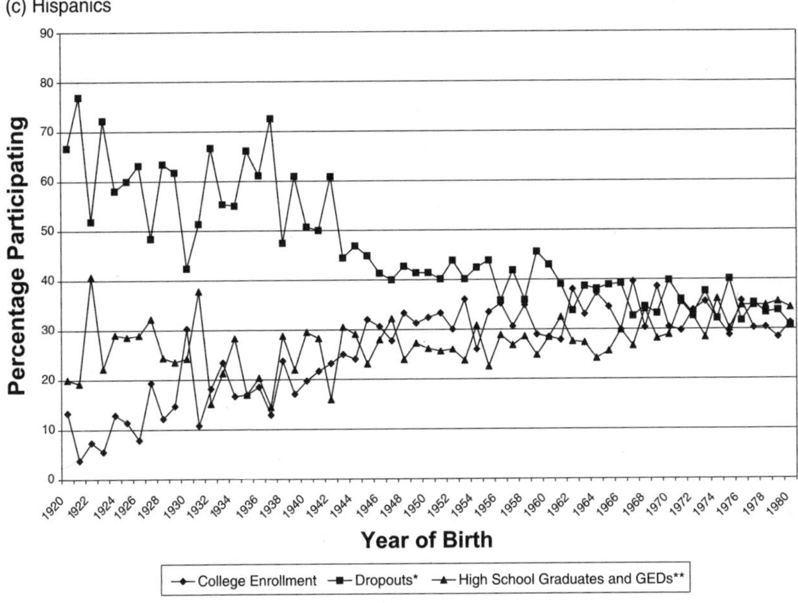

Figure 2.1
School participation rates by year of birth.
Source: Data from 2000 Current Population Survey.
*Dropouts excluding GED holders
**GED holders are known for the Birth cohort 1971–1982

Unpleasant as these numbers are, the official statistics paint an overly optimistic picture because they count those who have exam-certified high school equivalents (i.e., General Educational Development or "GED") as high school graduates. According to these statistics, the high school graduation rate is increasing and the high school dropout rate decreasing (see figure 2.3a). Recent studies (Cameron and Heckman 1993; Boesel, Alsalam, and Smith 1998; and Heckman 2003) show that those with GEDs perform the

(a) College participation rates by year of birth

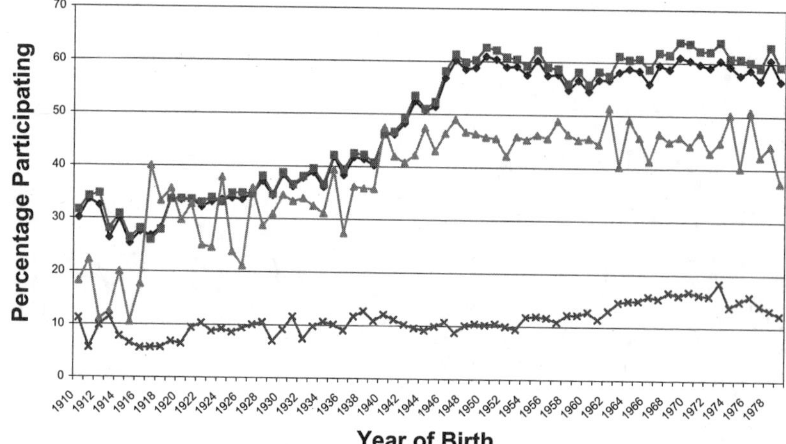

(b) High school dropout rates (excluding GED holders) by year of birth

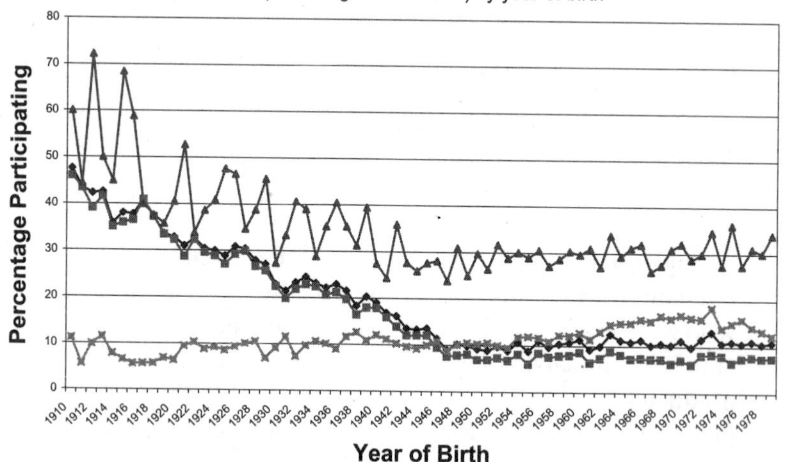

(c) Percentage of overall educational participation due to immigrants by year of birth

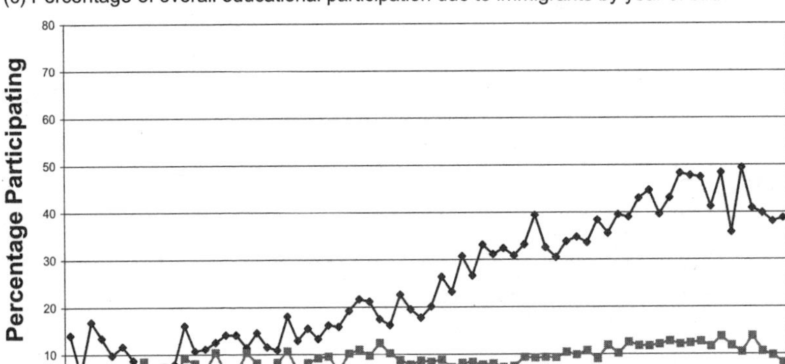

Figure 2.2
Educational participation rates by year of birth.
Source: Data from 2000 Current Population Survey.

same in the labor market as high school dropouts with comparable schooling levels. The percentage of measured high school graduates who receive the status by route of the GED is growing and is as high as 25 percent in some states (see figure 2.3b). As a result, the quality of measured high school graduates is declining. When GEDs are classified as dropouts, the U.S. high school dropout rate is increasing, and not decreasing as the official statistics indicate (see figure 2.3c).

The slowdown in the growth of the quality of the U.S. labor force comes in a period of increasing wage differentials between skilled and unskilled workers and contributes

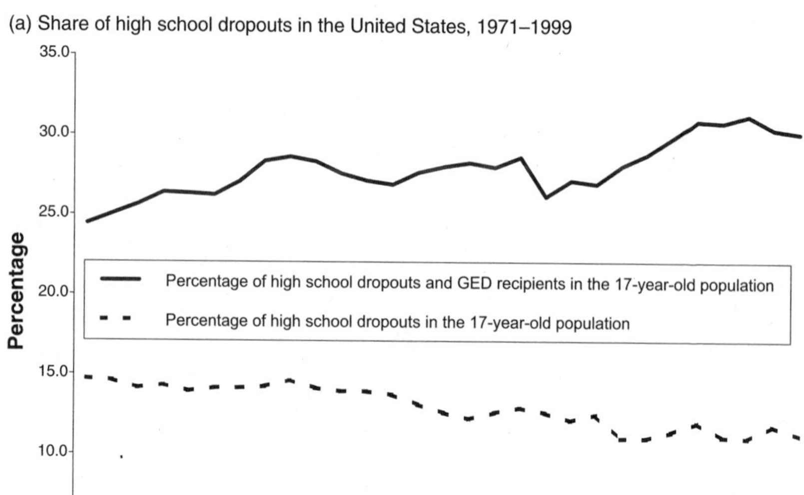
(a) Share of high school dropouts in the United States, 1971–1999
Percentage
Year
Percentage of high school dropouts and GED recipients in the 17-year-old population
Percentage of high school dropouts in the 17-year-old population

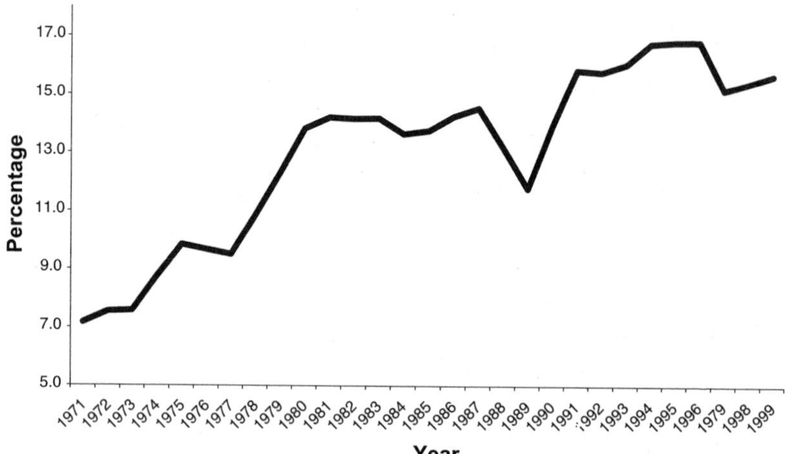
(b) Number of people receiving high school equivalency credentials as a percentage of total high school credentials issued by public schools, private schools, and the GED program, United States, 1971–1999
Percentage
Year

(c) High school graduates of regular day school programs, public and private, as a percentage of seventeen-year-old population, United States, 1971–1999

Figure 2.3
Educational statistics by category over time.
Source: Based on data from (1) The Department of Education National Center for Education Statistics and (2) American Council on Education, General Educational Development Testing Service

to the growth in those differentials and to overall wage inequality. The measured wage premium for higher-skilled workers began to increase substantially around 1980 (see Autor and Katz 1999). In response to the economic incentives provided by the increase in the wage premium, children from certain socioeconomic groups increased their college attendance in the 1980s. This response has not been uniform across racial, ethnic, or family income groups, however, even though the return to schooling has increased for all groups. Adolescent white male high school graduates from the top half of the family income distribution began to increase their college attendance rate in 1980 (see figure 2.4). Those from the third quartile of the family income distribution were less likely to attend college than those from the top half, and delayed their response to the rising wage premium for skill. The response to the wage premium was even more delayed for white male high school graduates at the bottom of the family income distribution. Thus already substantial gaps in college attendance among those from different income groups widened. Racial and ethnic gaps in attendance also widened (see figure 2.5).[2] Because education is a primary determinant of earnings, these differential

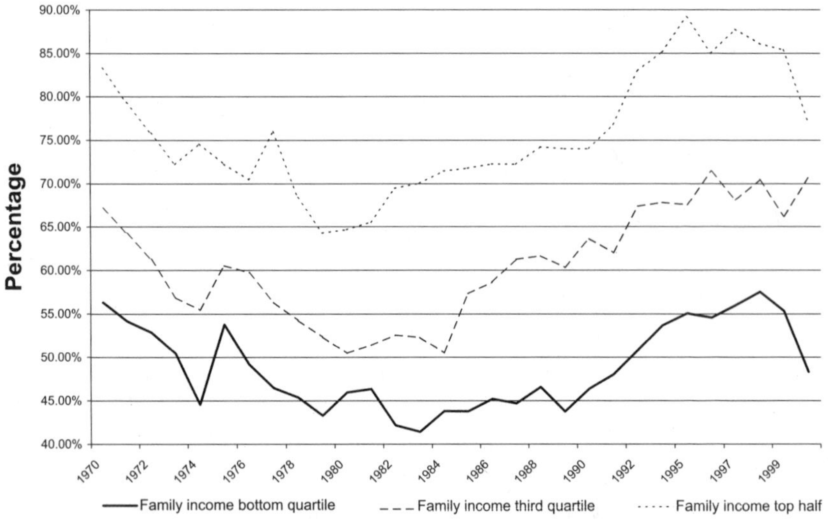

Figure 2.4
College participation of high school graduates and GED holders by family income quartile, dependent* white males, ages eighteen to twenty-four.
Source: Computed from the CPS P-20 School Reports and the October CPS.
* Dependent means living at parental home or supported by parental family while at college

responses to the increased market demand for skills will widen racial, ethnic, and family-origin wage differentials in the next generation, making the America of tomorrow even more unequal than the America of today and the America of the past.

In the face of declining real wages for low-skilled workers and increasing real returns to college graduation, a greater proportion of U.S. youth are low-skilled dropouts than thirty years ago. College enrollment responses to the increasing return to schooling have been weak. This is in spite of the growth in per pupil expenditure in public schools

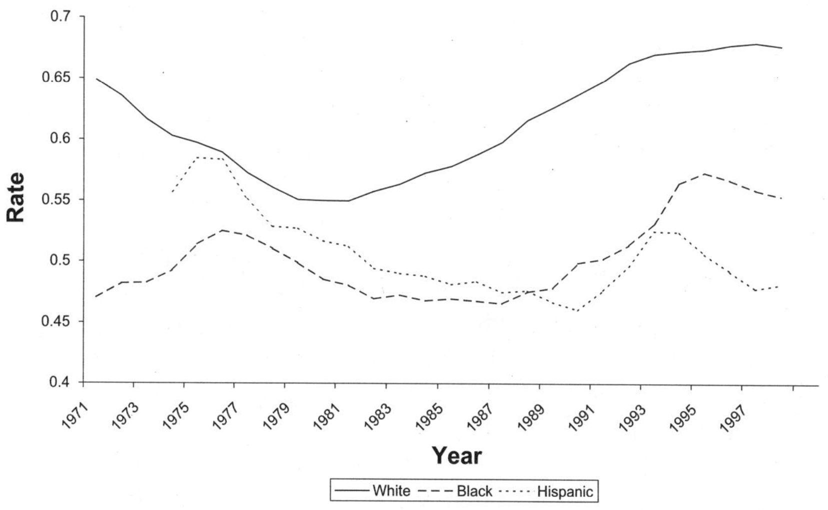

Figure 2.5
College participation by race for dependent* high school graduates and GED holders, males, ages eighteen to twenty-four.
Source: These numbers were computed from the CPS P-20 School Reports and the October CPS.
Note: Three-year moving averages are shown. * Dependent means living at parental home or supported by parental family while at college.

over the past thirty years. Together with the decline in high school graduation has come a decline in the academic performance of American students (see Hanushek 2003). America has an underclass of unskilled and illiterate persons with no counterpart in northern Europe (see Blau and Khan 2001).

The problem is clear. The supply of skilled workers is not keeping pace with demand. How to increase the supply of skilled workers in an economically efficient way is not so clear, and there are many advocates of fundamentally different policies that are difficult to compare because their costs and benefits have not been tabulated. Many recent discussions seize upon the gaps in schooling attainment by family income, evident in figure 2.4, as a major causal factor in the failure of the supply of skilled workers to increase. The growth in college tuition costs over the past twenty years and the decline in the earnings of families headed by low-skilled workers are often cited to explain college attendance patterns of their children (see Carnevale and Fry 2000, and Hauser 1993). Policies are proposed to reduce tuition or supplement family resources of children in the college-going years. Yet the evidence presented in this chapter suggests that longer-term factors such as parental environments and family income available to children over their entire life cycle are far more decisive in promoting college readiness and social attachment than family income in the adolescent years. This evidence suggests that factors operating during the early childhood years and culminating in adolescence in the form of crystallized cognitive abilities, attitudes, and social skills play far more important roles than tuition or family credit constraints during the college-going years in explaining minority-majority gaps in socioeconomic attainment. It suggests that tuition reduction may be much less effective in increasing college attendance rates than policies that foster cognitive abilities.

In this chapter we critically examine the claim that liquidity constraints in the college-going years play a fundamental role in explaining the gaps in college attendance evident in figure 2.4. We present evidence that a small group of people is credit-constrained in this short-run sense, and that policies that relieve the constraints this group faces may be cost effective. Nonetheless, according to our analysis, relieving all short-term credit constraints is unlikely to reduce gaps in schooling participation substantially.

We also suggest a variety of other policies to improve the quality of skills in the American economy. Policies to improve the quality of secondary schools are often put forward, and debates over such policies are intense. We argue that such policies are unlikely to have any substantial effect on the quality of the U.S. workforce unless more fundamental reforms in incentives in schools are made. Second-chance remediation programs such as publicly provided job training or exam certification as an alternative to conventional high school graduation (GED programs) are sometimes suggested as effective low-cost strategies to overcome early disadvantage. We show that the economic return to such programs is low. Tax and subsidy policies are also advocated to address early disadvantage. We find that such policies are likely to have only modest effects on skill formation. Policies to limit the immigration of the unskilled are also proposed to alleviate downward pressure on wages and to reduce inequality (see Borjas 1999). We argue that such policies are likely to be ineffective.

There is no shortage of policy proposals. There is, however, a shortage of empirical evidence on the efficacy of the proposed policies. No common framework has been used to evaluate them or compare them. The goal of this chapter is to provide evidence on the effectiveness of alternative policies within a common cost-benefit framework.

This chapter analyzes policies that are designed to foster skill formation in the American economy. A central premise of this chapter is that effective policy is based on empirically grounded studies of the sources of the problems that the proposed policies are intended to address. Although it is possible through trial and error to stumble onto effective policies without understanding the sources of the problems that motivate them, a more promising approach to human capital policy formulation is to understand the mechanisms and institutions that produce skill, how they are related, and where they have failed.

Human capital accumulation is a dynamic process. The skills acquired in one stage of the life cycle affect both the initial conditions and the technology of learning at the next stage. Human capital is produced over the life cycle by families, schools, and firms, although most discussions of skill formation focus on schools as the major producer of abilities and skills, despite a substantial body of evidence that families and firms are also major producers of abilities and skills.

A major determinant of successful schools is successful families. Schools work with what parents bring them. They operate more effectively if parents reinforce them by encouraging and motivating children. Job training programs, whether public or private, work with what families and schools supply them and cannot remedy twenty years of neglect.

Recent studies in child development (e.g., Shonkoff and Phillips 2000) emphasize that different stages of the life cycle are critical to the formation of different types of abilities.

When the opportunities for formation of these abilities are missed, remediation is costly, and full remediation is often prohibitively costly. These findings highlight the need to take a comprehensive view of skill formation over the life cycle that is grounded in the best science and economics so that effective policies for increasing the low level of skills in the workforce can be devised.

A study of human capital policy grounded in economic and scientific fundamentals improves on a purely empirical approach to policy evaluation that relies on evaluations of the programs and policies in place or previously experienced. Although any trustworthy study of economic policy must be grounded in data, it is also important to recognize that the policies that can be evaluated empirically are only a small subset of the policies that might be tried. If we base speculation about economic policies on economic fundamentals, rather than solely on estimated "treatment effects" that are only weakly related to economic fundamentals, we are in a better position to think beyond what has been tried to propose more innovative solutions to human capital problems. This chapter investigates the study of human capital policy by placing it in the context of economic models of life cycle learning and skill accumulation rather than focusing exclusively on which policies have "worked" in the past.

We use the rate of return, in cases where it is justified, to place different policies on a common footing. Our justification for using the marginal rate of return to human capital compared to the market return on physical capital in evaluating human capital projects is presented in appendix A. For many, but not all, human capital policies, the marginal rate of return is an accurate guide to determining where the next dollar should be spent. We also compute present values of alternative policies where possible. Present values are not subject to the criticisms that are directed toward rates of return.

Figure 2.6 summarizes the major theme of this chapter. It plots the rate of return to human capital at different stages of the life cycle for a person of given abilities. The horizontal axis represents age, which is a surrogate for the agent's position in the life cycle. The vertical axis represents the rate of return to investment assuming the same investment is made at each age. Ceteris paribus the rate of return to a dollar of investment made while a person is young is higher than the rate of return to the same dollar made at a later age. Early investments are harvested over a longer horizon than those made later in the life cycle. In addition, because early investments raise the productivity (lower the costs) of later investments, human capital is synergistic. This dynamic complementarity in human investment was ignored in the early work on human capital (Becker 1964).[3] Learning begets learning; skills (both cognitive and noncognitive) acquired early on facilitate later learning. For an externally specified opportunity cost of funds r (represented by the horizontal line with intercept r in figure 2.6a), an optimal investment strategy is to invest less in the old and more in the young. Figure 2.6b presents the optimal investment quantity counterpart of figure 2.6a.

We also develop a second interpretation of figure 2.6a in this chapter: that it is an empirical description of the economic returns to investment at current levels of spending in the American economy. The return to investment in the young is apparently quite high; the return to investment in the old and less able is quite low. A socially optimal investment strategy would equate returns across all investment levels. A central empirical conclusion of this chapter is that

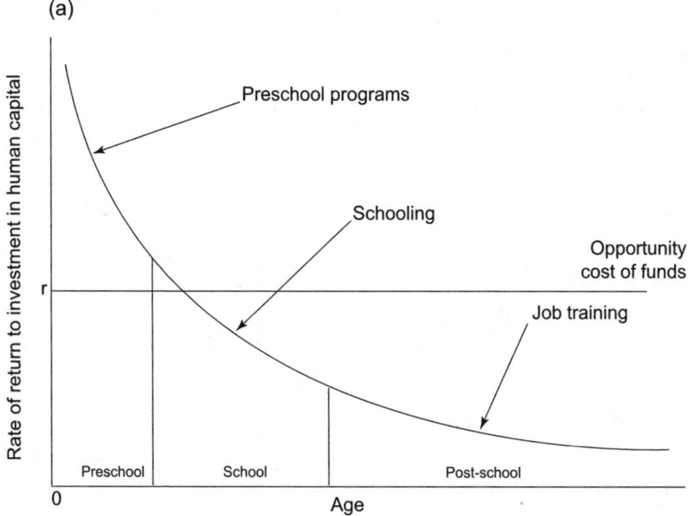

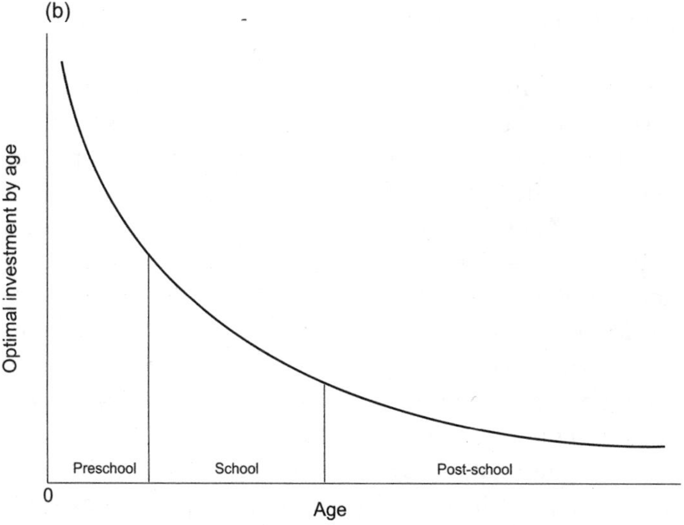

Figure 2.6
(a) Rates of return to human capital investment initially setting investment to be equal across all ages; (b) Optimal investment levels.

at *current* investment levels, efficiency in public spending would be enhanced if human capital investment were directed more toward the young and away from older, less-skilled, and illiterate persons for whom human capital is a poor investment.

Our analysis challenges the conventional point of view that equates skill with intelligence and draws on a body of research that demonstrates the importance of both cognitive and noncognitive skills in determining socioeconomic success. Both types of skills are affected by families and schools, but they differ in their malleability over the life cycle, with noncognitive skills being more malleable than cognitive skills at later ages. Differences in levels of cognitive and noncognitive skills by family income and family background emerge early and persist. If anything, schooling widens these early differences.

Current educational policy and economic analysis focuses on tested academic achievement as the major output of schools. Proposed systems for evaluating school performance are often premised on this idea. Economic models of signaling and screening assume that cognitive ability is an important determinant, if not *the* most important determinant, of academic and economic success. Recent evidence challenges this view. No doubt, cognitive ability is an important factor in schooling and labor market outcomes. At the same time, noncognitive abilities, although harder to measure, also play an important role.

Noncognitive abilities matter for success both in the labor market and in schooling. This finding is supported by studies of early childhood interventions that primarily improve noncognitive skills, with substantial effects on schooling and labor market outcomes, but only weakly affect cognitive ability. Mentoring programs in the early teenage years can also affect these skills. Current analyses of skill formation focus too much on cognitive ability and too little on noncognitive ability in evaluating human capital interventions.

We also depart from the conventional human capital literature in another respect. The early literature stressed that human capital theory was an alternative to ability-based models of earnings. In our analysis, while cognitive ability is affected by schooling and family background, schooling does not equalize differences in cognitive ability. Cognitive ability is thus a form of human capital and not a rival to it.

This chapter also stresses the need for clear analytical frameworks for comparing alternative policies. Good economic policy evaluation accounts for the limited size of the government budget and the opportunity costs of public funds. Saying that an educational project earns a 10 percent rate of return and should be supported is a meaningless statement unless the opportunities foregone, including the other projects that could have been funded and the costs of tax revenues, are properly accounted for. We emphasize the importance of cost-benefit analyses that properly account for the full costs of policies, including the social-opportunity costs of funds for public projects. Many analyses of human capital programs ignore direct costs and the costs of taxation in presenting cost-benefit calculations. When these costs are counted properly, many apparently successful policies are shown to be economically unprofitable.

It is important to account for policies in place when one is evaluating new policies that are introduced to supplement existing efforts. One should distinguish statements about a world in which there is no human capital policy from the world in which we live. The relevant question for this chapter is whether we should increase current subsidies to education and job training, and not whether there should be any subsidies at all. At a very low level of expenditure, increasing schooling quality is known to improve schooling outcomes. Increasing the level of schooling undoubtedly produces externalities when schooling is at a low level. The current subsidy of direct costs to students at major public universities in the U.S. is around 80 percent, however, and the rate of subsidization is even higher for secondary and primary schools. The scope for further subsidies is correspondingly reduced.

One topic we do not discuss is the case for subsidies arising from human capital externalities. Although such externalities have received prominent play in the recent revival of growth theory, no evidence for them at *the current level of spending* has been found. An accumulating body of evidence (e.g., Acemoglu and Angrist 2001; Heckman, Layne-Farrar, and Todd 1996; Heckman and Klenow 1998) suggests that these theoretical possibilities are empirically irrelevant.

This chapter is organized in four parts, of which this introduction is the first. The second part lays the foundation for our policy analysis by examining the sources of skill disparities. A major premise of our chapter is that good policy is based on a clear understanding of the problems that policies are intended to address. We seek to elevate the discussion of skill formation policy above the level of the standard treatment effect approach that discusses what "works" and what does not. In the first section of this part, we present evidence on the relative importance of short-term credit constraints and cognitive ability in accounting for disparities in educational attainment (evidence on job training is presented in the third part). In the second section, we present evidence on the early origin of cognitive-ability differentials and their determinants. In the third section, we present a similar analysis of noncognitive skills.

This chapter's third part draws on the analysis of the second part and discusses specific policies. The first section of this part discusses policies designed to improve primary and secondary schooling. We demonstrate the ineffectiveness of policies designed to improve schooling quality at existing levels of expenditure without reforms in incentives and choices in schools. Such policies are ineffective in terms of a cost-benefit analysis. The second section discusses the evidence on early childhood policies. The greatest effect of early childhood programs is on noncognitive skills, motivation and achievement, not on IQ. The third section discusses adolescent-mentoring policies. We know that adolescent-mentoring programs are effective and operate primarily through motivation of participants. The fourth section discusses the evidence on the effectiveness of both public and private job training programs. Although some public job training programs are successful, most are not. The ones that are successful provide classroom education. Private training is much more successful. We present evidence that private training reinforces early differentials in ability and schooling but compensates for early disadvantages in access to funds. This latter feature of private training tends to offset the dynamic complementarity of the former feature. On net, job training is neutral with respect to family background. The fifth section discusses tax and subsidy policy. Tax policy is an unlikely strategy for eliminating skill differentials. The sixth section discusses the problem of the transition and the likely effectiveness of wage subsidies. The seventh section briefly discusses migration policy. The separation of topics into the paper's second and third parts is far from exact. Some of the evidence on the skill formation process is obtained from analyzing specific policies. This chapter's fourth part concludes. We then present two appendices; one discusses rates of return and discount rates and the other complements the computations reported in part 2.

2. Sources of Skill Differences

The Evidence on Credit Constraints

There is a strong relationship between family income and college attendance. Figure 2.4 displays aggregate time series college participation rates for eighteen- to twenty-four-year-old American males classified by their parental income, as measured in the child's late adolescent years. There are substantial differences in college participation rates across family income classes in each year. This pattern is found in many other countries (see Blossfeld and Shavit 1993). In the late 1970s or early 1980s, college participation rates started to increase in response to increasing returns to schooling, but only for youth from the top family income groups. This differential educational response by income class promises to perpetuate or widen income inequality across generations and among racial and ethnic groups.

There are two, not necessarily mutually exclusive, interpretations of this evidence. The first, more common interpretation of the evidence, and the one that guides current policy, is the obvious one: credit constraints facing families in a child's adolescent years affect the resources required to finance a college education. A second interpretation emphasizes more long-run factors associated with higher family income. It notes that family income is strongly correlated over the child's life cycle. Families with high income in a child's adolescent years are more likely to have high income throughout the child's life at home. Better family resources in a child's formative years are associated with higher quality of education and better environments that foster cognitive and noncognitive skills.

Both interpretations of the evidence are consistent with a form of credit constraint. The first interpretation is clearly consistent with the notion of short-term credit constraints. But the second interpretation is consistent with another type of credit constraint: the inability of the child to buy the parental environment and genes that form the cognitive and noncognitive abilities required for success in school. This interpretation renders a market failure as a type of credit constraint.[4]

This chapter argues on quantitative grounds that the second interpretation of figure 2.4 is by far the more important one. Controlling for ability formed by the early teenage years, parental income plays only a minor role in explaining education gaps. The evidence from the United States presented in this chapter suggests that at most 8 percent of American youth are subject to short-term liquidity constraints that affect their postsecondary schooling. Most of the family income gap in enrollment is due to long-term factors that produce the abilities needed to benefit from participation in college.

In this section, we first summarize the evidence against an influential argument advanced by Card (1999, 2001) and others. That argument claims that the evidence that instrumental variables (IV) estimates of the wage returns to schooling (the Mincer coefficient) exceed ordinary least squares (OLS) estimates demonstrates the importance of short-term credit constraints. We discuss why this argument is uninformative about the presence or absence of short-term credit constraints in explaining educational attainment differentials or skill deficits.

We also consider a number of other arguments advanced in the literature in support of the empirical importance of short-term credit constraints.

- Kane (1994) claims that college enrollment is more sensitive to tuition for people from poorer families. Greater tuition sensitivity of the poor, even if empirically true, does not prove that they are constrained. Kane's empirical evidence has been challenged by Cameron and Heckman (1999, 2001). Conditioning on ability, responses to tuition are uniform across income groups.
- Cameron and Heckman also show that adjusting for long-term family factors (measured by ability or parental background) mostly eliminates ethnic or racial gaps in schooling. We extend Cameron and Heckman's analysis and eliminate most of the family income gaps in enrollment by conditioning on long-term factors.
- We also examine a recent qualification of the Cameron and Heckman analysis by Ellwood and Kane (2000), who claim to produce evidence of substantial credit constraints. For several dimensions of college attendance, adjusting for long-term factors in their type of analysis eliminates any role for short-term credit constraints associated with family income.
- We also scrutinize the arguments advanced in support of short-term credit constraints that (a) the rate of return to human capital is higher than that to physical capital and (b) rates of return to education are higher for individuals from low-income families or for individuals with low ability.

The evidence assembled in this section suggests that the first-order explanation for gaps in enrollment in college by family income is long-run family factors that are crystallized in ability. Short-run income constraints do play a role in creating these gaps, albeit a quantitatively minor one. There is scope for intervention to alleviate these short-term constraints, but one should not expect to reduce the enrollment gaps in figure 2.4 substantially by eliminating such constraints.

Family Income and Enrollment in College The argument that short-term family credit constraints are the most plausible explanation for the relationship depicted in figure 2.4 starts by noting that human capital is different from physical capital. With the abolition of slavery and indentured servitude, there is no asset market for human capital. People cannot sell rights to their future labor earnings to potential lenders to secure financing for their human capital investments. Even if they could, there would be substantial problems in enforcing performance of contracts on future earnings given that persons control their own labor supply and the effort and quality of their work. The lack of collateral on the part of borrowers and the inability to monitor effort by lenders are widely cited reasons for current large-scale government interventions to finance education.

If people had to rely on their own resources to finance all of their schooling costs, undoubtedly the level of educational attainment in society would decline. To the extent that subsidies do not cover the full costs of college tuition, persons are forced to raise funds to pay tuition through private loans, through work while in college, or through foregone consumption. This may affect the choice of college quality, the content of the educational experience, the decision of when to enter college, the length of time it takes to complete schooling, and even graduation from college. Children from families with higher incomes have access to resources that are not available to children from low-income families, although children from higher-income families still depend on the good will of their parents to gain access to those resources. Limited access to credit markets means that the costs of funds are higher for the children of the poor, and this limits their enrollment in college.[5] This view apparently explains the evidence that shows that the enrollment response to the rising educational premium that began in the late 1970s or early 1980s was concentrated in the top half of the family income distribution. Low-income whites and minorities began to respond to the rise in the return to college education only in the 1990s. The reduction in the real incomes of parents in the bottom half of the family income distribution, coupled with a growth in real tuition costs, apparently contributes to growing disparity between the college attendance of the children of the rich and of the poor.

An alternative interpretation of the same evidence is that long-run family and environmental factors play a decisive role in shaping the ability and expectations of children. Families with higher levels of resources produce higher-quality children who are better able to perform in school and take advantage of the new market for skills.

Children whose parents have higher incomes have access to better-quality primary and secondary schools. Children's tastes for education and their expectations about their life chances are shaped by those of their parents. Educated parents are better able to develop scholastic aptitude in their children by assisting and directing their studies. It is known that cognitive ability is formed relatively early in life and becomes less malleable as children age. By age 8, intelligence as measured by IQ tests seems to be fairly well set (see the evidence summarized in Heckman 1995). Noncognitive skills are more malleable until the late adolescent years (Heckman 2000). The influences of family factors present from birth through adolescence accumulate to produce ability and college readiness. By the time individuals finish high school and their scholastic ability is determined, the scope of tuition policy for promoting college attendance through boosting cognitive and noncognitive skills is greatly diminished.

The interpretation that stresses the role of family and the environment does not necessarily rule out short-term borrowing constraints as a partial explanation for the patterns revealed in figure 2.4. However, if the finances of poor but motivated families hinder them from providing decent elementary and secondary schooling for their children, and produce a low level of college readiness, government policy aimed at reducing the short-term borrowing constraints for the college expenses of those children during their college-going years is unlikely to be effective in substantially closing the gaps in figure 2.4. In such circumstances, policy that improves the environments that shape ability will be more effective in increasing college enrollment in the long run. The issue can be settled empirically. Surprisingly, until recently there have been few empirical investigations of this topic.

The following experiment captures the essence of the distinction we are making. Suppose families participate in lotteries that are adjusted to have the same expected present value (at age zero of the child) but have different award dates. Credit markets are assumed to be imperfect, at least in part, so the timing of receipts matters. A family that wins the lottery in the child's adolescent years is compared to a family that wins in the child's early formative years. The child from the family that wins late would lack all of the benefits of investment in the early years of the child that the child from the family that wins early would receive. The child from the late-winning family would be likely to have lower levels of cognitive and noncognitive abilities than the child from the early-winning family. Although none of the data we possess are as clean as the data generated by this hypothetical experiment, taken as a whole they point in the general predicted direction.

In this subsection, we critically examine the evidence in the literature and present new arguments and evidence of our own. Evidence exists for both short-run and long-run credit constraints. Long-run family influence factors produce both cognitive and noncognitive abilities that vitally affect schooling. Differences in levels of these skills among children emerge early and, if anything, are strengthened in school. Conditioning on long-term factors eliminates, for all except for a small fraction of young people, most of the effect of family income in the adolescent years on college enrollment decisions. We reach similar conclusions about other dimensions of college participation: delay of entry, final graduation, length of time to complete school, and college quality. For some of these dimensions, adjusting for long-run factors eliminates or even over-adjusts for family income gaps. At most, 8 percent of American youth are constrained in the short-run sense. Credit constraints in the late adolescent years play a role for a small group of youth who can be targeted.

Before turning to our main evidence, we briefly review and criticize the argument that comparisons between IV and OLS estimates of the returns to schooling are informative about the importance of credit constraints.

OLS, IV, and Evidence On Credit-Constrained Schooling

A large body of literature devoted to the estimation of

"causal" effects of schooling has found that in many applications, instrumental-variables (IV) estimates of the return to schooling exceed ordinary-least-squares estimates (see Griliches 1977; Card 1999, 2001). Researchers have used compulsory-schooling laws, distance to the nearest college, and tuition as their instruments to estimate the return to schooling.

Since IV can sometimes be interpreted as estimating the return to schooling for those induced by the selected instrument to change their schooling status, finding higher returns for changers suggests that they are credit-constrained persons who face higher marginal costs of schooling. This argument has become very popular in recent research in the economics of education (see, e.g., Kane 2001; DeLong, Goldin, and Katz 2003).

For three reasons, this evidence is not convincing on the issue of the existence of credit constraints. First, the validity of the instruments used in this literature is questionable (Carneiro and Heckman 2002). These instruments systematically bias upward the estimated return to schooling. Second, even granting the validity of the instruments, the IV-OLS evidence is consistent with empirically well-established models of self-selection or comparative advantage in the labor market even in the absence of credit constraints (Carneiro, Heckman, and Vytlacil 2003; Carneiro and Heckman 2002). Third, the argument ignores the quality margin. One manifestation of credit constraints is lower-quality schooling. Students will attend two-year schools instead of four-year schools, or will attend lower-quality schools at any level of attained years of schooling. This leads to a *lower* Mincer return for credit-constrained people induced to attend college. For further elaboration of these arguments, see Carneiro and Heckman (2002).

An additional criticism of this literature is that, in general, IV does not identify the credit-constrained people for whom it would be useful to target an intervention. Using a direct method like the one described next, we can identify a group of high-ability people who are not going to college, and we can target policy interventions toward them.

Adjusting Family Income Gaps Using Ability or Other Long-Term Family Factors A more direct approach to testing the relative importance of long-run factors versus short-run credit constraints in accounting for the evidence in figure 2.4 is to condition on long-run factors and examine if there is any additional role for short-run credit constraints. Conditioning on observed variables also identifies specific subgroups of persons who might be constrained and who might be targeted advantageously by policies.

Cameron and Heckman (1998, 1999, 2001) compare the estimated effects of family background and family income on college attendance, controlling for scholastic ability (as measured by the Armed Forces Qualifying Test, or AFQT). Measured scholastic ability is influenced by long-term family and environmental factors, which are in turn produced by the long-term permanent income of families. To the extent that the influence of family income on college attendance is diminished by the inclusion of scholastic ability in an analysis of college attendance, one would conclude that long-run family factors crystallized in AFQT scores are the driving forces behind schooling attainment, and not short-term credit constraints. Fitting a life cycle model of schooling to a subsample of the National Longitudinal Survey of Youth (NLSY) data with AFQT measured before high school graduation, Cameron and Heckman examine what portion of the gap between minority youth and whites in school attendance at various levels is due to family income, to tuition costs, and to family background.[6] They find that when they do not control for ability measured at an early age, about half (five points) of the eleven-point gap between black and white college attendance rates is due to family income; more than half (four points) of the seven-point difference between Hispanics and whites is due to family income. When scholastic ability is accounted for, only one half of one point of the eleven-point black-white gap is explained by family income. The gap between Hispanics and whites actually widens when family income is included in the empirical model. Equalizing ability more than accounts for minority-majority college attendance gaps. Cameron and Heckman obtain comparable results when they adjust for parental education and family structure.[7] The effects of tuition on college entry are also greatly weakened when measures of ability are included. Ability and not financial resources in the teenage years accounts for pronounced minority-majority differences in schooling attainment. The disincentive effects of college tuition on college attendance are dramatically weakened when ability is included in the analysis of college attendance. This analysis suggests that long-run factors determine college attendance, not short-term borrowing constraints.

It is sometimes claimed that the enrollment responses to tuition should be larger for constrained (low-income) persons (see Kane 1994 and the survey in Ellwood and Kane 2000). This does not follow from any rigorous argument.[8] Table 2.1, taken from Cameron and Heckman 1999, explicitly addresses this issue empirically. It reports estimates of tuition responses by family income in the adolescent years

Table 2.1
Effects of a $1,000 increase in gross tuition (both two and four year) on the college entry probabilities of high school completers by family income quartile and by AFQT quartile

	Whites (1)	Blacks (2)	Hispanics (3)
A. Overall gross tuition effects			
(1) No explanatory variables except tuition in the model	−.17	−.10	−.10
(2) Baseline specification	−.06	−.04	−.06
(3) Adding AFQT to the row (2) specification	−.05	−.03	−.06
B. By family income quartiles (panel A, row (2) specification)			
(4) Top quartile	−.04	−.01	−.04
(5) Second quartile	−.06	−.03	−.05
(6) Third quartile	−.07	−.07	−.08
(7) Bottom quartile	−.06	−.05	−.08
(8) Joint test of equal effects Across quartiles (*p*-values)	.49	.23	.66
C. By family income quartiles (panel A, row (3) specification)			
(9) Top quartile	−.02	−.02	−.02
(10) Second quartile	−.06	.00	−.05
(11) Third quartile	−.07	−.05	−.09
(12) Bottom quartile	−.04	−.04	−.07
(13) Joint test of equal effects Across quartiles (*p*-values)	.34	.45	.49
D. By AFQT quartiles (panel A, row (3) specification plus tuition-AFQT interaction terms)			
(14) Top quartile	−.03	−.02	−.03
(15) Second quartile	−.06	−.01	−.05
(16) Third quartile	−.06	−.03	−.07
(17) Bottom quartile	−.05	−.03	−.05
(18) Joint test of equal effects Across quartiles (*p*-values)	.60	.84	.68

Table 2.1
(continued)

Source: Cameron and Heckman (1999).
Notes: Gross tuition is the nominal sticker-price of college and excludes scholarship and loan support. These simulations assume both two-year and four-year college tuition increase by $1,000 for the population of high school completers. The baseline specification used in row (2) of panel A and rows (4) through (7) of panel B includes controls for family background, family income, average wages in the local labor market, tuition at local colleges, controls for urban and southern residence, tuition-family income interactions, estimated Pell grant award eligibility, and dummy variables, that indicate the proximity of two- and four-year colleges. Panel D specification adds AFQT and an AFQT-Tuition interaction to the baseline specification.

of the child, not adjusting and adjusting for AFQT (see panels B and C of the table, respectively).[9] Even without adjusting for AFQT, there is no pattern in the estimated tuition response by family income level. When the authors condition on ability, tuition effects become smaller (in absolute value), and no pattern by family income is apparent. Even if the argument that enrollment responses to tuition should be larger for those with low incomes had theoretical validity, there is no empirical support for it.

Ellwood and Kane (2000) accept Cameron and Heckman's main point, that academic ability is a major determinant of college entry. At the same time, they argue that family income operates as an additional constraint, not as powerful as academic ability, but more easily addressed by policy than ability. The left-hand portion of figures 2.7 and 2.8 present our version of Ellwood and Kane's case using data from the NLSY for 1979. Classifying people by ability results in a clear ordering that shows that more able people are more likely to go to college than those who are less able.

(a) Percentage enrolled in two-year and four-year colleges

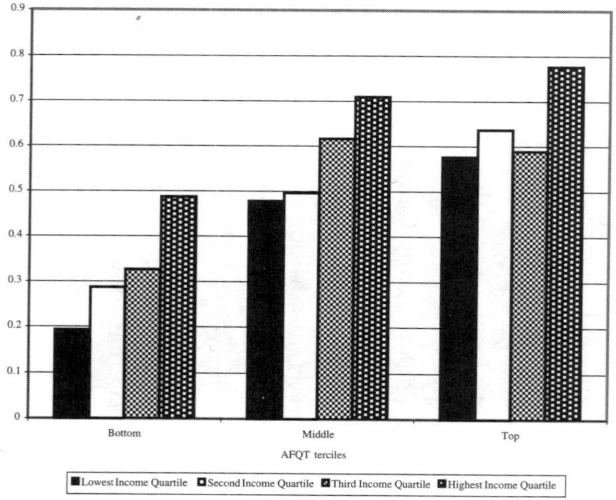

(b) Adjusted percentage enrolled in two-year and four-year colleges

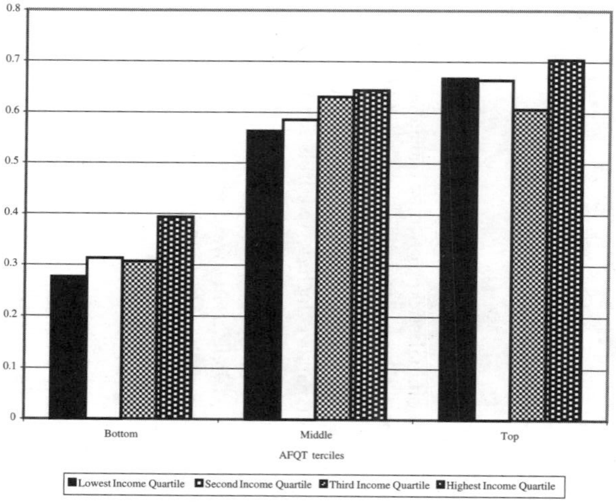

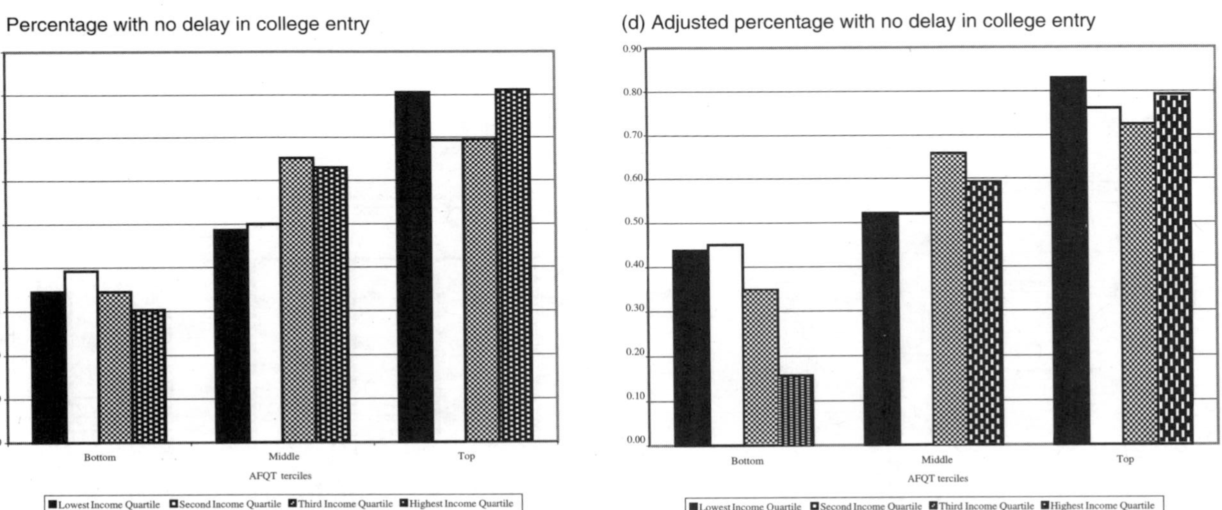
(c) Percentage with no delay in college entry
0.90
0.80
0.70
0.60
0.50
0.40
0.30
0.20
0.10
0.00
Bottom
Middle
Top
AFQT terciles
Lowest Income Quartile
Second Income Quartile
Third Income Quartile
Highest Income Quartile
(d) Adjusted percentage with no delay in college entry
0.90
0.80
0.70
0.60
0.50
0.40
0.30
0.20
0.10
0.00
Bottom
Middle
Top
AFQT terciles
Lowest Income Quartile
Second Income Quartile
Third Income Quartile
Highest Income Quartile

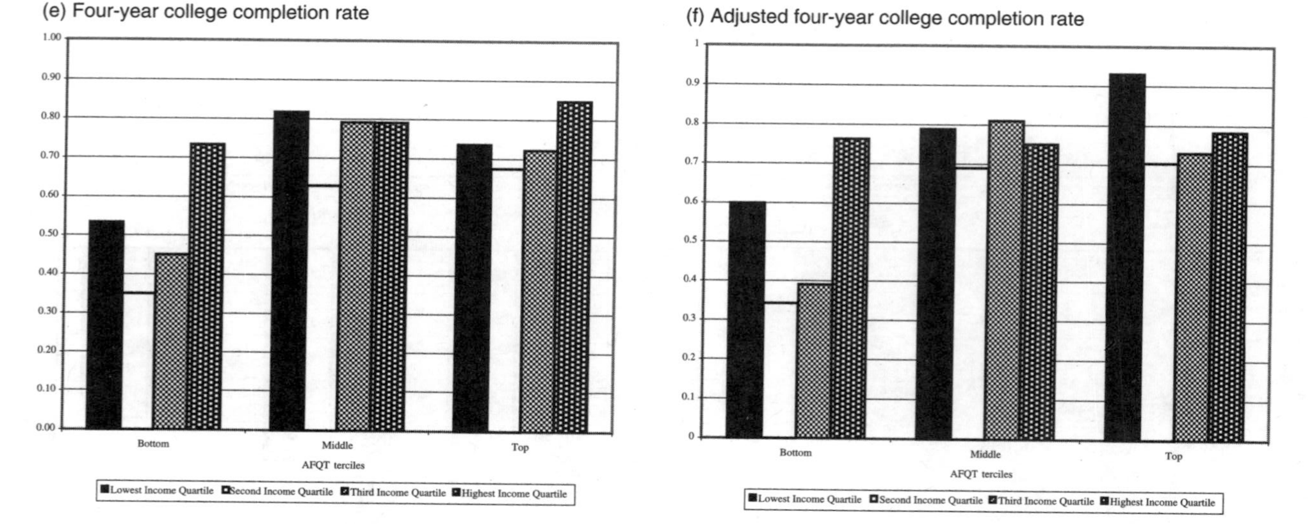

(e) Four-year college completion rate
1.00
0.90
0.80
0.70
0.60
0.50
0.40
0.30
0.20
0.10
0.00
Bottom
Middle
Top
AFQT terciles
Lowest Income Quartile
Second Income Quartile
Third Income Quartile
Highest Income Quartile
(f) Adjusted four-year college completion rate
1
0.9
0.8
0.7
0.6
0.5
0.4
0.3
0.2
0.1
0
Bottom
Middle
Top
AFQT terciles
Lowest Income Quartile
Second Income Quartile
Third Income Quartile
Highest Income Quartile

Figure 2.7
Enrollment, completion, and no-delay rates by family income quartiles and age-adjusted AFQT terciles, white males, NLSY79

Note: To draw these graphs we performed the following steps. (1) Within each AFQT tercile, we regress percentage enrolled, completion rate, and percentage with no delay on family background: $y = a + \mathbf{F}\gamma + Q_1\beta_1 + Q_2\beta_2 + Q_3\beta_3$, where y is percentage enrolled, completion rate, or percentage with no delay, $\mathbf{F}$ is a vector of family background variables (southern origin, broken home, urban origin, mother's education and father's education), Q_1 is a dummy for being in the first quartile of the distribution of family income at 17, Q_2 is for being in the second quartile and Q_3 is for being in the third quartile. (2) Then, within each AFQT tercile, the height of the first bar is given by $a + \overline{\mathbf{F}}\gamma + \beta_1$, the second is given by $a + \overline{\mathbf{F}}\gamma + \beta_2$, the third by $a + \overline{\mathbf{F}}\gamma + \beta_3$ and the fourth by $a + \overline{\mathbf{F}}\gamma$ (where $\overline{\mathbf{F}}$ is a vector of the mean values for the variables in $\mathbf{F}$). The coefficients for the regression are given in the appendix table 2B.2. We correct for the effect of schooling on AFQT.

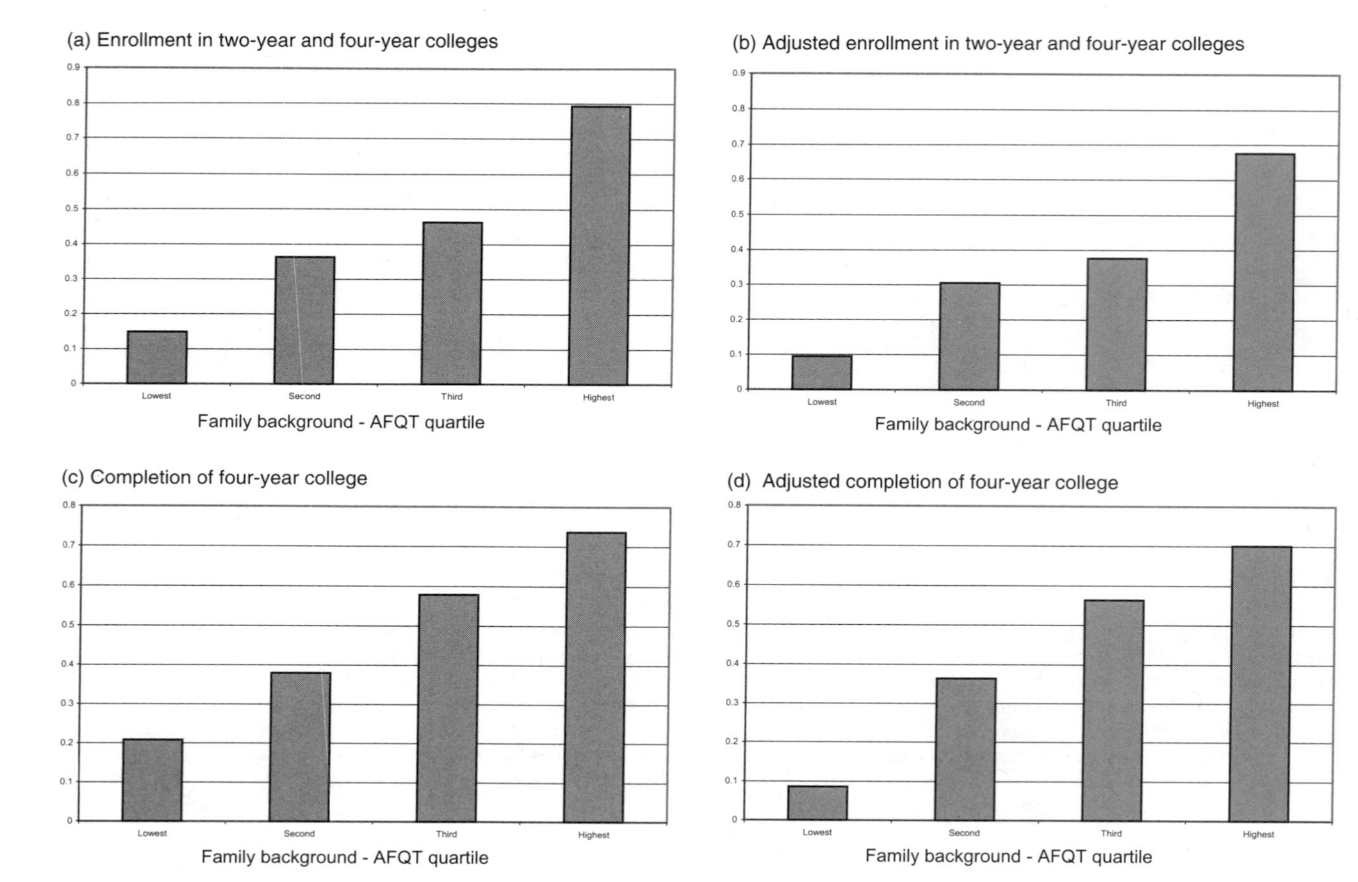
(a) Enrollment in two-year and four-year colleges
0.9
0.8
0.7
0.6
0.5
0.4
0.3
0.2
0.1
0
Lowest
Second
Third
Highest
Family background - AFQT quartile
(b) Adjusted enrollment in two-year and four-year colleges
0.9
0.8
0.7
0.6
0.5
0.4
0.3
0.2
0.1
0
Lowest
Second
Third
Highest
Family background - AFQT quartile
(c) Completion of four-year college
0.8
0.7
0.6
0.5
0.4
0.3
0.2
0.1
0
Lowest
Second
Third
Highest
Family background - AFQT quartile
(d) Adjusted completion of four-year college
0.8
0.7
0.6
0.5
0.4
0.3
0.2
0.1
0
Lowest
Second
Third
Highest
Family background - AFQT quartile

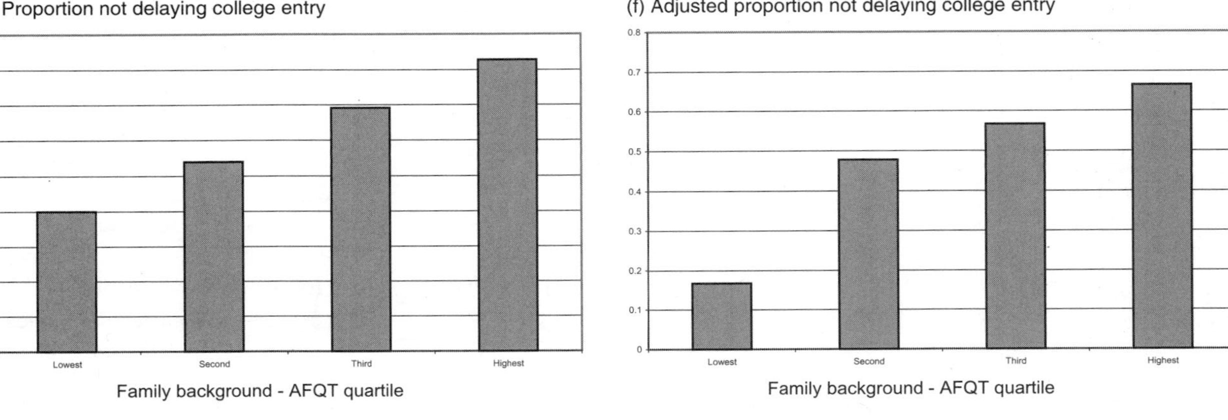

Figure 2.8
Enrollment, completion, and delay by family background–AFQT quartiles, NLSY79 white males. We correct for the effect of schooling at the test date on AFQT. The family background–AFQT index is based on a linear combination of south, broken home, urban, mother's education, father's education and AFQT. For the residual plots, we condition on family income at age 17. See table B2.3 in the appendix for the coefficients on the linear combination of variables forming this index.

Table 2.2
Adjusted gaps in college participation

	White males	White females	Black males	Black females	Hispanic males	Hispanic females	Overall
A. Percentage of population credit constrained							
Enrollment	.0515	.0449	−.0047	.0543	.0433	−.0789	.0419
Complete four-year college	−.0621	.0579	−.0612	−.0106	.0910	.0908	−.0438
Complete two-year college	.0901	.0436	−.0684	−.0514	.2285	.0680	.0774
Proportion of people not delaying college entry	.0872	−.0197	−.1125	−.1128	.1253	−.0053	.0594
Enrollment in four-year versus two-year college	.0646	.0491	.1088	.0024	.1229	−.0915	.0587
B. Percentage of the population credit constrained: Only statistically significant gaps							
Enrollment	0	.0095	0	.0164	.0278	−.0139	.0018
Complete four-year college	−.0545	.0089	−.0596	0	0	0	.0461
Complete two-year college	0	0	0	0	0	.0409	.0020
Proportion of people not delaying college entry	.0714	−.0318	−.0190	.0459	.0487	0	.0538
Enrollment in four-year versus two-year college	.0530	0	0	0	0	−.0451	.0391

C. Percentage of population family constrained							
Enrollment	.3123	.3280	.2658	.2420	.3210	.2923	.2623
Complete four-year college	.2723	.2338	.1435	.0738	.4950	.0205	.1958
Complete two-year college	−.1718	−.0350	−.0763	−.0565	−.1945	.2168	−.0785
Proportion of people not delaying college entry	.1965	.1898	.1910	.0460	.1950	.1360	.1135
Enrollment in four-year versus two-year college	.0568	.2423	.1643	.1143	.1533	.0738	.1155
D. Percentage of population family constrained: Only statistically significant gaps							
Enrollment	.3123	.3280	.2378	.2420	.3210	.2923	.2623
Complete four-year college	.2723	.2338	.0960	0	.4950	0	.1958
Complete two-year college	−.1408	0	0	0	0	.1678	−.0730
Proportion of people not delaying college entry	.1718	.1328	.1403	0	.1560	0	.1135
Enrollment in four-year versus two-year college	.0333	.2423	.1350	.0848	.1225	0	.1155

Notes: Credit constraints are measured in the following way. Within each AFQT tercile, we regress enrollment (completion, delay) on quartiles of the distribution of family income at age 17 and family background variables (south, broken, urban, mother's education, father's education): $y = a + \mathrm{F}\gamma + Q_1\beta_1 + Q_2\beta_2 + Q_3\beta_3$, where y is enrollment (completion, delay), **F** is a vector of family background variables, Q_1 is a dummy for being in the first quartile of the family income distribution, Q_2 for being in the second and Q_3 for being in the third. Within each AFQT tertile, the percentage of people constrained in each quartile of family income is measured by β_1, β_2 and β_3, which are gaps in average enrollment (completion, delay) between each quartile and the top quartile of the family income. To get the numbers in the table, we multiply the measured gap in

Table 2.2
(continued)

enrollment (completion, delay) for each quartile relative to the highest quartile by the percentage of people in that AFQT tercile-family income quartile. Within each AFQT tercile we add over the three bottom quartiles of family income and then add over the three tertiles of AFQT to get the number of credit-constrained people in the population. When computing family constraints we use a family background index that is a linear combination of south, broken, urban, mother's education, father's education, and AFQT. The coefficients for this linear combination are obtained by linearly regressing enrollment (completion, delay) on the variables composing the index. We then construct quartiles of this index. Family constraints are measured in the following way. We regress enrollment (completion, delay) on the family background quartile and family income at age 17: $y = a + Q_1\gamma_1 + Q_2\gamma_2 + Q_3\gamma_3 + Inc17\beta$, where y is enrollment (completion, delay), Q_1 is a dummy for being in the first quartile of the family background index, Q_2 for being in the second and Q_3 for being in the third, and $Inc17$ is family income at age 17. The percentage of people constrained in each quartile of the family background index is measured by γ_1, γ_2, and γ_3, which are gaps in average enrollment (completion, delay) between each quartile and the top quartile of the family background index. To get the numbers in the table, we multiply the measured gap in enrollment (completion, delay) for each quartile relative to the highest quartile by the percentage of people in that quartile. Then we add over the three bottom quartiles to get the number of family-constrained people in the population. The coefficients for these regressions for white males are presented in the appendix tables 2B.1 (unadjusted gaps) and 2B.2 (adjusted gaps). Regression coefficients for the other demographic groups are available on request from the authors.

Classifying white males by their test score terciles, we further display college enrollment rates by family income. There is a clear ordering in the high-ability group and in other ability groups as well. Persons from families with higher income are more likely to enroll in college. This ordering occurs in other data sets, even for low-ability groups.

The graphs on the left-hand side of figure 2.7 indicate a subsidiary, but still quantitatively important role for family income in accounting for schooling enrollment. This does not necessarily mean that short-run credit constraints are operative in the college-going years. Family income in the adolescent years is strongly correlated with family income throughout the life cycle. In addition, long-run family resources are likely to produce many skills that are not fully captured by a single test score.

When we control for early family background factors (parental education, family structure, and place of residence), we greatly weaken the relationship between family income and school enrollment. Table 2.2 panels A and B report overall adjusted gaps for the five measures of college participation listed in the table's first column. For each measure, within each AFQT tercile and income quartile, we adjust the raw rates for the background variables listed in the note to the table. Plots of the adjusted rates for three of these measures are presented in figures 2.7b, 2.7d, and 2.7f, corresponding to figures 2.7a, 2.7c, and 2.7e, respectively. The estimates in table 2.2 are weighted averages of the differences in adjusted rates of enrollment, completion, and delay for each income quartile with respect to the highest income quartiles within each ability tercile averaged over all three ability terciles.[10] The weights used are the population proportion in each cell. The numbers reported in each table are measures of the adjusted discrepancy in participation rates by income, controlling for long-term factors, and are estimates of the importance of short-term credit constraints. Focusing on enrollment in college (first row), as does most of the literature, we find that by this measure only 5.15 percent of all white males are constrained relative to the top income group. Figure 2.7b plots the adjusted family income gaps according to the three different ability terciles for college enrollment using the regressors reported in table 2.2A. Table 2.2B reports the results for the statistically significant gaps alone.[11] They are generally much smaller.

Most of the analysis in the literature focuses on college enrollment and much less on other dimensions of college attendance, such as completion, quality of school, and delay of entry into college.[12] In part, this emphasis on enrollment is due to reliance on Current Population Survey data, which are much more reliable for studying enrollment-family income relationships than for studying completion-family income relationships.

Using the NLSY79 data we look at four other measures of college participation. The remaining panels of table 2.2 report estimates of the credit constrained for these measures. When we perform a parallel analysis for completion of four-year college, we find no evidence of constraints for white males and in fact overadjust the gaps in college enrollment. Figures 2.7c and 2.7d present the raw and adjusted gaps respectively, for completion of four-year college. Figures 2.7e and 2.7f show the raw and adjusted gaps respectively, for delay of entry into college.[13] There is no evidence of short-run credit constraints in these measures. In results available from the authors on request, there is evidence of short-run credit constraints for the "dumb poor" in completing two years of college, but not for the "bright poor." There is weak evidence in certain cells of the table for short-term credit constraints in years of delay of entry and for choice of two-year versus four-year colleges, which is a measure of school quality. Depending on the measure of college participation selected, the estimated percentage of white males constrained ranges from 0 to 9 percent. Setting statistically insignificant gaps to zero, we obtain a smaller range of values (0 to 7 percent). We obtain comparable results for other demographic groups.

Overall, the estimated percentage constrained ranges from 8 percent (for completion of two-year college) to 0 percent for completion of four-year college. The strongest evidence for short-term credit constraints is for Hispanic males. The illegality of many Hispanics may make them appear, as a group, to be constrained because Hispanics who are in the country illegally do not have the same eligibility for schooling aid as those who are legal residents. The weakest evidence for credit constraints is for black males. On many measures, the effective constraint for this group is zero. There is little evidence that short-term credit constraints explain much of their gap in college participation relative to other groups.

Our analysis might be faulted on the following grounds. Many of the variables on which we condition to control for long-term family factors also predict family income in the adolescent years, so the preceding analysis may just project family income in the adolescent year into "long-term family factors." In response, it is important to note that the prediction of family income in the adolescent years on long-term factors is not perfect. There is still independent variation in family income when these variables are controlled for.

We present two additional pieces of evidence to bolster the point made in table 2.2 panels A and B. First, in panels

Table 2.3
Regression of enrollment in college on per capita permanent income, per capita early income, and per capita late income: Children of the NLSY

Variable	(1)	(2)	(3)	(4)
Family Income 0–18 (permanent income)	0.0839	0.0747	0.0902	0.0779
(Standard error)	(0.0121)	(0.0184)	(0.0185)	(0.0284)
Family Income 0–5	—	0.0158	—	0.0149
(Standard error)	—	(0.0238)	—	(0.0261)
Family Income 16–18	—	—	−0.0069	−0.0023
(Standard error)	—	—	(0.0177)	(0.0194)
PIAT-Math at Age 12	0.0077	0.0076	0.0076	0.0075
(Standard error)	(0.0017)	(0.0018)	(0.0018)	(0.0018)
Constant	0.1447	0.1404	0.1410	0.1380
(Standard error)	(0.0264)	(0.0272)	(0.0268)	(0.0273)
Observations	863	863	861	861
R^2	0.10	0.10	0.11	0.11

Note: Family income (permanent income) 0–18 is average family income between the ages of 0 and 18. Family income 0–5 is average family income between the ages of 0 and 5. Family income 16–18 is average family income between the ages of 16 and 18. Income is measured in per capita terms (dividing family income by family size, year by year) in tens of thousands of 1993 dollars. To construct average discounted family income (or permanent income), we used a discount rate of 5 percent. PIAT-Math is a math test score. For details on this sample, see BLS (2001). Let $Y_{i,t}$ be the per capita family income at age t for child i. Family income 0–18 is:

$$\sum_{t=0}^{18} \frac{Y_{i,t}}{(1+r)^t} \cdot \frac{\frac{1}{1+r} - 1}{\left(\frac{1}{1+r}\right)^{19} - 1} \cdot \frac{1}{19};$$

resources in present value terms over the life of the child, where r is the interest rate $=0.05$. Family income 0–5 is:

$$\sum_{t=0}^{5} \frac{Y_{i,t}}{(1+r)^t} \cdot \frac{\frac{1}{1+r} - 1}{\left(\frac{1}{1+r}\right)^{6} - 1} \cdot \frac{1}{6}.$$

Table 2.3
(continued)

Family income 16–18 is:

$$\frac{1}{(1+r)^{15}}\sum_{t=16}^{18}\frac{Y_{i,t}}{(1+r)^{t}}\cdot\frac{\frac{1}{1+r}-1}{\left(\frac{1}{1+r}\right)^{3}-1}\cdot\frac{1}{3}.$$

C and D, we reverse the roles of family income in the adolescent years and family background. We create an index of family background, defined precisely in the note to table 2.2 (and in appendix table 2B.4), and classify persons on the basis of quartiles of this index. The index includes a child's ability, parental education, and location. It strongly predicts various college participation decisions. When we condition further on family income in the adolescent years (table 2.2C), a strong long run family background effect remains. This is true even if we report only statistically significant estimates (table 2.2D).[14] Figure 2.8 graphically presents the results of this analysis. The gaps by family status are not substantially affected by adjusting for family income in the adolescent years.

Table 2.3 reports further evidence on the unimportance of short-run credit constraints on college attendance. The table presents estimates of child enrollment in college on family per capita permanent income and on family per capita income flows received at various stages of the life cycle (transitory income). Permanent income is formed as an average discounted income flow to the family over the life of the child at home (ages 0 to 18).[15]

Two features are clear from this table: (a) permanent income matters a lot for college enrollment and (b) given permanent income, transitory income flows matter little. Early income and late income have positive but small and statistically insignificant effects (see column 4), but late income has, if anything, a slight *negative* effect on college enrollment. The evidence in table 2.3 suggests that short-term income constraints are not binding.[16]

Policies that improve the financing of the education of identified constrained subgroups will increase their human capital and may well be justified on objective cost-benefit criteria. The potential economic loss from delay in entering college can be substantial. If V is the economic value of attending school, and schooling is delayed one year, then the costs of delaying schooling by one year are $rV/(1 + r)$, where r is the interest rate. For $r = .10$, which is not out of line with estimates in the literature, this delay is 9 percent of the lifetime value of schooling (roughly \$20,000). For the identified constrained subgroups, the benefits to reducing delay and promoting earlier college completion, higher college quality and graduation are likely to be substantial.

In designing policies to harvest these benefits, it is important to target the interventions toward the constrained. Broad-based policies generate deadweight. For example, Dynarski (2001) and Cameron and Heckman (1999) estimate that 93 percent of President Clinton's Hope Scholarship funds, which were directed toward middle-class families, were given to children who would have attended school even without the program.

While targeting those identified as constrained may be good policy, it is important not to lose sight of the main factors accounting for the gaps in figure 2.4. Family background factors crystallized in ability are the first-order factors explaining college attendance and completion gaps.

Differences in average ability by family income groups appear at early ages and persist. We discuss the sources of these differences in the next section. A major conclusion of this chapter is that the ability that is decisive in producing schooling differentials is shaped early in life. If we are to substantially eliminate ethnic and income differentials in schooling, we must start early. We cannot rely on tuition policy applied in the child's adolescent years, job training, or GED programs to compensate for the neglect the child experienced in the early years.

At the same time, policies to foster early abilities are known to be costly. The mechanisms through which ability is generated remain to be fully explored. Policies that efficiently target the short-run constrained are likely to pass a rigorous cost-benefit test. We next consider other arguments used to support the claim of pervasive short-term credit constraints.

High Rate of Return to Schooling Compared to the Return on Physical Capital Estimates of the rate of return to schooling, based on the Mincer earnings function, are often above 10 percent and sometimes are as high as 17 to 20 percent. Estimates based on instrumental variables are especially high. (See, for example, the evidence surveyed by Card 1999, 2001 and the discussion of the quality of the instruments used in this literature presented in Carneiro and Heckman 2002.) It is sometimes claimed that the returns to schooling are very high and therefore people are credit-constrained or some other market failure is present.

The cross-section Mincerian rate of return to schooling does not, in general, estimate the marginal internal rate of return to schooling. (See Heckman, Lochner, and Todd 2003; and Heckman, Lochner, and Taber 1998a for an example in which cross-section rates of return are uninformative about the return to schooling that any person experiences.) Willis (1986) and Heckman, Lochner, and Todd (2001) state the conditions under which the Mincerian rate of return will be equal to the marginal internal rate of return to schooling. Even if these conditions are satisfied, implicit comparisons are usually made against a risk-free interest rate. However this is not the relevant comparison for evaluating schooling decisions. Carneiro, Hansen, and Heckman (2001, 2003) estimate considerable uncertainty in the returns to schooling. We discuss this evidence in the paper's third part. The illiquidity and irreversibility of human capital investments drive the premium on human capital far above the safe interest rate (see Judd 2000). Comparisons of Mincer returns and returns to capital are intrinsically uninformative about the existence of credit constraints or the need for intervention in human capital markets.

Are Rates of Return to Schooling Higher for Persons from Low-Income Families? Assuming the same technology of educational investment across families and no comparative advantage in the labor market, if low-income families are credit-constrained, then at the margin the returns to schooling for constrained children should be higher, since they are investing less than the efficient amount. Carneiro and Heckman (2002) establish that if choices are made at the quality margin, the estimated Mincer return may be *lower* for constrained persons, unless adjustments are made for quality. The empirical literature, which does not adjust for quality, finds that returns to schooling are higher for high-ability people than for low-ability people. (See, for example, Meghir and Palme 1999; Cawley et al. 2000; Taber 2001, or the evidence presented in part 3 below.) Family income and child ability are positively correlated, so one would expect higher returns to schooling for children of high-income families for this reason alone. Altonji and Dunn (1996) find in their preferred empirical specification that the returns to schooling are higher for children of more-educated families than for children of less-educated families. There is no evidence that rates of return to schooling are higher for children from low-income families than for children from high-income families.[17]

Additional Evidence from the Literature Cameron and Heckman (1998) analyze the determinants of grade-by-grade schooling attainment for cohorts of American males born between 1908 and 1964. Consistent with the notion that family income and family background factors reflect long-run and not short-term influences on schooling attainment, they find that ability and family background factors are powerful determinants of schooling completion from elementary school through graduate school. An appeal to borrowing constraints operating in the college years is not necessary to explain the relationship between family income and college attendance decisions and the stability of the relationship over long periods of time.

Cameron and Taber (2000) examine the empirical importance of borrowing constraints in a model that incorporates the insight that borrowing constraints will influence both schooling choices and returns to schooling. Using a variety of methods, they find no evidence that borrowing constraints play a role in explaining the years of schooling attained by recent cohorts of American youth. Keane and Wolpin (2001) estimate a more explicit sequential dynamic model and reach the same conclusion. Students are estimated to be short-run constrained, but alleviate the constraints they face through working. Relaxing the budget constraint barely budges schooling decisions but affects work while in school. Neither study looks at delay or quality effects, which have been found to be quantitatively important.

Stanley (1999) studies the impact of the GI Bill on the college-going decisions of Korean War veterans. Consistent with our analysis, he finds that most college subsidies under the bill were used by veterans from families in the top half of the socioeconomic distribution. When she studies the effects of the HOPE (Help Outstanding Students Educationally) Scholarship program in Georgia, Dynarski (2000) finds that it benefits mostly middle- and higher-income students. The elasticity of enrollment to tuition subsidies in her sample is as high as other estimates found in the literature: middle- and higher-income people do not seem to respond less elastically to education subsidies than do lower-income people. This is consistent with the evidence from Cameron and Heckman (1999) previously discussed. Shea (2000) estimates the effect of a measure of parental income on schooling using the Panel Survey of Income Dynamics (see Hill 1992 for a description of this data set). Controlling for parental background variables, he finds an effect of his measure of family income on schooling, controlling for ability. Using instrumental variables, however, he estimates no effect of his measure of family income on schooling attainment, and he interprets this result as evidence of no credit constraints.[18]

Summary In this section we have examined arguments made in the literature about the strength of credit constraints in schooling. We have evaluated the available evidence and presented new evidence using American data.

Some of the evidence in the literature is uninformative on this issue. The leading example is the evidence from IV and OLS estimation of the returns to schooling discussed in detail in Carneiro and Heckman (2002). The literature on price effects and tuition subsidies generally is also not very informative on this matter, since it does not separate price effects from borrowing constraints.

The observed correlation between family income and college attendance can be interpreted as arising in two different ways: from short-run credit constraints or from long-run family effects. The latter are quantitatively more important, even though we identify a group of people (at most 8 percent of the population) who seem to be facing short-run credit constraints. The first-order factors accounting for the gaps in figure 2.4 are long-term factors that cannot easily be offset by tuition policy or supplements to family income in the adolescent years of prospective students.

It is important to stress that all of the empirical analyses reported in this section are for contemporary American society, in which a substantial edifice of financial aid to support postsecondary education is in place. The limited role short-run credit constraints play in explaining contemporary American educational gaps is, no doubt, in part due to the successful operation of policies that were designed to eliminate such constraints. Substantial reductions in the generosity of educational benefits would undoubtedly affect participation in college, although they would operate primarily through price effects. The evidence in Blossfeld and Shavit 1993, Cameron and Heckman 1998, and Cossa 2000, however, suggests the universal first-order importance of long-term family influences on educational attainment. Gaps in educational attainment related to family background arise in many different environments, including those with free tuition and no restrictions on college entry. This evidence points to the powerful role of the long-term factors that we have emphasized in this section of our paper. We next turn to evidence on the sources of these long-term factors.

Early Test Score Differentials

Important differences in ability across family types appear at early ages and persist. Figure 2.9a plots average percentile rank in PIAT (Peabody Individual Achievement Test) Math scores by age and family income quartile.

Constructing the graph in figure 2.9a, we computed for each person his or her percentile rank in the distribution of test scores at each age. Then we grouped individuals in different quartiles of family income and computed the average percentile rank within each group at each age the test was taken. We used ranks because the absolute values of test scores or their growth have no meaning. Any monotonic transformation of a test score is also a valid test score. Use of ranks avoids this difficulty. For all race and ethnic groups, there are important differences by family income quartile in how children rank in cognitive test scores as early as age 6. These gaps in ranks across income quartile remain stable as children grow, and for some test scores they widen. At the same time, just as racial differences in schooling participation rates are evident, racial differences in early test scores also emerge. Figure 2.9c presents evidence on the emergence of racial gaps in ranks of test scores, as measured by PIAT-Math test scores.

The ability that drives schooling participation is shaped early in life. The available evidence indicates that cognitive ability is relatively more malleable early in the life cycle (see Heckman 1995). Having access to more and higher-quality resources that contribute to improving cognitive ability early in life affects skill acquisition later in life.

Figure 2.10 presents ranks of adjusted test score gaps in figure 2.9, controlling for the long-term family factors listed at the base of the figure. The gaps in rank across racial and income groups are significantly reduced when we control for mother's education, mother's ability, and family structure in the test score equation.[19] The gaps at age 12 do not disappear, however, when we compare the highest and lowest income quartiles or whites with blacks. Measured long-term family factors play a powerful role but do not fully eliminate the gaps.

Other analysts have also focused their attention on these gaps in cognitive ability and have attempted to eliminate them by controlling for more factors. Using data from the Early Childhood Longitudinal Survey (ECLS), Fryer and Levitt (2002) eliminate the black-white gap in math and reading test scores in early kindergarten by controlling for measures of family background, birth weight, and number of books a child has.[20] They also find that both the raw and the residualized test score gaps widen with age. If anything, schooling widens these gaps, a point emphasized in Fryer and Levitt's paper. They cannot account for the increase in these gaps using available measures of school quality. Their evidence indicates that socioeconomic background at early ages is a very important determinant of a child's test score. Using data on the Children of the NLSY, Phillips et al. (1998) also study the black-white test score gap.[21] They analyze only the PIAT-Math and the Peabody Picture Vocabulary Tests at ages 3 to 4. They cannot fully eliminate the test score

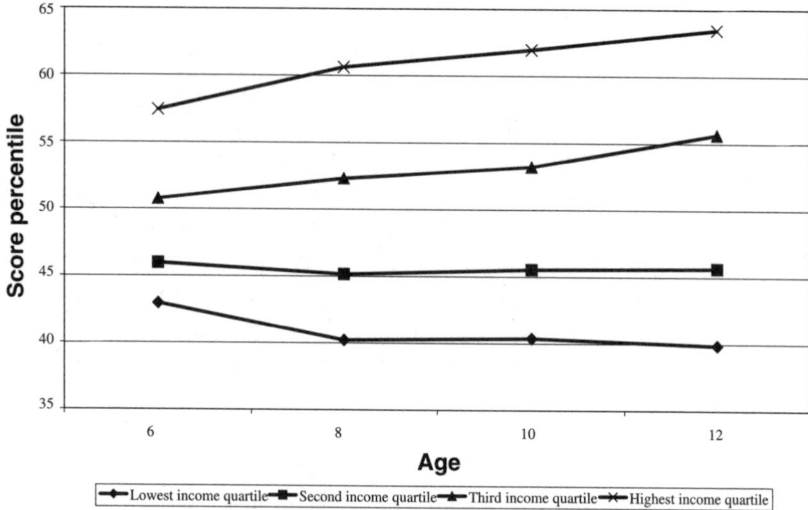
(a) Average percentile rank on PIAT-Math score by income quartile
Score percentile
65
60
55
50
45
40
35
6
8
10
12
Age
Lowest income quartile
Second income quartile
Third income quartile
Highest income quartile

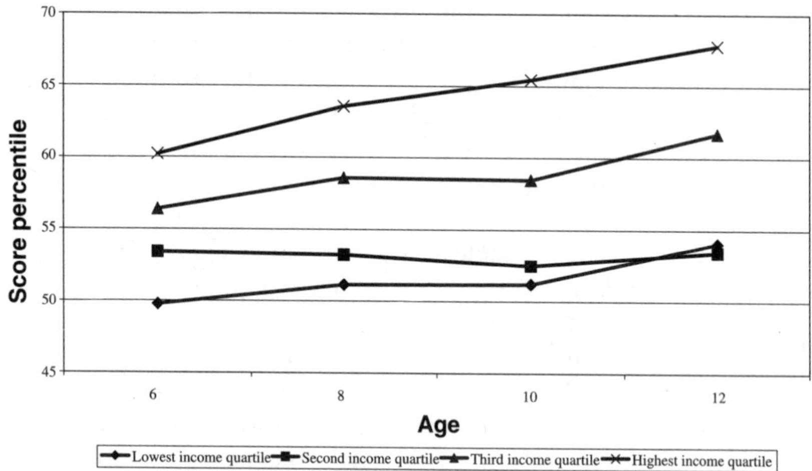
(b) Average percentile rank on PIAT-Math score by income quartile, whites only
Score percentile
70
65
60
55
50
45
6
8
10
12
Age
Lowest income quartile
Second income quartile
Third income quartile
Highest income quartile

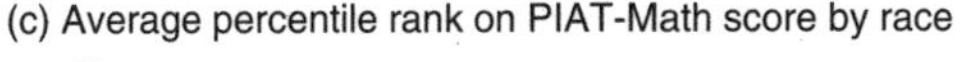

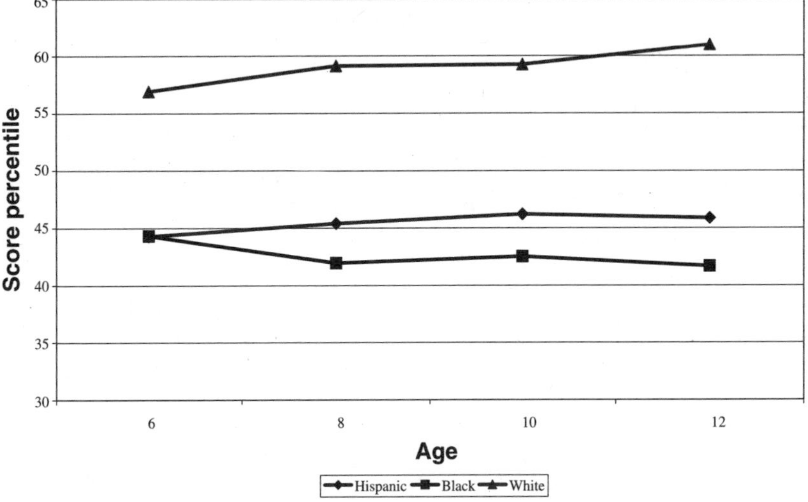

Figure 2.9
PIAT-Math score by income quartile and race, Children of NLSY.

gap using family background, mother's AFQT, and rich measures of family environment, although controlling for these factors substantially reduces the gap.

The emergence of early test score differentials is not limited to cognitive measures. At early ages, differences in children's behaviors and attitudes across income and racial groups are also evident, as figure 2.11a illustrates. The figure presents differences in ranks of indices of Anti-Social behavior across different income and racial groups.[22] It is common knowledge that motivation, trustworthiness, and other behavioral skills are important traits for success in life. We consider evidence on the importance of noncognitive skills in the next section. Hence, understanding the gaps in

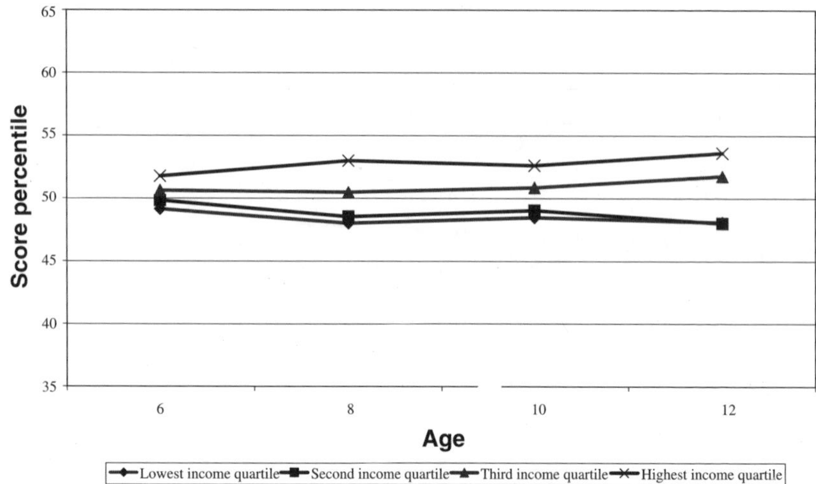
(a) Residualized average percentile rank on PIAT-Math score by income quartile
Score percentile
65
60
55
50
45
40
35
6
8
10
12
Age
Lowest income quartile
Second income quartile
Third income quartile
Highest income quartile

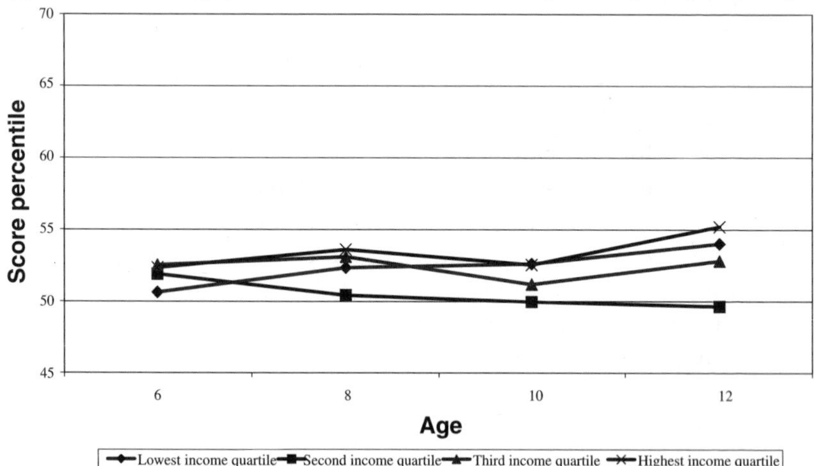
(b) Residualized average percentile rank on PIAT-Math score by income quartile, whites only
Score percentile
70
65
60
55
50
45
6
8
10
12
Age
Lowest income quartile
Second income quartile
Third income quartile
Highest income quartile

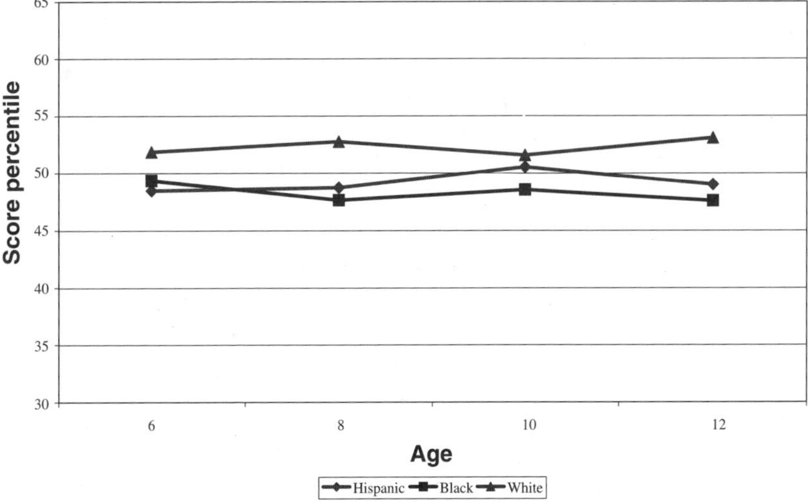

Figure 2.10
Residualized PIAT-Math score by income quartile and race, Children of NLSY.
Note: Residualized on maternal education, maternal AFQT (corrected for the effect of schooling) and broken home at each age.

these behavioral skills across different income and racial groups and how to eliminate them is also important for understanding the determinants of economic success. Figure 2.12 presents adjusted ranks of test scores for behavioral measures for mother's ability, mother's AFQT, and broken home.[23] Adjusting for early family background factors substantially reduces gaps in ranks in noncognitive skills across income and racial groups. Comparing adjusted cognitive and noncognitive test scores reveals the importance of long-term factors in reducing the gaps in behavioral scores across

(a) Average percentile rank on anti-social score by income quartile

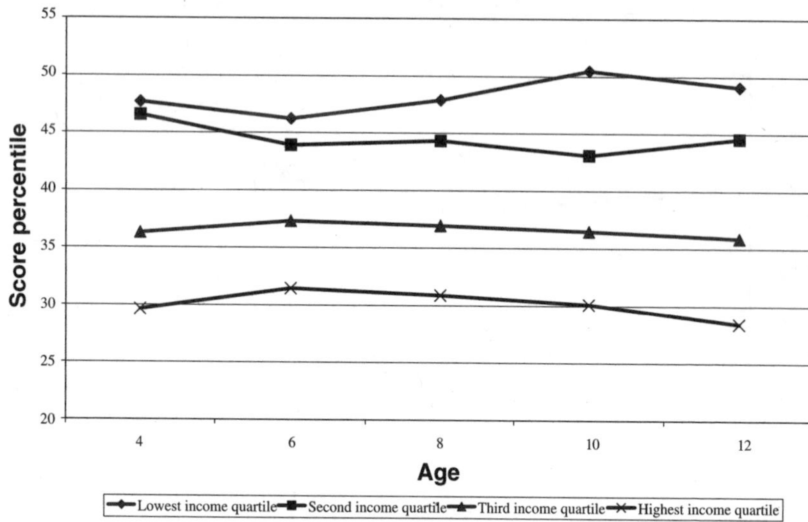

(b) Average percentile rank on anti-social score by income quartile, whites only

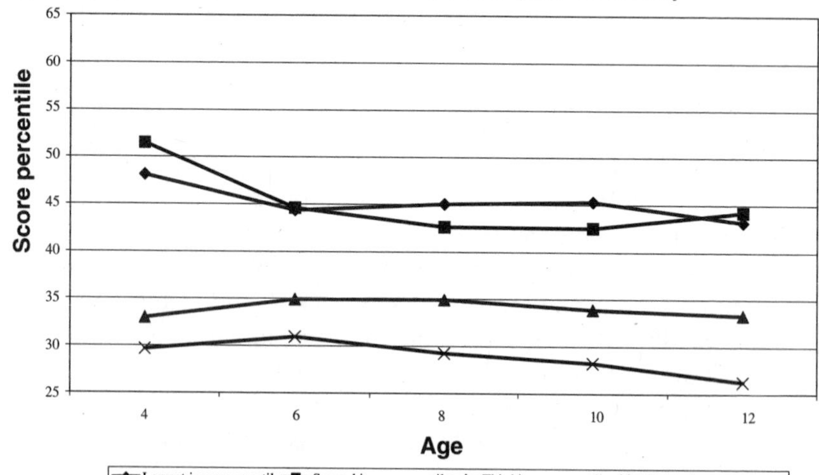

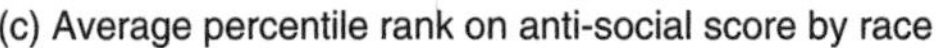

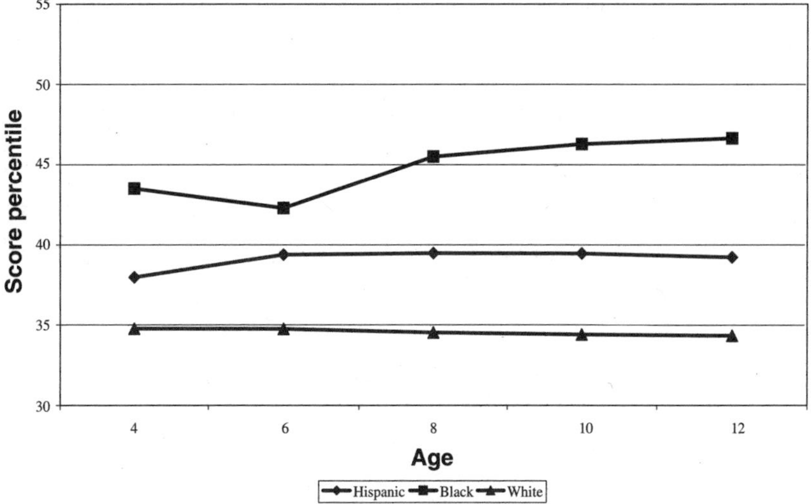

Figure 2.11
Anti-social score by income quartile and race, Children of NLSY.
Note: Income quartiles are computed from average family income between the ages of 6 and 10.

these groups. Although noncognitive ability gaps across income and racial groups cannot be eliminated at later ages, controlling for mother's ability, family income, family structure, and location significantly reduces the gaps in ranks in noncognitive abilities across these groups at both early and later ages.[24]

This evidence, like that of the entire literature, is very crude. Good families promote cognitive, social, and behavioral skills. Bad families do not. The relevant policy issue is to determine what interventions in bad families are successful. We present evidence on this question after presenting

(a) Residualized average percentile rank on anti-social score by income quartile

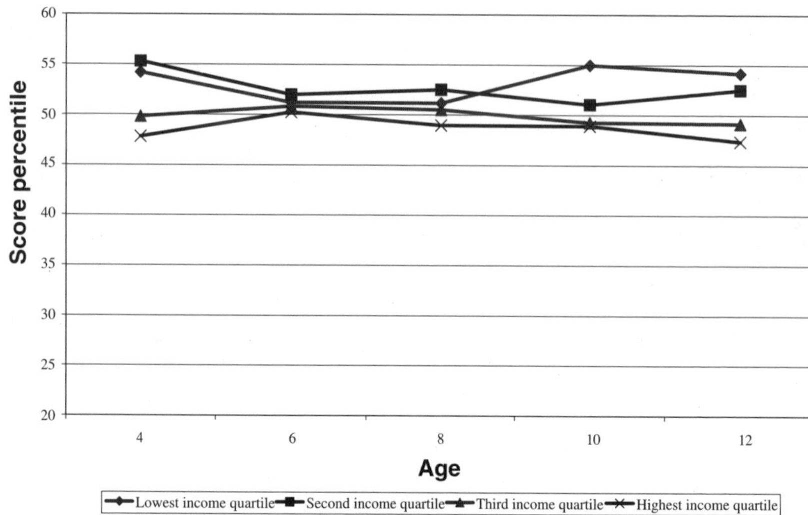

(b) Residualized average percentile rank on anti-social score by income quartile, whites only

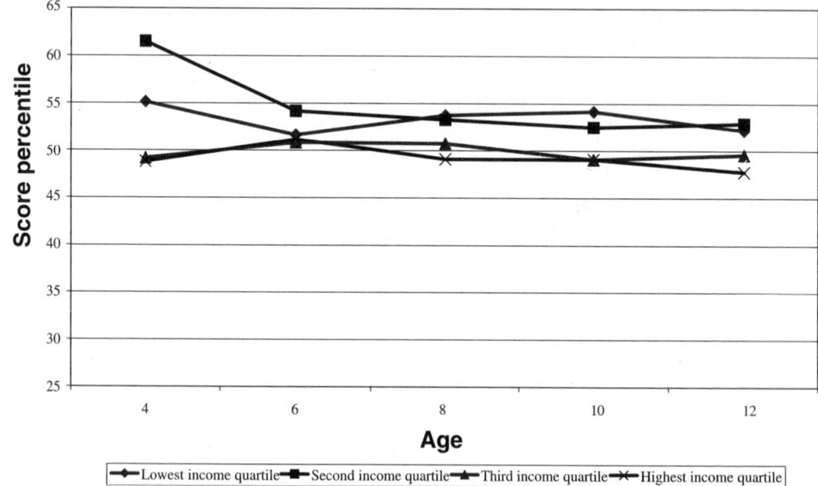

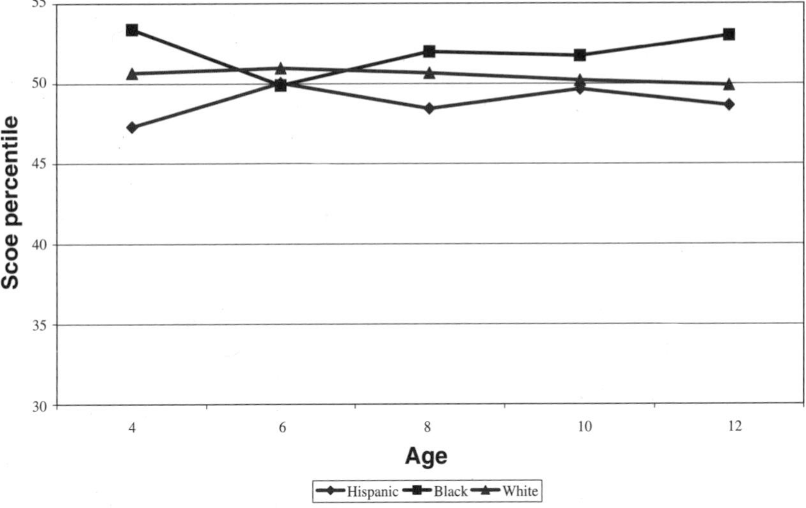

Figure 2.12
Residualized anti-social score by income quartile and race, Children of NLSY.
Note: Residualized on maternal education, maternal AFQT (corrected for the effect of schooling), and broken home at each age.

further evidence on the importance of noncognitive skills for economic success. We show in the paper's third part that manipulating noncognitive skills is more feasible (less costly) than manipulating cognitive skills. In addition, remediation efforts for noncognitive skills are effective at later ages. But first we discuss the evidence on the importance of noncognitive skills for economic success.

The Evidence on the Importance of Noncognitive Skills

Numerous instances can be cited of high-IQ people who fail to achieve success in life because they lack self-discipline and of low-IQ people who succeed by virtue of persistence, reliability, and self-discipline. It is thus surprising that academic discussions of skill and skill formation focus almost exclusively on measures of cognitive ability and ignore noncognitive skills. The early literature on human capital (Becker 1964) contrasted cognitive-ability models of earnings with human capital models, ignoring noncognitive traits entirely. The signaling literature (Spence 1974) emphasized that education was a signal of a one-dimensional ability, usually interpreted as a cognitive skill. Most discussions of ability bias in the estimated return to education treat omitted ability as cognitive ability and attempt to proxy the missing ability using cognitive tests. Most assessments of school reforms stress the gain from reforms as measured by the ability of students to perform on a standardized achievement test. Widespread use of standardized achievement and ability tests for admissions and educational evaluation are premised on the belief that the skills that can be tested are essential for success in schooling and in the workplace, a central premise of the educational-testing movement since its inception.

Much of the neglect of noncognitive skills in analyses of earnings, schooling, and other life outcomes is due to the lack of any reliable means of measuring them. Many different personality and motivational traits are lumped into the category of noncognitive skills. Psychologists have developed batteries of tests to measure these skills (Sternberg 1985). Companies use these tests to screen workers, but they are not yet used to assess college readiness or to evaluate the effectiveness of schools or reforms of schools. The literature on cognitive tests ascertains that one dominant factor ("g") summarizes cognitive tests and their effects on outcomes.

No single factor has emerged as dominant in the literature on noncognitive skills and it is unlikely that one will ever be found, given the diversity of traits subsumed under the category of noncognitive skills.

Studies by Bowles and Gintis (1976), Edwards (1976), and Klein, Spady, and Weiss (1991) demonstrate that job stability and dependability are traits most valued by employers as ascertained by supervisor ratings and questions of employers, although they present no direct evidence on wages and educational attainment. Perseverance, dependability and consistency are the most important predictors of grades in school (Bowles and Gintis 1976).

Self-reported measures of persistence, self-esteem, optimism, future orientedness, and the like are now being collected, and some recent papers discuss estimates of the effects of these measures on earnings and schooling outcomes (see Bowles, Gintis, and Osborne 2001). These studies shed new light on the importance of noncognitive skills for success in social life. Yet these studies are not without controversy. For example, ex post assessments of self-esteem may be as much the consequence as the cause of the measures being investigated.

Heckman and Rubinstein (2001) avoid the problems inherent in these ex post assessments by using evidence from the GED testing program in the United States to demonstrate the quantitative importance of noncognitive skills in determining earnings and educational attainment. The GED program is a second-chance program that administers a battery of cognitive tests to self-selected high school dropouts to determine whether or not their level of academic attainment is equivalent to that of high school graduates. Study of the GED program is of interest in its own right. GEDs are a major output of government training programs, including the Job Corps program, as we note in the chapter's third part. Those awarded the GED constitute 15 percent of all persons certified with new high school credentials.

In this section of the chapter we summarize findings reported in Heckman (2003) and Heckman and Rubinstein (2001). The GED examination is successful in psychometrically equating GED test takers with ordinary high school graduates who do not go on to college. Recipients are as smart as ordinary high school graduates who do not go on to college, where cognitive ability is measured by an average of cognitive components of the AFQT or by the first principal component ("g"). According to these same measures, GED recipients are smarter than other high school dropouts who do not obtain a GED (see figure 2.13, which plots AFQT scores by race for high school graduates who do not go on to college and GED recipients). The pattern is the same for all demographic groups. GED recipients earn more than other high school dropouts, have higher hourly wages, and finish more years of high school before they drop out. This is entirely consistent with the literature that emphasizes the importance of cognitive skills in determining labor market outcomes.

When measured ability is controlled for, however, GED recipients earn *less*, have lower hourly wages, and obtain lower levels of schooling than other high school dropouts. Some unmeasured factors therefore account for their relatively poor performance compared to other dropouts. Heckman and Rubinstein (2001) identify these factors as noncognitive skills noting that a subsequent analysis should parcel out which specific noncognitive skills are the most important.

The fact that someone has received the GED sends a mixed signal. Dropouts who pass the GED test are smarter (have higher cognitive skills) than other high school dropouts and yet at the same time have lower levels of noncognitive skills. Both types of skill are valued in the market and affect schooling choices. The findings of Heckman and Rubinstein (2001) challenge the conventional signaling literature, which assumes there is a single skill that determines socioeconomic success. It also demonstrates the folly of a psychometrically oriented educational evaluation policy that assumes that cognitive skills are all that matter for success in life. Inadvertently, the GED has become a test that separates bright but nonpersistent and undisciplined dropouts from other dropouts. It is, then, no surprise that GED recipients are the ones who drop out of school, fail to complete college (Cameron and Heckman 1993), and fail to persist in the military (Laurence 2000). GED holders are "wise guys" who lack the ability to think ahead, persist in tasks, or to adapt to their environments. The performance of GED recipients compared to that of both high school dropouts of the same ability and high school graduates demonstrates the importance of noncognitive skills in economic life.

Evidence from the GED Program The performance of GED recipients compared to that of both high school dropouts of the same ability and high school graduates demonstrates the importance of noncognitive skills in economic life. Boesel, Alsalam, and Smith (1998) present a comprehensive review of evidence on the GED program. Currently one in two high school dropouts and one in five high school graduates, as classified by the U.S. Census, is a GED recipient.[25]

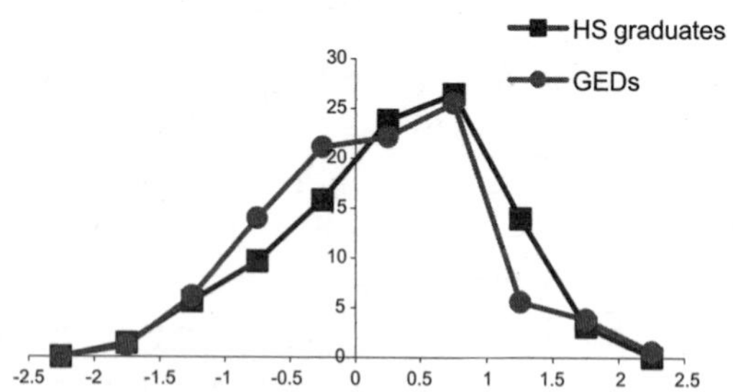

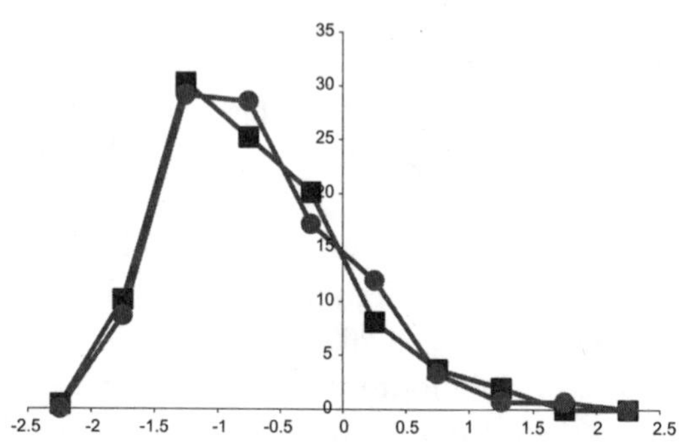

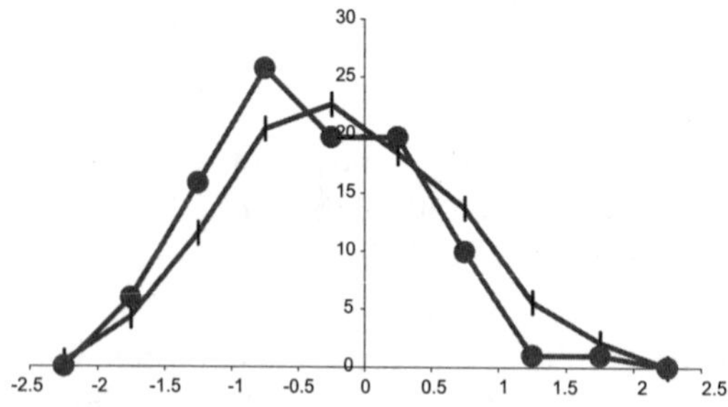

Figure 2.13
Density of age-adjusted AFQT scores, GED recipients, and high school graduates with twelve years of schooling.
Source: Heckman, Hsee, and Rubinstein 2001.

(b) White females

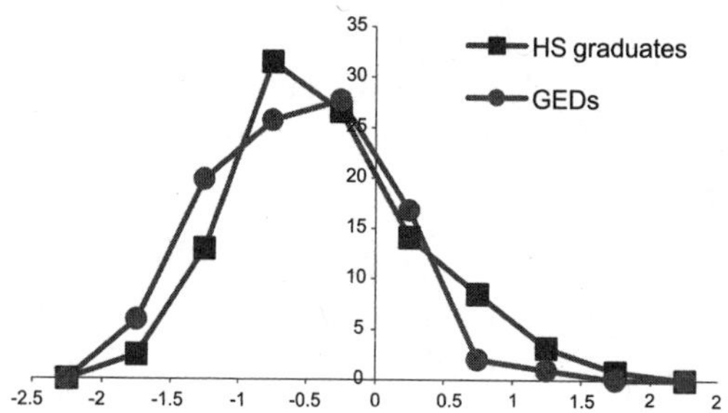

(d) Black females

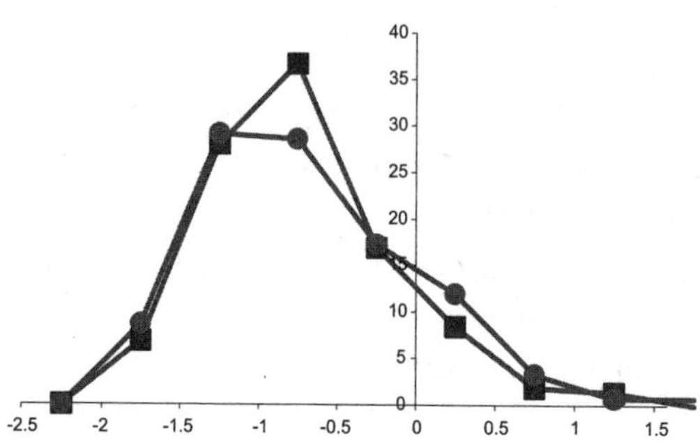

(f) Hispanic females

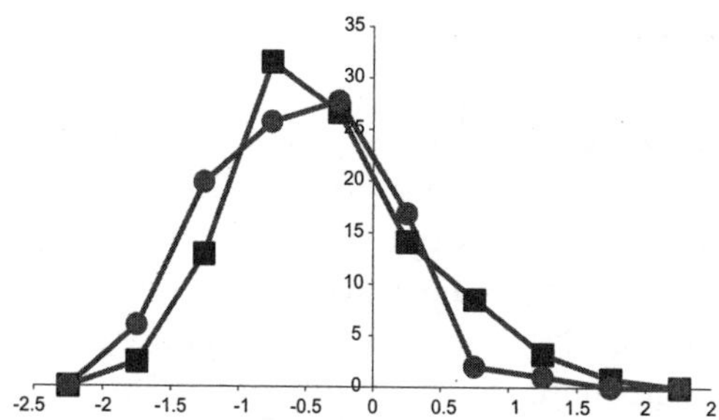

Figure 2.13 (continued)

A series of papers using NLSY data (Cameron and Heckman 1993; Heckman 2003), have yielded the following findings regarding white males:

- In unadjusted cross-sectional comparisons, GED recipients have hourly wage rates and annual earnings substantially less than those of high school graduates and earn slightly more than other high school dropouts. The number of years of schooling is also slightly higher for GED recipients than for other dropouts. When their higher levels of schooling and their higher AFQT scores are accounted for, GED recipients earn less than other high school dropouts and have lower hourly wages. Similar results for other demographic groups are reported in Heckman (2003). These results are statistically significant.
- Controlling for individual fixed effects (person-specific unobservables), longitudinal studies reveal no evidence of a permanent effect of GED certification on wages, employment, or job turnover for persons who take the GED after age 17. GED recipients are more likely to change jobs than high school dropouts both before and after taking the exam.
- Both cognitive and noncognitive skills promote educational attainment.
- In a model that explicitly accounts for both unmeasured (or badly measured) cognitive and noncognitive skills, in the short run GED certification appears to have the effect of boosting wages for persons who take the GED at young ages (younger than age 20), holding constant noncognitive skills by signaling greater cognitive ability of workers. This effect fades quickly, however, as employers rapidly learn about noncognitive ability. In the long run, holding ability constant, GED recipients earn lower wages as their adverse noncognitive characteristics are revealed.

• Persons with higher AFQT scores take the GED earlier. This accounts for a larger initial positive effect of GED certification on earnings for younger recipients that disappears with age.

• There is some suggestion that white male GED recipients show the highest level among high-school dropouts of participation in (almost) every category of illegal activity. This is true even when the outcomes are not adjusted for differences in AFQT scores and educational attainment. It remains true even when we drop persons who acquire the GED in prison, or all persons who have been in prison, to avoid a spurious causal relationship arising from the inclusion of prisoners, and hence people with a greater rate of participation in crime, acquiring the GED. The same applies for white females except for teenage mothers, who are much less likely to get the GED in prison. GED recipients are more likely to participate in illegal drug use, drug selling, fighting in school, vandalism, shoplifting, theft, robberies, and school absenteeism than are other dropouts.[26]

• The labor force participation and employment rates of GED recipients are lower than those of other dropouts (conditional on AFQT scores and years of schooling completed). Their turnover rates are higher. These rates do not change with the acquisition of the GED. Hence GED recipients accumulate less work experience over the life cycle.

• The correlation between AFQT scores and an index of participation in illicit activity defined in Heckman, Hsee, and Rubinstein (2001) is statistically significant and negative in the population at large. Individuals with higher AFQT scores are less likely to participate in illicit behavior. Yet this relationship does not hold within education groups. The correlation between AFQT scores and an index among all high school dropouts and one among high school graduates (with twelve years of schooling) is positive and statistically significant. It is especially strong for all dropouts, suggesting that among high school dropouts, the higher the AFQT score, the more likely is participation in illicit activity. Such a correlation is consistent with the view that both cognitive and noncognitive traits play important roles in determining graduation from high school.

- The story for white females is slightly different. Girls who drop out of school because of pregnancy typically do so with fewer years of schooling attained than other girls who drop out. Findings for girls who drop out for reasons other than pregnancy, however, are like those for teenage boys who drop out (i.e., they earn less than other dropouts conditioning on AFQT or schooling). Teenage mothers who are GED recipients have the same level of earnings as other high school dropouts once AFQT scores and years of schooling are accounted for.

Implications for Policy We draw two main conclusions from our analysis of the importance of noncognitive skills in determining educational and life outcomes apart from the specific conclusion that holding a GED sends a mixed signal about the holder that characterizes him or her as smart but unreliable. Current systems of evaluating educational reforms are based on changes in scores on cognitive tests. These tests capture only one of the many skills required for a successful life (see Heckman 1999). Our first conclusion is therefore that more comprehensive evaluations of educational systems would account for their effects on producing the noncognitive traits that are also valued in the market. There is substantial evidence that mentoring and motivational programs oriented toward disadvantaged teenagers are effective. We discuss this evidence in the paper's third part. Much of the effectiveness of early childhood interventions comes from boosting noncognitive skills and from fostering motivation. (See Heckman 2000 for a comprehensive review of the literature.) It has long been conjectured that the greater effectiveness of Catholic schools comes in producing more motivated and self-disciplined students (Coleman and Hoffer 1983). It has also been conjectured that the decline in discipline in inner-city public schools is a major source of their failure. It would be valuable to gather more systematic information on noncognitive effects of alternative education systems. IQ is fairly well set by age 8. Motivation and self-discipline are more malleable at later ages (Heckman 2000). Given the evidence on the quantitative importance of noncognitive traits, the second conclusion we draw from our analysis in this section is that social policy should be more active in attempting to alter noncognitive traits, especially in children from disadvantaged environments who receive poor discipline and little encouragement at home. This more active social-policy approach would include mentoring programs and stricter enforcement of discipline in the schools. We present evidence on the value of such interventions in the paper's third part. Such interventions would benefit the child and the larger society but at the same time might conflict with widely held values of sanctity of the family for those families that undervalue self-discipline and motivation and resent the imposition of what are perceived as middle-class values on their children.

Summary

The evidence presented in this part of the paper demonstrates that long-term environmental factors crystallized in cognitive and noncognitive abilities play a major role in accounting for gaps in schooling attainment across socioeconomic groups, where the short-term credit constraints and tuition factors that receive prominent attention in current policy discussions do not. Short-term credit constraints do, however, affect a small group of persons, and targeted subsidy policies appear to be cost effective for those persons. We cannot expect tuition reduction policies to eliminate the substantial gaps in schooling attainment according to socioeconomic background. Gaps in levels of cognitive and noncognitive skills open up early and are linked to family environments at early ages, not parental income in the adolescent years. Noncognitive skills substantially determine socioeconomic success later in life.

In the next part of the chapter, we apply these lessons and add to them in our analyses of specific policies designed to foster skills in children and youth.

3. Analyses of Specific Policies

In this part of the chapter, we analyze the returns to schooling and schooling quality and the returns to job training, early childhood interventions, and mentoring programs. We also consider tax and subsidy policy, immigration policy, and problems associated with the transition to new technologies that demand new skills and make old skills obsolete.

The Returns to Schooling and Schooling Quality

Few topics in empirical economics have received more attention than the economic return to schooling. By now there is a firmly established consensus that the mean rate of return to a year of schooling, as of the 1990s, exceeds 10 percent and may be as high as 17 to 20 percent (Carneiro, Heckman, and Vytlacil 2003). This return is higher for more able people (Taber 2001) and for children from better backgrounds (Altonji and Dunn 1996). Those from better backgrounds and with higher ability are also more likely to attend college and earn a higher rate of return from it. This evidence is robust to alternative choices of instrumental variables and to the use of alternative methods for controlling for self-selection. The synergy or complementarity suggested in figure 2.6a is confirmed in estimates of ability and background on earnings. Both cognitive and noncognitive skills raise earnings through promoting schooling and through their direct effects on earnings. (See the evidence in Taber 2001; Heckman, Hsee, and Rubinstein 2001; Carneiro 2002; Carneiro, Hansen, and Heckman 2001, 2003.) Table 2.4 presents our summary of the mean rate of return to schooling for different ability groups. The annual return to college is higher for persons with greater ability.

Means mask a lot of important information about the distribution of returns. Even if the mean returns to participants in schooling are high, marginal entrants attracted into schooling may have low returns. Economic analysis is all about persons at the margin. Although Mincer (1974) emphasized heterogeneity in the returns to education in his pioneering research on earnings functions and reported estimates of the dispersion of these returns, only recently have full distributions of returns and the returns to marginal entrants attracted into schooling been estimated (Carneiro, Hansen, and Heckman 2001, 2003). We summarize the main findings of this body of work.

The heterogeneity in rates of return can arise from cross-sectional differences known to agents but not to observing

Table 2.4
Return to one year of college for individuals at different percentiles of the math test score distribution, white males from High School and Beyond

	5%	25%	50%	75%	95%
Average return in the population	0.1121 (0.0400)	0.1374 (0.0328)	0.1606 (0.0357)	0.1831 (0.0458)	0.2101 (0.0622)
Return for those who attend college	0.1640 (0.0503)	0.1893 (0.0582)	0.2125 (0.0676)	0.2350 (0.0801)	0.2621 (0.0962)
Return for those who do not attend college	0.0702 (0.0536)	0.0954 (0.0385)	0.1187 (0.0298)	0.1411 (0.0305)	0.1682 (0.0425)
Return for those at the margin	0.1203 (0.0364)	0.1456 (0.0300)	0.1689 (0.0345)	0.1913 (0.0453)	0.2184 (0.0631)

Note: Wages are measured in 1991 by dividing annual earnings by hours worked per week multiplied by 52. The math test score is an average of two 10th grade math test scores. There are no dropouts in the sample and the schooling variable is binary (high school–college). The gross returns to college are divided by 3.5 (this is the average difference in years of schooling between high school graduates who go to college and high school graduates who do not in a sample of white males in the similar NLSY data). To construct the numbers in the table, we proceed in two steps. First we compute the marginal treatment effect using the method of local instrumental variables as in Carneiro, Heckman, and Vytlacil (2001). The parameters in the table are different weighted averages of the marginal treatment effect. Therefore, in the second step we compute the appropriate weight for each parameter and use it to construct a weighted average of the marginal treatment effect (see also Carneiro 2002). Individuals at the margin are indifferent between attending college or not. Standard errors are in parentheses.

economists or from genuine uncertainty that agents face in making their schooling decisions. Both anticipated heterogeneity in returns and the components of genuine uncertainty unknown to agents when they make their schooling decisions are estimated in recent research by Carneiro, Hansen, and Heckman (2001, 2003), who distinguish ex ante components of gains to schooling known to agents at the

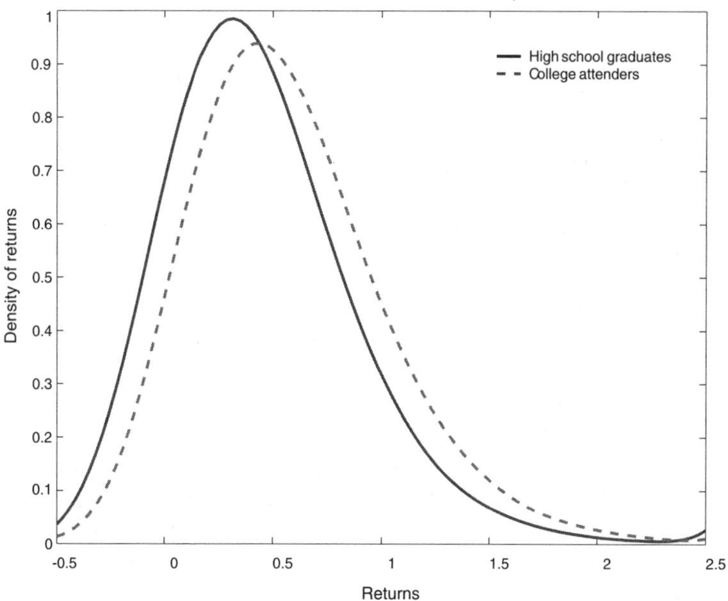

Figure 2.14
Distribution of returns to college versus high school, white males, NLSY79. *Source:* Carneiro, Hansen, and Heckman 2003.

time they make their decisions from ex post realizations of those gains.[27]

Carneiro, Hansen, and Heckman's research extends the analysis of Willis and Rosen (1979) to identify distributions of outcomes of schooling. Figure 2.14 plots the ex post (realized) counterfactual distribution of the returns to college graduation (compared to high school graduation) for both college graduates and high school graduates who do not go on to college. About 7 percent of college graduates earn ex post negative returns. For them, going to college turns out to be a financial mistake. It would be a mistake for a greater proportion (14 percent) of those who stay in high school and do not go on to college.[28]

Carneiro, Hansen, and Heckman (2003) estimate that only a small amount of the variance in the utility returns to schooling is forecastable at the time college attendance decisions are made. One way to summarize their findings is presented in figure 2.15. It shows the reduction in the ex ante dispersion of the distribution of returns to college versus high school under a no-information assumption (no predictors) and a rich information set using all the information

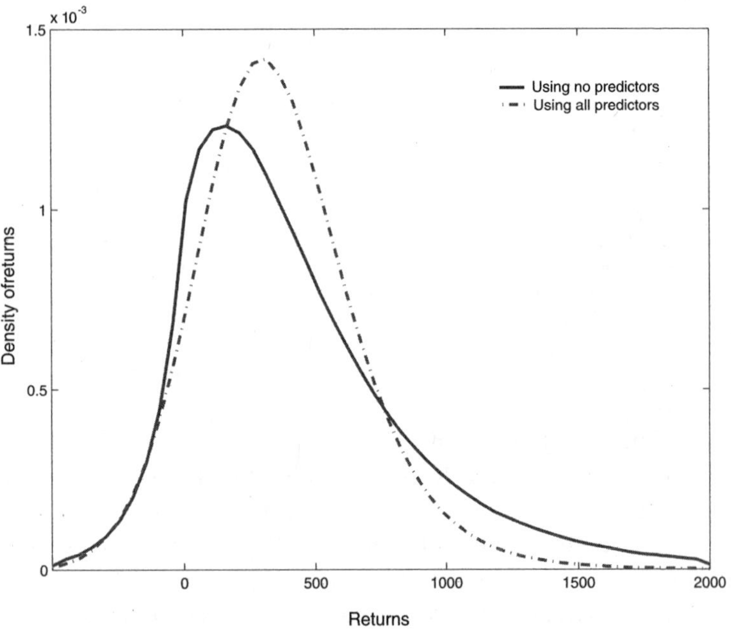

Figure 2.15
Returns to college under different information sets, white males, NLSY79.
Source: Carneiro, Hansen, and Heckman 2003.

that agents act on in making schooling choices. Even under an information set that Carneiro, Hansen, and Heckman argue is implausibly rich, there is a great deal of intrinsic uncertainty about future returns at the time schooling decisions are made. This intrinsic uncertainty, coupled with the risk aversion that is estimated in Carneiro, Hansen, and Heckman's model helps to explain some of the apparent puzzle, discussed by Ellwood and Kane (2000), among others, that students react more strongly to costs than to returns. Direct costs (such as tuition) are known with near certainty. Future returns are uncertain. Risk aversion leads agents to discount returns relative to costs.

The evidence presented above suggests that there are great potential benefits to gathering information to reduce uncertainty about future payoffs to schooling. Greater dispersion in ex ante returns among minorities and low-income majority groups in comparison to those of majority groups partially explains the sluggish response of minorities and low-income majority whites to changes in the returns to schooling over time.

However, risk aversion is not the whole story or even the main story explaining the sluggish college enrollment rates. When they simulate an environment of full information, they find that only a small fraction of people regret their schooling choices ex post. Carneiro, Hansen, and Heckman (2003) show that nonpecuniary factors (associated with psychic costs, motivations, and the like) play a major role in explaining why minorities and persons from low-income families do not attend college even though it is financially profitable to do so.

Returns to schooling for marginal entrants attracted into college by changes in tuition are below those of the average participant. Figure 2.16, taken from the work of Carneiro,

Hansen, and Heckman (2001, 2003), shows that returns to schooling are lower for people less likely to attend college.[29] Carneiro (2002) and Carneiro, Heckman, and Vytlacil (2003) also establish that the marginal returns are lowest for the least able persons, underscoring our emphasis on early ability. They analyze different American datasets and find that, for most of them, the return to one year of college for the average college student (a high-ability individual) is 4 to 15 percent larger than the return to one year of college for the average individual at the margin between attending college or not (a low-ability individual). Ability greatly affects rates of return.

The Effects of Schooling on Measured Test Scores and the Effects of Test Scores on Wages In recent work, Hansen, Heckman, and Mullen (2003) estimate the effect of schooling on test scores, accounting for the joint determination of schooling and tests.[30] It is well known that test scores predict schooling. It is more controversial that schooling raises measured test scores. Herrnstein and Murray (1994) claim that the effects of schooling on test scores are weak. Winship and Korenman (1997) survey the literature on this subject. Hansen, Heckman, and Mullen (2003) estimate the effect of additional years of schooling on standardized test scores for persons age 14 and over at different levels of latent ability.[31] Schooling is found to raise measured achievement (AFQT) by two-tenths of a standard deviation per year. This effect is uniform across latent ability levels. There are substantial gains in test scores in the early high school years. But because of parallelism across ability levels in the effects of schooling on achievement test scores, schooling does not eliminate initial disadvantages in test scores across latent ability levels. Because the relationship between log wages and test scores is nonlinear

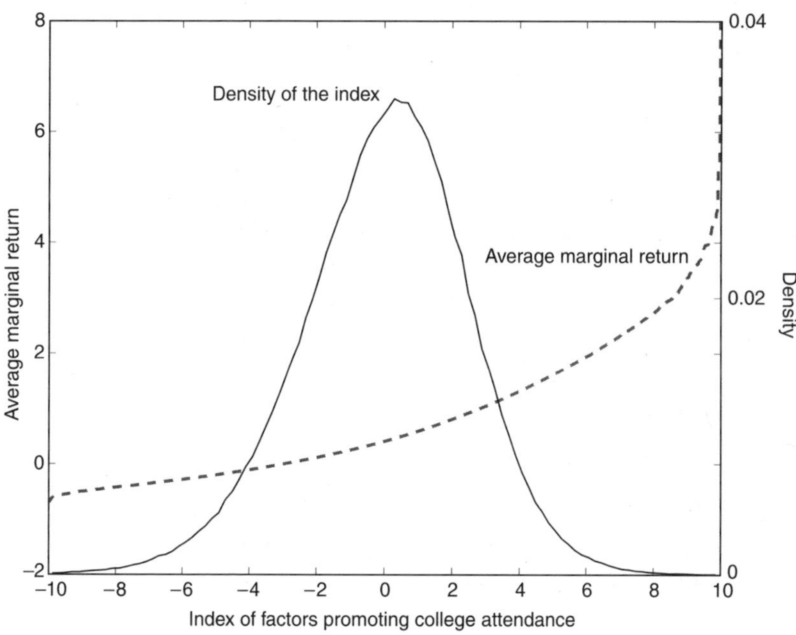

Figure 2.16
Average marginal returns for those at the margin of indifference between college and high school.
Source: Carneiro, Hansen, and Heckman 2003.
Notes: Average marginal return is for the return to college for persons at the margin of indifference to attending college for a given level of index. Factors promoting schooling refer to variables related to schooling (a higher level of the index leads to a higher probability of attending college). The density in the figure corresponds to the density of individuals at each level of the index.

(see Heckman and Vytlacil 2001), schooling tends to equalize wages for those at the bottom of the latent test score distribution.

The research of Hansen, Heckman, and Mullen shows that schooling has an additional effect on earnings through raising ability beyond its direct effect on earnings. Estimates of returns to schooling that condition on measured test scores that are reported in the literature lead to downward-biased estimates of the return to schooling.

Raising Schooling Quality The most commonly suggested reforms for schools are class size reductions, institution of summer school programs, and increases in teacher salaries and per-student expenditures. Krueger (1999) suggests that these interventions are likely to be cost effective. Some of the evidence on the success of such initiatives is based on experimental evidence, such as that from the Tennessee Student-Teacher Achievement Ratio (STAR) program. Evidence on the results of this program has been mixed; kindergarten students in smaller classes initially have higher test scores than those in larger classes, but in later grades, treatment and control group students' test scores move much closer together, although there is still a small positive effect of the program (see Hanushek 2000; for an opposing view, see Krueger 1999). There is no evidence that class size reductions of the sort reported in the Tennessee STAR experiment will substantially affect earnings or reduce the substantial skill gaps across socioeconomic groups in American society. Even if the test score gains from class size reduction can be shown to be persistent, test scores are only weakly linked to earnings later in life (Cawley, Heckman, and Vytlacil 1999; Heckman and Vytlacil 2001).

Studies linking measures of schooling quality to lifetime earnings and occupational achievement have recently appeared, making unnecessary reliance on inherently arbitrarily scaled test scores for evaluating the effectiveness of interventions in schooling quality. There is a growing consensus as a result of these studies that within current ranges in most developed economies, changes in measured inputs such as class size and spending per pupil have weak effects on the future earnings of students (see Heckman, Layne-Farrar, and Todd 1996; Hanushek 1998, 2003). Even if one takes the most favorable estimates from the literature and combines them with the best-case scenario for the costs of raising schooling quality, decreasing the pupil-teacher ratio by 5 pupils per teacher does not turn out to be a wise investment. Such a reduction in the pupil-teacher ratio, while keeping the number of students enrolled the same, would require the addition of new teachers, not to mention the addition of new classroom and school facilities. Accounting only for the costs of adding new teachers, we estimate that decreasing the pupil-teacher ratio by 5 pupils per teacher would cost about $790 per student.[32] Table 2.5 presents estimates of the net returns for such a reduction in the pupil-teacher ratio under different assumptions about productivity growth, discount rates, and the social opportunity costs of funds.[33] Taking a high estimate (relative to the estimates reported in the literature) of a 4 percent increase in future earnings resulting from a decrease in the pupil-teacher ratio by 5 pupils per teacher yields a *loss* of lifetime earnings of between $2,600 and $5,500 per 1990 high school graduate at standard discount rates (5 to 7 percent).

Card and Krueger (1997) argue that productivity growth in wages should be included in calculations of returns to reductions in the pupil-teacher ratio. Using a 1 percent productivity growth rate, which is consistent with historical experience, does not reverse the conclusion reached as a result of such calculations. Even using a 3 percent productivity growth rate in wages (calculations not shown), which is a high estimate outside of historical experience, does not offset the costs unless one uses a 3 percent discount rate.[34] Estimates of the net returns to reductions in the pupil-teacher ratio are even more negative after the social costs of taxation

Table 2.5
Evaluating school quality policies: discounted net returns to decreasing pupil-teacher ratio by 5 pupils per teacher for people with 12 years of schooling in 1990

	Productivity growth rate	Includes 50% social cost of funds	Annual rate of return to earnings from school quality change		
			1%	2%	4%
7% discount rate	0%	Yes	−9056	−8092	−6163
	0%	No	−5716	−4752	−2823
	1%	Yes	−8878	−7736	−5451
	1%	No	−5538	−4396	−2111
5% discount rate	0%	Yes	−9255	−7537	−4103
	0%	No	−5597	−3880	−445
	1%	Yes	−8887	−6802	−2632
	1%	No	−5230	−3145	1025
3% discount rate	0%	Yes	−8840	−5591	905
	0%	No	−4810	−1562	4934
	1%	Yes	−8036	−3984	4119
	1%	No	−4007	45	8149

Note: All values, in 1990 dollars, are given as net present values at age 6 of an individual; costs of schooling improvements are incurred between ages 6 and 18 and benefits from increased earnings occur between ages 19 and 65. Data for costs are from NCES 1993. Costs of adding new teachers include salaries and capital, administrative, and maintenance expenditures. Estimates of increases in earnings resulting from a decrease in the pupil-teacher ratio by 5 pupils per teacher come from Card and Krueger (1992), table 3, which produces a range of estimated earnings increases from about 1 to 4 percent, whereas most of the estimates in the literature are in the 1 to 2 percent range. To capture the benefits of smaller class sizes, students must attend twelve years of higher quality of schooling. We calculate the costs for one year of improvements and then calculate the present value of the costs over the twelve years of school attendance.

are accounted for. Only if we take very high-end estimates of the effect of schooling quality on earnings and discount costs by a very low rate (3 percent) do we find any sizeable positive effect of schooling quality on future earnings.

The evidence presented here regarding the returns to reductions in pupil-teacher ratios indicates that the United States may be spending too much on students given the current organization of educational production. Pouring more funds into schools to lower class sizes by one or two pupils or to raise spending per pupil by a few hundred dollars will not solve the problems of the American primary and secondary school system, nor will it stimulate the college going of minorities and the poor. This is not to say that school quality does not matter. Hanushek (1971, 1997), Murnane (1975), and Hanushek and Luque (2000) all show that individual teachers matter in the sense of raising the test scores of students. Conventional measures of teacher quality do not, however, predict who are the good teachers. Giving principals more discretion in rewarding and punishing teachers would be an effective way to use local knowledge. Bureaucratization hinders use of this knowledge.

Although the effects of schooling quality vary across environments and additional funding for some schools may be justified, marginal improvements in school quality are likely to be ineffective in raising lifetime earnings and more fundamental changes are required if we hope to see a significant improvement in our educational system.

Improving School Quality through Choice in Schooling

It is commonly perceived that despite the high estimated returns to schooling, American primary and secondary schools as a whole are failing. The evidence for this failure is both the dismal ranking of the performance of American high school students on standardized achievement tests compared to that of students from other nations and stagnant test scores among American students over time (see the evidence presented in Blau and Kahn 2001; OECD and Statistics Canada 1995; and Hanushek 2000). Determining how to fix this problem requires an understanding of how American schools are organized. By and large, public school systems in the United States are local monopolies with few competitors. The incentives of many principals and teachers to produce knowledge are weak, although there are many dedicated professionals in these schools who work hard without reward. Educational bureaucracies are often unresponsive to the changing demand for skills or to the market realities that will confront their students when they leave schools. They are not accountable to anyone because it is not easy to monitor them. One valuable source of information—parental and student perception of the qualities of teachers and schools—is rarely used to punish poor teaching.

School choice has been advocated as a reform to improve the quality of educational services for students. Proponents of school choice argue that competition among schools to attract students will force schools to decrease costs and increase the quality of services provided. Additionally, by having parents actively choose the schools attended by their children, school choice systems would likely increase the degree of parental involvement in children's schooling. On the other hand, opponents of school choice argue that increased competition among schools will lead to increased stratification and inequality among students as well as a dilution of basic schooling standards and that poor parents lack the information and the ability to make informed decisions for their children. Hence, school choice systems would be most beneficial to those already able to exercise choice in the current system, the richer families.

Most of the research on this topic has been theoretical. Although there is some degree of choice within the current U.S. schooling system that can be explored to understand the mechanisms of school choice, the data are often lacking and when available are generally inconclusive.

Voucher experiments provide data for empirical studies concerning school choice. Experiments that give tuition vouchers to public-school students so that they may attend private schools have been conducted in several U.S. cities, including Milwaukee, Cleveland, Minneapolis, and New York.[35] These experiments have been studied, but the conclusions of these studies have been controversial. Researchers do not agree on whether vouchers have any impact on students' educational achievement. Recent research (see Peterson and Hassel 1998) shows important differences in student and parental satisfaction. Relative to parents not allowed to exercise choice, parents under school choice systems are more likely than other parents to report satisfaction with their children's school. These voucher experiments are often limited in their scale, and it is difficult to generalize any findings from them to the national level. Any national voucher program will most likely have large general-equilibrium effects that cannot be estimated from these small-scale experiments (see Urquiola and Hsieh 2002).

Other researchers have studied the effect of introducing competition among public schools into the monopolistic setting of the U.S. public school system. Evidence from these studies indicates that increased school competition and student and parental choice improves the quality of schools, as measured by test scores and by parental and student satisfaction with learning. Contrary to the view that competition siphons resources away from the public sector to its detriment, Caroline Hoxby's (2000) research suggests that when public schools are subject to greater competition both from parochial and other private schools, the performance of all schools increases. Higher levels of achievement are produced at lower cost.

Cullen, Jacob, and Levitt (2000) present evidence on competition among schools in the Chicago Public Schools. They find that those students who change schools given the choice have higher high school graduation rates than observationally identical students who remain at their assigned schools. They explain this outcome as resulting from student sorting. School choice allows higher-ability students to sort to higher-quality schools and increase their likelihood of high school graduation. Even though choice helps high-quality students, it does not seem to hurt low-ability students.

A study by Derek Neal (1997) demonstrates that the higher schooling attainment of students in Catholic schools compared to those in public schools is largely a consequence of gains registered by inner-city students who choose Catholic schools over inferior inner-city public schools. In the suburbs, where districts are smaller and competition among school districts is more intense, the Catholic schools have little advantage over the public schools, and the performance of both school systems is higher than that of the inner-city schools. Grogger and Neal (2000) present substantial evidence confirmatory of the original Neal study using a broader set of outcome measures, including measured achievement and attainment.

It is remarkable that in a society as committed to consumer sovereignty and choice as the American society, there is so much resistance to permitting choice and instituting incentives in education. The conventional argument of educational planners is that parents and students are not able to make wise choices. The available evidence points to better outcomes from increased school competition but it is far from definitive. Policies that promote such competition are much more likely to raise schooling performance than policies that increase schooling quality and do not change the organization of schools. Exact quantitative trade-offs, however, are not available (see Hanushek 2000, 2002).

Early Childhood Investments

The evidence presented in the second part of this chapter suggests that both cognitive and noncognitive abilities affect schooling and economic success and that socioeconomic differences in cognitive and noncognitive skills appear early and, if anything, widen over the life cycle of the child. We demonstrate there that parental inputs are important correlates of these skills. Yet the policy intervention indicated by this evidence is far from obvious, because the exact causal mechanisms through which good families produce good children are not yet well understood. Perhaps for this reason, American society has been reluctant to intervene in family life, especially in the early years.

There is a profound asymmetry in popular views about family life and schooling. On the one hand, there is a widespread belief that parents cannot make wise choices about their children's schooling. If that is true, then how can parents be trusted to make correct decisions in the preschool years, which recent research has demonstrated to be so important for lifetime success? The logical extension of the paternalistic argument that denies the wisdom of parental sovereignty in choosing schools would suggest that the state should play a far more active role in the preschool life of the child. That is a position that few would accept.

Paternalistic interventions in the early life of children in certain dysfunctional families may be appropriate. If we are to violate the principle of family sovereignty anywhere in the life cycle process of learning, the case for doing so is strongest at the preschool stage (and only for some groups) and not at later stages of formal schooling, for which the argument for paternalism is most often made. Dysfunctional families and environments are major sources of social problems. Paternalistic interventions into the life of such families may be warranted on efficiency grounds, although such interventions raise serious questions about the need to protect the sanctity of family life.

Recent small-scale studies of early-childhood investments in children from disadvantaged environments have shown remarkable success. They indicate that interventions in the early years can effectively promote learning and that external interventions can enrich child environments. They demonstrate the value of good families by showing that interventions can remedy the failings of bad families. Early-childhood interventions of high quality have lasting effects on learning and motivation. They raise achievement and noncognitive skills, but they do not raise IQ. Disadvantaged subnormal IQ children (average IQ = 80) in Ypsilanti, Michigan, were randomly assigned to the Perry Preschool program, and intensive treatment was administered to them at ages 4 to 5. Treatment was then discontinued, and the children were followed over their life cycle. Evidence on the treatment group, which is now about thirty-five years old, indicates that those enrolled in the program have higher earnings and lower levels of criminal behavior in their late twenties than did comparable children randomized out of the program. Reported benefit-cost ratios for the program are substantial. Measured through age 27, the program returns $5.70 for every dollar spent. When returns are projected for the remainder of the lives of program participants, the return on the dollar rises to $8.70. A substantial fraction (65 percent) of the return to the program has been attributed to reductions in crime (Schweinhart, Barnes, and Weikart 1993). The Syracuse Preschool program provided family development support for disadvantaged children, from prenatal care for their mothers through age 5 of the children's lives. Reductions in problems with probation and criminal offenses ten years later were as large as 70 percent among children randomly assigned to the program. Girls who participated in the program also showed greater school achievement (Lally, Mangione, and Honig 1988). Studies have found short-term increases in test scores, less in-grade retention, and higher high school graduation rates among children enrolled in early intervention programs. Of those studies that examine predelinquent or criminal behavior, most have found lower rates of such behavior among program participants. Table 2.6 summarizes the effects of selected early intervention programs on student test scores, schooling, earnings, and delinquency. Table 2.7 recounts the findings of studies on the Perry Preschool program, and a cost-benefit analysis of that program. The benefit-cost ratio is substantially greater than one. Recent estimates of the internal rate of return to the program are 13 percent (Barnett, personal communication, 2002). This number looks low relative to the 15 to 20 percent return for schooling reported by Carneiro (2002). It should be compared to the return for low-ability students, because the Perry program only recruited low-ability children. Table 2.4 shows that the

Table 2.6
Effects of early intervention programs

Program/Study	Costs[a]	Program description
Abecedarian Project[b] (Ramey et al. 1988)	N/A	Full-time year-round classes for children from infancy through preschool
Early Training[b] (Gray, Ramey, and Klaus 1982)	N/A	Part-time classes for children in summer; weekly home visits during school year
Harlem Study (Palmer 1983)	N/A	Individual teacher-child sessions twice weekly for young males
Houston PCDC[b] (Johnson 1988)	N/A	Home visits for parents for two years; child nursery care four days per week in year 2 (Mexican Americans)
Milwaukee Project[b] (Garber 1988)	N/A	Full-time year-round classes for children through first grade; job training for mothers
Mother-Child Home Program (Levenstein, O'Hara, and Madden 1983)	N/A	Home visits with mothers and children twice weekly
Perry Preschool Program[b] (Schweinhart, Barnes, and Weikart 1993)	$13,400	Weekly home visits with parents; intensive, high-quality preschool services for one to two years
Rome Head Start (Monroe and McDonald 1981)	$5,400 (2 years)	Part-time classes for children; parent involvement
Syracuse University Family Development (Lally, Mangione, and Honig 1988)	$38,100	Weekly home visits for family; day care year round
Yale experiment	$23,300	Family support; home visits and day care as needed for thirty months

Source: Heckman, Lochner, Smith, and Taber (1997). Data from Donohue and Siegelman (1998), Schweinhart, Barnes, and Weikart (1993), and Seitz (1990) for the impacts reported here.
Note: All comparisons are for program participants versus nonparticipants. N/A indicates not available.

Test scores	Schooling	Predelinquency crime
Higher scores at ages 1–4	34% less in-grade retention by second grade; better reading and math proficiency	N/A
Higher scores at ages 5–10	16% less in-grade retention; 21% higher high school graduation	N/A
Higher scores at ages 3–5	21% less in-grade retention	N/A
Higher scores at age 3	N/A	Rated less aggressive and hostile by mothers (ages 8–11)
Higher scores at ages 2–10	27% less in-grade retention	N/A
Higher scores at ages 3–4	6% less in-grade retention	N/A
Higher scores in all studied years (ages 5–27)	21% less in-grade retention or special services; 21% higher HS graduation rates	2.3 versus 4.6 lifetime arrests by age 27.7% versus 35% arrested five or more times
N/A	12% less in-grade retention; 17% higher HS graduation rates	N/A
Higher scores at ages 3–4	N/A	6% versus 22% had probation files; offenses were less severe
Better language development at thirty months	Better school attendance and adjustment; fewer special adjustments; school services (ages 12 1/2)	Rated less aggressive and predelinquent by teachers and parents (ages 12 1/2)

a. Costs valued in 1990 dollars.

b. Studies used a random assignment experimental design to determine program impacts.

Table 2.7
Perry Preschool: Net present values of costs and benefits through age 27

1. Cost of preschool for child, ages 3–4	12,148
2. Decrease in cost to government of K–12 special education courses for child, ages 5 to 18	6,365
3. Decrease in direct criminal justice system costs[a] of child's criminal activity, ages 15 to 28	7,378
4. Decrease in direct criminal justice system costs[a] of child's projected criminal activity, ages 29 to 44	2,817
5. Income from child's increased employment, ages 19 to 27	8,380
6. Projected income from child's increased employment, ages 28 to 65	7,565
7. Decrease in tangible losses to crime victims, ages 15 to 44	10,690
Total benefits:	43,195
Total benefits excluding projections[b]	32,813
Benefits minus costs	31,047
Benefits minus costs excluding projections[b]	20,665

Sources: Karoly et al. 1998 and Barnett 1993.
Notes: All values are net present values in 1996 dollars at age 0 calculated using a 4 percent discount rate.
a. Direct criminal justice system costs are the administrative costs of incarceration.
b. Benefits from projected decreased criminal activity (4) and projected income from increased employment (6) are excluded.

return to one year of college for the average individual in the fifth percentile of the ability distribution is 11 percent and the return to college for the average individual in the fifth percentile of the ability distribution not attending college is 7 percent. (Most of the population at this percentile of the ability distribution is not attending college, so the latter is the relevant number for the comparison.) If we examine individuals at the twenty-fifth percentile of the ability distribution, higher than the percentile for the Perry participants, this return rises to 9.5 percent. We conjecture that the returns to maternal inputs at early ages are very high for normal children and that 13 percent is a lower bound on the return for normal children, although there is no direct evidence on this issue. At the same time, the gap between schooling and preschooling returns might widen if there are substantial noncognitive returns to schooling that we have not enumerated.

Evidence on the more universal Head Start program is less clear, but the program is quite heterogeneous and is much less well funded than the Perry Preschool program. Currie and Thomas (1995) find short-term gains in test scores for all children participating in Head Start; most of those gains decayed quickly, however, for African American children after they left the program. Currie and Thomas conclude that either differences in local-program administration or in quality of schooling subsequent to the Head Start program are at the root of the differences between the outcomes for black and white children. Ramey et al. (1988) note that the schools attended by the Perry Preschool children were of substantially higher quality than those attended by the typical Head Start child. In addition, the Perry program also taught parenting skills and arguably put better long-term environments in place for the children. The failure to support in subsequent years the initial positive stimulus of Head Start may account for the decline in the impact of Head Start over time, and may account for its apparent ineffectiveness compared to the Perry Preschool program. In a more recent paper, Garces, Thomas, and Currie (2002) find substantial long-term effects of Head Start on high school graduation, college attendance, earnings, and crime. The largest effects are for individuals whose mothers have less than a high school education. Among whites in this group, attending Head Start leads to a 28 percent increase in the probability of high school graduation, a 27 percent increase in the probability of college attendance, and a 100 percent increase in earnings measured in the early twenties. For blacks, the likelihood of being booked or charged with crime is 12 percent lower for those who attended Head Start than for those who did not.

In light of our discussion in the chapter's second part, an exclusive emphasis on cognitive test scores is misplaced. It appears that early childhood programs are most effective in changing noncognitive skills, although they also raise achievement test scores (as opposed to IQ). We also note that eventual decay of initial gains in test scores, like those found in regard to the Head Start program, were found for programs like Perry Preschool as well, but the long-term evaluations of these programs are quite favorable in terms of participants' success in school and society at large. The psychometric test score literature is not clear about the relationship between early test scores and success in school, graduation rates, socialization, and labor market outcomes. The fade-out effects in test scores found for the Head Start program do not imply that participation in the program has no long-term beneficial effects. Head Start may improve the lifetime prospects of its participants, despite yielding only short-term gains in test scores, which may not measure many relevant dimensions of social and emotional skills.

The Perry intervention affected both children and parents. Parents in the program improved their education and labor force activity and reduced their participation in welfare. Successful enrichment programs like Perry Preschool foster long-term improvements in the home environment that carry over to the child long after the program has terminated. Head Start offers a staff of much lower quality (and much lower paid), part-time classes for children, and limited parental involvement. The program terminates without any substantial intervention into or improvement in the home environments of the disadvantaged children. Improvements in Head Start, proponents argue, are likely to produce effects closer to those observed in more-successful small-scale programs. Given the potential for success of such programs (as exhibited by the Perry Preschool experiment), more studies of the long-term impacts of various types of small-scale and broad-based early intervention programs are certainly warranted. Provocative calculations by John Donohue and Peter Siegelman (1998) indicate that if enriched early intervention programs were targeted toward high-risk, disadvantaged minority male youth, the expected savings in incarceration costs alone would more than repay the substantial costs of these enriched programs.

An important lesson to draw from the Perry Preschool program, and indeed from the entire literature on successful early interventions, is that the social skills and motivation of the child are more easily altered than his or her IQ. These social and emotional skills affect performance in school and in the workplace. Academics have a bias toward believing that cognitive skills are of fundamental importance to success in life. Because of this, the relatively low malleability of IQs after early ages has led many to proclaim a variety of interventions to be ineffective. Yet the evidence from the Perry Preschool program and the evidence presented in table 2.8 reveals that early intervention programs are highly effective in reducing criminal activity, promoting social skills, and integrating disadvantaged children into mainstream society. The greatest benefits of these programs are their effects on socialization and not those on IQ. Social skills and motivation have large payoffs in the labor market, so these programs have the potential for a large payoff.

Table 2.8
Outcomes of early intervention programs

	Program (years of operation)	Outcome
Cognitive measures	Early Training Project (1962–1965)	IQ
	Perry Preschool Project (1962–1967)	IQ
	Houston PCDC (1970–1980)	IQ
	Syracuse FDRP (1969–1970)	IQ
	Carolina Abecedarian (1972–1985)	IQ
	Project CARE (1978–1984)	IQ
	IHDP (1985–1988)	IQ (HLBW[a] sample)
Educational outcomes	Early Training Project	Special education
	Perry Preschool Project	Special education High school graduation
	Chicago CPC (1967–present)	Special education Grade retention High school graduation
	Carolina Abecedarian	College enrollment
Economic outcomes	Perry Preschool Project	Arrest rate Employment rate Monthly earnings Welfare use
	Chicago CPC (preschool vs. no preschool)	Juvenile arrests
	Syracuse FDRP	Probation referral
	Elmira PEIP (1978–1982)	Arrests (High risk sample)

Source: Karoly 2001.
Notes: Cognitive measures include Stanford-Binet and Wechsler Intelligence Scales, California Achievement Tests, and other IQ and achievement tests measuring cognitive ability. All results significant at .05 level or higher. For a discussion of the specific treatments offered under each program see Heckman 2000 and Karoly 2001.

Followed up to age	Age when treatment effect last statistically significant	Control group	Change in treated group
16–20	6	82.8	+12.2
27	7	87.1	+4.0
8–11	2	90.8	+8.0
15	3	90.6	+19.7
21	12	88.4	+5.3
4.5	3	92.6	+11.6
8	8	92.1	+4.4
16–20	18	29%	−26%
27	19	28%	−12%
	27	45%	+21%
20	18	25%	−10%
	15	38%	−15%
	20	39%	+11%
21	21	14%	+22%
27	27	69%	−12%
	27	32%	+18%
	27	$766	+$453
	27	32%	−17%
20	18	25%	−8%
15	15	22%	−16%
15	15	0.53	−45%

Houston PCDC is the Houston Parent-Child Development Center. Syracuse FDRP is the Syracuse Family Development Research Program. Project Care is the Carolina Approach to Responsive Education. IHDP is the Infant Health and Development Project. Chicago CPC is the Child-Parent Center. Elmira PEIP is the Elmira (New York) Prenatal/Early Infancy Project.

a. HLBW = heavier, low birth weight sample.

At the same time, it is important to be cautious about the evidence from these programs. Whether they can be replicated on a large scale is an issue. Like those in the Tennessee STAR program, teachers in the early intervention programs studied may have been motivated more than would be possible in a permanent large-scale program. Proper accounting for future benefits is required before strong conclusions can be drawn. The substantial gap in time between the payment in terms of costs and the harvest of benefits requires that these benefits be substantial to justify early intervention programs. Prima facie the benefits are there, but a stronger case would be desirable.

We next turn to the evidence on the effectiveness of interventions for older children. Programs aimed at intervening in the lives of children in their teen years attempt to redress the damage of bad childhoods. Although these programs do not raise participants' IQ, there is some evidence that they can affect their social skills (noncognitive abilities), because the prefrontal cortex, which controls emotion and behavior, is malleable until the late teenage years (Shonkoff and Phillips 2000).

Interventions in the Adolescent Years

How effective are interventions in the adolescent years? Is it possible to remedy the consequences of neglect in the early years? These questions are relevant because cognitive abilities are fairly well determined and stable by age 8 in the sense that IQ at later ages is highly correlated with IQ at that ages. Just as early intervention programs have a high payoff primarily because of the social skills and motivation they impart to the child and the improved home environment they produce, interventions during the adolescent years also have high payoffs for many of the same reasons.

Table 2.9 summarizes evidence on the effects of adolescent interventions on education, earnings, and crime rates. There are few estimates of rates of return for these programs. School-based and training-based programs are compared in the table. We briefly discuss here what is known about school-based interventions during the adolescent years. A few recent studies of mentoring programs, like the Big Brothers/Big Sisters (BB/BS) and the Philadelphia Futures Sponsor-A-Scholar (SAS) programs, have shown that these programs have broad positive social and academic impacts on participating school-aged children and adolescents. BB/BS pairs unrelated adult volunteers with youth from single-parent households for the purpose of providing youth with an adult friend. This promotes private youth development and surrogate parenthood. No specific attempts are made to ameliorate particular deficiencies or to reach specific educational goals; a broad, supportive role is envisioned for the mentor. In a random-assignment study, Tierney and Grossman (1995) found that eighteen months after being matched with a mentor, Little Brothers and Sisters (ages 10 to 16 at the time of the match) were less likely to have initiated drug or alcohol use, to hit someone, to skip class or a day of school, or to lie to their parents; they had higher average grades and were more likely to feel competent in their school work and report a better relationship with their parents.

The primary goal of SAS is to help students from Philadelphia public high schools make it to college. The program provides long-term mentoring (throughout high school and for one year beyond), substantial academic support, help with college application and financial-aid procedures, and financial support for college-related expenses. Individually matched mentors serve as surrogate parents, provide

Table 2.9
Estimated benefits of mentoring programs (treatment group compared to control group)

Program	Outcome measure	Change	Program costs per participant
Big Brother/ Big Sister	Initiating drug use	−45.8%	\$500–\$1500[a]
	Initiation alcohol use	−27.4%	
	Number of times hit someone	−31.7%	
	Number of times stole something	−19.2%	
	Grade point average (GPA)	3.0%	
	Skipped class	−36.7%	
	Skipped day of school	−52.2%	
	Trust in parent	2.7%	
	Lying to parent	−36.6%	
	Peer emotional support	2.3%	
Sponsor-A-Scholar	Tenth-grade GPA (100-point scale)	2.9	\$1485
	Eleventh-grade GPA (100-point scale)	2.5	
	% Attending college (1 year after HS)	32.8%	
	% Attending college (2 years after HS)	28.1%	
Quantum Opportunity Program	Graduated HS or obtained GED	+26%	N/A
	Enrolled in 4-year college	+15%	
	Enrolled in 2-year college	+24%	
	Currently employed full time	+13%	
	Self receiving welfare	−22%	
	Percentage ever arrested	−4%	

Table 2.9
(continued)

Sources: Benefits from Heckman 1999 and Taggart 1995, costs from Johnson 1996 and Herrera et al. 2000.
a. Costs, in 1996 dollars, for school-based programs are as low as $500 per participant and more expensive community-based mentoring programs cost as much as $1,500. HS = high school.

a successful role model, monitor student progress, and provide encouragement and support. SAS provides students with $6,000 in financial assistance throughout college for those choosing to enroll in an accredited two- or four-year postsecondary institution. The program also provides a coordinator for groups of about thirty students to ensure a successful relationship is built between mentors and students. Using a matched sample of non-SAS students in Philadelphia high schools,[36] Johnson (1996) estimates statistically significant increases in grade point averages for tenth and eleventh grades, as well as a 22 percent (16 percent) increase in college attendance one year (two years) after graduation from high school. Because the primary goal of SAS is to increase college enrollment, Johnson did not collect other social and psychological measures.

Much like SAS, the Quantum Opportunity Program (QOP) offered disadvantaged minority students counseling and financial incentives (one dollar up front and one dollar put in a college fund) for every hour spent in activities aimed at improving social and market skills. Students who were randomly chosen to participate in the program were provided with a mentor at the beginning of ninth grade. All participants were kept in the program for four years regardless of whether they stayed in school. Over four years, the average participant logged 1,286 hours of educational activities like studying with tutors or visiting museums. Two years after program completion, about a third more participating students graduated from high school (or obtained a GED) than similar nonparticipants. Since many participants were enrolled in postsecondary schooling at the time of the follow-up study, it is difficult to determine the program's effect on earnings. Arrest rates for program participants, however, were one-half those for nonparticipants. These benefits did not come without substantial expenditures, however, as the average four-year cost per participant was $10,600. Still, a cost-benefit analysis estimated positive net social returns to QOP. (See Taggart 1995 for a more detailed description of the program and an evaluation of its impacts). Tables 2.9–2.10 present evidence from a randomized-trial evaluation of the Quantum program. Again, the evidence shows that QOP and programs like it can dramatically improve social skills and the adaptation of adolescents to society.

Two other studies provide additional evidence that creative programs designed to keep adolescents in school can be effective. These are discussed more extensively in Heckman 2000 and Heckman and Lochner 2000, and we merely summarize these discussions here. Ohio's Learning, Earning, and Parenting (LEAP) program and the Teenage Parent Demonstration (TPD) provided financial incentives for teenage parents on welfare to stay in school or take GED classes (or, alternatively, imposed financial penalties for nonenrollment). LEAP showed increases in high school graduation or GED rates among randomly assigned participants who were still enrolled in school when they entered the program. TPD showed mixed results on education depending on the program site. Young women who had already dropped out of school at the time of enrollment in the program (and, to a lesser extent, those who were still attending school when they entered the program) may have substituted GED training for high school graduation as an easier way to meet program requirements, raising concerns about an unintended, potentially negative effect.[37] Both of these programs show positive post-program effects on earnings and employment for students who were still in school when they entered the program. The effects were often negative, however, for participants who had already dropped out of school before entering the program. Both studies thus show more positive impacts for individuals still enrolled in school than for dropouts.[38] It is still unknown whether the effects of the programs are more positive for those still in school because, on average, they are of higher ability than those who have already dropped out, or because there is some advantage to intervening before adolescents leave school.

The available schooling literature demonstrates that providing disadvantaged students with financial incentives to stay in school and participate in learning activities can increase schooling and improve employment outcomes. It should be noted that although programs providing such incentives have proven to influence employment and earnings positively (and, in the case of QOP, to reduce crime), they do not perform miracles. The impacts they achieve are modest, but positive. (See the estimates in table 2.9)

The Summer Training and Employment Program (STEP) provided remedial academic education and summer jobs to disadvantaged youth ages 14 and 15. Each summer, participants enrolled in 110 hours of classes and 90 hours of part-time work. Although program participants achieved modest short-term gains in reading and math skills, those

Table 2.10
Effects of selected adolescent social programs on schooling and crime

Program/Study	Costs[a]	Program description	Schooling	Crime
STEP (Walker and Viella-Velez 1992)	N/A	Two summers of employment, academic remediation and life skills for 14- to 15-year-olds	Short-run gains in test scores; no effect on school completion rates	N/A
Quantum Opportunities Program[b] (Taggart 1995)	$10,600	Counseling; educational, community, and development services; financial incentives for four years beginning in ninth grade	34% higher high school graduation and GED reception rates (two years after program)	4% versus 16% convicted; .28 versus .56 average. number of arrests (2 years after program)

Source: Heckman, Lochner, Smith, and Taber 1997.
Notes: All comparisons are for program participants vs. nonparticipants. N/A indicated not available.
a. All dollar figures are in 1990 values.
b. Studies used a random assignment experimental design to determine program impacts.

gains did not last. Two to three years after program completion, program participation was found to have no effects on high school graduation rates, grades, or employment. The program has been criticized for not attempting to follow up on its summer program with a school year curriculum. Maryland's Tomorrow program did just that: it combined an intensive summer program with a school year follow-up, offering participants summer jobs and academic instruction, career guidance, and counseling through adult mentors, peer support, or tutoring. Although the program did not reduce final dropout rates, it did seem to delay dropout (dropout rates were lower for program participants during the ninth grade but not by the end of the twelfth grade). The program also increased the pass rate for twelfth grade students taking the Maryland Functional Tests, a series of tests of basic skills (see Heckman and Lochner 2000).

The evidence on programs aimed at increasing the skills and earnings of disadvantaged youth suggests that sustained interventions targeted at adolescents still enrolled in school can positively affect learning and subsequent employment and earnings.[39] The studies discussed in this section also suggest that interventions for dropouts are much less successful. Unfortunately, they do not reveal why. We do not know whether there is some advantage to intervening in a young person's life if he or she has already made the decision to drop out, or whether those who choose to drop out have less motivation and lower ability, making programs less effective for them regardless of when the intervention takes place. It is important to remember, however, that the interventions conducted by such programs only alleviate and do not reverse early damage caused by bad family environments.

Public and Private Job Training

Because of a lack of data and a bias in favor of the funding of studies of government training, the returns to private-sector training are less well studied than the returns to public-sector training. Studies by Lynch (1992, 1993), Lillard and Tan (1986), Bishop (1994), and Bartel (1992) find sizable effects of private-sector training on earnings. In comparison with studies of public-sector training, most of these studies do not attempt to control for the bias that arises because more-able persons are more likely to undertake training, so estimated rates of return overstate the true returns to training by combining them with the return to ability. Part of the measured return may result from the fact that more-motivated and able persons undertake training. Upper-bound estimates of the return to training for marginal entrants range from 16 to 26 percent and are comparable to those obtained from education (see table 2.11).

An important feature of private sector training is that the more-skilled participants in such training do more investing in human capital even after they attain high skill levels. Different types of training and learning have strong complementarities with respect to one another. The hypothesis of

Table 2.11
Rates of return on investment in private job training

Data set	Return
PSID, all males	23.5%
NLS (new young cohort)	16.0%
NLS (old young cohort)	26.0%

Source: Mincer 1993.
Note: PSID is the Panel Study of Income Dynamics. NLS is the National Longitudinal Survey.

universal complementarity that underlies figures 2.6a and 2.6b receives support in recent U.S. data. Table 2.12 analyzes participation in training for different demographic groups. As shown in column 1, more-able people (as measured by AFQT) and people with more schooling are more likely to participate in company training. This is further evidence on dynamic complementarity that supports our thesis that skill begets skill and that motivates figure 2.6a and 2.6b. Those with higher parental income, however, (as measured by family income at age 14 and by father's education), after their own education and their own ability are controlled for, are more likely to train in companies after completing their schooling. Private financing arrangements between workers and firms appear to offset family income constraints and partially offset initial disadvantages. On net, however, postschool training is neither equalizing nor disequalizing. Column 2 of the table reports the net effect of parental background and family income, with neither schooling nor ability controlled for. For most demographic groups, private job training is neutral with respect to family background after its effects on ability and schooling are netted out.

Low-skilled persons typically do not participate in private-sector training. Firms can be exclusive regarding participation in programs they fund in ways that government training programs for disadvantaged workers are designed not to be. The lack of interest of private firms in training disadvantaged workers indicates the difficulty of the task and the likely low return to this activity. The best available evidence indicates that public training programs are an inefficient transfer mechanism and an inefficient investment policy for low-skilled adult workers. We present that evidence next.

Table 2.12
Average marginal effect of AFQT, family income, grade completed, and father's education on participation in company training

Variables	Average marginal effect					
	White males		Black males		Hispanic males	
	(1)	(2)	(1)	(2)	(1)	(2)
Age-adjusted AFQT	0.0149	—	0.0182	—	0.0066	—
	(0.0024)	—	(0.0033)	—	(0.0037)	—
Family income in 1979 (in $10,000)	−0.0021	−0.0005	−0.0047	−0.0019	0.0011	0.0015
	(0.0012)	(0.0011)	(0.0024)	(0.0023)	(0.0024)	(0.0023)
Grade completed	0.0382	—	0.0060	—	0.0036	—
	(0.001)	—	(0.0014)	—	(0.0014)	—
Father's education	−0.0014	0.0007	0.0003	0.0010	0.0002	0.0008
	(0.0006)	(0.0005)	(0.0008)	(0.0008)	(0.0007)	(0.0007)
	White females		Black females		Hispanic females	
	(1)	(2)	(1)	(2)	(1)	(2)
Age-adjusted AFQT	0.0076	—	0.0169	—	0.0159	—
	(0.0025)	—	(0.0038)	—	(0.0045)	—
Family income in 1979 (in $10,000)	−0.0007	0.0001	−0.0006	0.0014	−0.0065	−0.0043
	(0.0011)	(0.0011)	(0.0024)	(0.0023)	(0.0031)	(0.0029)

Grade completed	0.0027	—	0.0014	—	0.0013	—
	(0.0010)	—	(0.0016)	—	(0.0016)	—
Father's education	0.0001	0.0009	0.0015	0.0021	−0.00001	0.0007
	(0.0006)	(0.0006)	(0.0008)	(0.0008)	(0.0009)	(0.0008)

Note: The panel was constructed using NLSY79 data from 1979–1994. Data on training in 1987 is combined with 1988 in the original data set. Company training consists of formal training conducted by employer, and military training excluding basic training.

Specification (1) includes a constant, age, father's education, mother's education, number of siblings, southern residence at age 14 dummy, urban residence at age 14 dummy, and year dummies.

Specification (2) drops age-adjusted AFQT and grade completed. Average marginal effect is estimated using average derivatives from a probit regression. Standard errors are reported in parentheses.

Evidence about Conventional Public Training and Work-Welfare Programs Before we turn to a discussion of the benefits of specific training programs, it is important to reiterate a few general points that critically affect how we interpret the evidence on training. In evaluating any public project, it is necessary to account for the welfare costs of raising public funds as well as the direct costs of providing the services.[40] In accounting for human capital projects (or any other type of investment project), it is necessary to estimate accurately the time series of the returns and to discount it appropriately to compare with project costs. Table 2.13 shows the importance of applying these principles. It takes experimental estimates from the evaluation of the JTPA program (see Bloom et al. 1993) and makes alternative assumptions about benefit duration, costs, welfare costs, interest rates for discounting, and the welfare cost of public funds. Accounting for these factors vitally affects the estimates of the economic return to training. Especially important is the assumption about benefit duration. The JTPA evaluation followed participants for only thirty months. When the benefits of the training provided are assumed to persist for seven years, the estimated effects are larger in absolute value.[41] On the other hand, Ashenfelter (1978) estimated a 13 percent annual depreciation rate of the first round impact on earnings, which suggests that an assumption of no depreciation is grossly at odds with the evidence. Heckman, LaLonde, and Smith (1999) present a comprehensive survey of the economic return to public-sector training, so it is unnecessary to restate their evidence here. Table 2.14, taken from a recent survey by Martin and Grubb (2001), suggests some general lessons from the empirical literature on job training.

Table 2.13

Effects of accounting for discounting, expected horizon and welfare costs of taxes: Benefit-minus-cost estimates for JTPA under alternative assumptions regarding benefit persistence, discounting, and welfare costs of taxation (National JTPA study, thirty-month impact sample)

Benefit duration	Direct costs included?	Six-month interest rate	Welfare cost of taxes	Adult males	Adult females	Male youth	Female youth
Thirty Months	No	0.000	0.00	1,345	1,703	−967	136
Thirty Months	Yes	0.000	0.00	523	532	−2,922	−1,180
Thirty Months	Yes	0.000	0.50	108	−54	−3,900	−1,838
Thirty Months	Yes	0.025	0.00	433	432	−2,859	−1,195
Thirty Months	Yes	0.025	0.50	17	−154	−3,836	−1,853
Seven Years	No	0.000	0.00	5,206	5,515	−3,843	865
Seven Years	Yes	0.000	0.00	4,375	4,344	−5,798	−451
Seven Years	Yes	0.000	0.50	3,960	3,758	−6,775	1,109
Seven Years	Yes	0.025	0.00	3,523	3,490	−5,166	−610
Seven Years	Yes	0.025	0.50	3,108	2,905	−6,143	−1,268

Source: Heckman and Smith 1998.

Note: "Benefit duration" indicates how long the estimated benefits from JTPA are assumed to persist. Actual estimates are used for the first thirty months. For the seven-year duration case, the average of the amount of benefits in months 18–24 and 25–30 is used as the amount of benefits in each future period. "Welfare cost of taxes" indicates the additional cost in terms of lost output due to each additional dollar of taxes raised. The value 0.50 lies in the range suggested by Browning (1987).

Estimates are constructed by breaking up the time after random assignment into six-month periods.

All costs are assumed to be paid in the first six-month period, whereas benefits are received in each six-month period and discounted by the amount indicated for each row of the table.

Table 2.14
Lessons from the evaluation literature

Program	Appears to help	Appears not to help	General observations on effectiveness
Formal classroom training	Women reentrants	Prime-aged men and older workers with low initial education	Important that courses have strong labor market relevance or signal "high" quality to employers. Should lead to a qualification that is recognized and valued by employers. Keep programs relatively small in scale.
On-the-job training	Women reentrants; single mothers	Prime-aged men	Must directly meet labor market needs. Hence, need to establish strong links with local employers, but this increases the risk of displacement.
Job search assistance (job clubs, individual counseling, etc.)	Most unemployed but in particular, women and sole parents		Must be combined with increased monitoring of the job-search behaviour of the unemployed and enforcement of work tests.
Of which: Reemployment bonuses	Most adult unemployed		Requires careful monitoring and controls on both recipients and their former employers.

Special youth measures (training, employment subsidies, direct job creation measures)		Disadvantaged youths	Effective programs need to combine an appropriate and integrated mix of education, occupational skills, work-based learning, and supportive services to young people and their families. Early and sustained interventions are likely to be most effective. Need to deal with inappropriate attitudes to work on the part of youths. Adult mentors can help.
Subsidies to employment	Long-term unemployed; women reentrants		Require careful targeting and adequate controls to maximize net employment gains, but there is a trade-off with employer take-up.
Of which: Aid to unemployed starting enterprises	Men (below age 40, relatively better educated)		Works only for a small subset of the population.
Direct job creation		Most adult and youth unemployed	Typically provides few long-run benefits and principle of additionality usually implies low marginal-product jobs.

Source: Martin and Grubb 2001.

Job training is a heterogeneous activity. It includes classroom education, make work, subsidized employment and job search. The rate of return to classroom training is sizeable (Heckman et al. 2000). The rates of return for other components of training, however, are generally lower, although subsidized work (as in the National Supported Work study) appears to have a large payoff. Even when an activity such as job search assistance is profitable, the scale of and gains from the activity are low. One cannot expect substantial benefits from job training. Missing from the literature is a detailed cost-benefit analysis of specific activities of training programs, although Heckman, LaLonde, and Smith (1999) and Martin and Grubb (2001) go part of the way toward developing such an analysis. Such assessments of the empirical evidence move the discussion beyond blanket statements about entire programs and allow discussions of public policy to focus on parts of the programs that are targeted to specific populations and are effective.

Like the heterogeneity found in studies of the earnings response to education, there is considerable evidence of heterogeneity in response to treatment in job training (Heckman, Smith, and Clements 1997). Treatment is found to be most effective for those at the high end of the wage distribution. It has no effect for those at the bottom. There are substantial gains to be realized from targeting treatment. The information required to do so effectively, however, is generally not available (see Heckman, Heinrich, and Smith 2002). The returns to job training for older workers and displaced workers are very low, a consistent finding of the literature on this subject that is also consistent with the general picture presented in figure 2.6a.

The Recent Job Corps Study Job Corps has recently been evaluated using experimental methods, and the results have been widely trumpeted as evidence of success for government training (Burghardt and Schochet 2001). Although the results of the evaluation for some groups are encouraging, the findings from the new Job Corps study are consistent with the previous literature on job training programs. Except for white teenagers ages 16 to 17, the results for earnings and employment are in line with the disappointing results found for most job training programs. It would be surprising to find a substantial impact of Job Corps on labor market outcomes, given that it is a GED factory and the economic return to the GED is low (see figure 2.17). Among

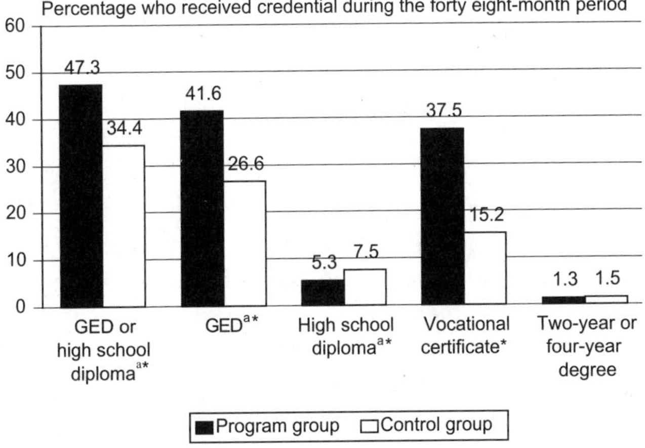

Figure 2.17
Job Corps evaluation: degrees, diplomas, and certificates received.
Source: Baseline and 12-, 30-, and 48-month follow-up interview data for those who completed 48-month interviews. See Schochet et al. 2001.
a. Figures pertain to those who did not have a high school credential at random assignment.
*Difference between the mean outcome for program and control group members is statistically significant at the 5 percent level. This difference is the estimated impact per eligible applicant.

white and black males ages 20 to 24, the annualized impacts of Job Corps participation are substantial. Over the four-year course of the experiment, however, the net benefit is only $624 (over four years) and not statistically significant. The large positive results for Job Corps training reported in the popular press (Krueger 2000) are based on out-of-sample forecasts that assume that benefits of participation last indefinitely. Table 2.15 is taken from the recent Job Corps study. The substantial excess of benefit over cost reported in line labeled *Benefits minus costs* is a consequence of the assumption by the Job Corps analysts that benefits last indefinitely. Making the opposite assumption, that benefits do not last at all, the net return is negative (see the line labeled *Benefits minus costs excluding extrapolation beyond observation*). It is also negative if one uses Ashenfelter's 13 percent estimated depreciation rate for males. Accounting for the social costs of taxation required to finance the Job Corps would make these negative benefit-cost accounts even more negative. There is no empirical support for the assumption that benefits of program participation last indefinitely, and no social-welfare cost of taxation is used to adjust costs in the main Job Corps report. As previously noted, many other programs have substantial rates of return if we assume that benefits persist into the indefinite future and if social costs of taxation are ignored. Before serious policy can be based on the Job Corps study, its assumptions must be more strongly defended. The most accurate assessment of what the Job Corps study shows is best summarized by a quotation from the final report:

> Over the whole period Job Corps participants earned about $3 per week (or about $624 overall) more than they would have if they had not enrolled in Job Corps. This impact, however, is not statistically significant. (Burghardt and Schochet 2001, p. xlii)

Table 2.15
Benefits and costs of Job Corps from different perspectives

	Perspective		
Benefits or costs	Society	Participants	Rest of society
Year 1	−$1,933	−$1,621	−$313
Years 2–4	$2,462	$1,626	$836
After observation period	$26,678	$17,768	$9,009
Output produced during vocational training in Job Corps	$225	$0	$225
Benefits from increased output	$27,531	$17,773	$9,758
Benefits from increased output excluding extrapolation beyond observation	$754	$5	$749
Benefits from reduced use of other programs and services	$2,186	−$780	$2,966
Benefits from reduced crime	$1,240	$643	$597
Program costs	−$14,128	$2,361	−$16,489
Benefits minus costs	$16,829	$19,997	−$3,168
(2) Benefits minus costs excluding extrapolation beyond observation	−$9,949	$2,229	−$12,177
Net benefits per dollar of program expenditures[a]	$2.02		
Net benefits per dollar of program expenditures excluding extrapolation beyond observation[a]	$0.40		

Source: Glazerman, Schochet, and Burghart 2001.
Note: All figures in 1995 dollars.
a. The ratio's denominator is the operating cost of the program ($16,489). The ratio's numerator is the benefit to society plus the cost of student pay, food, and clothing ($2,361). The cost of student pay, food, and clothing is included in the numerator to offset the fact that it is included in the denominator even though it is not a cost to society.

Summary of Training Impacts A comparison of the job training programs discussed in this section suggests a few important lessons. First, you get what you pay for. The recently terminated JTPA program cost very little per recipient but produced very few results. An exception to the rule is classroom training, the returns to which are substantial (Heckman et al. 2000). Second, the effects of treatment vary substantially among subgroups (Heckman, LaLonde, and Smith 1999). Third, job training programs also have effects on behavior beyond schooling and work that should be considered in evaluating their full effects. Reductions in crime may be an important impact of programs targeted at male youth. The evidence summarized in Heckman, LaLonde, and Smith 1999 indicates that the rate of return to most U.S. and European training programs is far below 10 percent, although the benefits to certain groups may be substantial, and some may pass cost-benefit tests. We cannot look to public job training to remedy or alleviate substantially skill deficits that arise at early ages. We next consider tax policy.

Tax and Subsidy Policy

The United States' progressive income tax system retards skill formation. Tax rules in the United States also tend to promote human capital formation over physical capital formation (Quigley and Smolensky 1990). There is some evidence that U.S. tax laws are more favorable toward investment by more-skilled and wealthier workers, although there are elements in the tax code that favor low-skilled workers as well. U.S. tax rules also tend to encourage investments made on the job over investments in formal schooling, especially schooling that requires substantial out-of-pocket or tuition costs. Although many of the effects of the current tax system on human capital investment may be unintended, they may nevertheless be substantial and may favor certain workers as well as certain types of investment over others.

To understand how taxes influence human capital investment, it is helpful to understand the costs of and returns to such investment. The costs of investment in human capital are foregone earnings net of taxes plus any additional tuition or out-of-pocket expenses. Higher proportional taxes reduce the costs of spending an hour in school by the amount they reduce the return of working an hour in the market.

The simplest case to consider is a regime with flat (proportional) taxes in which the only human capital investment cost is foregone income. In this case, changes in the level of the flat wage tax will have no effect on human capital accumulation. Increases in the tax rate reduce the return by the same proportion as they reduce the cost, so there is no change in the incentive to invest. The ratio of marginal returns to marginal costs remains unaffected. Hence, proportional taxes on labor income have no effect on investment in human capital. On the other hand, if there are tuition expenses that are not tax deductible, a higher tax rate discourages investment in human capital, because it lowers the returns to investment more than the costs. In the case of a 10 percent increase in the tax rate, the return to investment decreases by 10 percent, and the cost of foregone income declines by 10 percent, but the tuition cost remains unchanged if tuition cannot be deducted from taxable income. Thus, the return to investment declines by more than the costs, so human capital investment is discouraged.

The intuition behind the neutrality of flat labor income taxes on human capital investment arises from the fact that the cost of time inputs to investment is foregone earnings, which are tax deductible. If tax rates are 10 percent and one earns $10 less, one pays $1 less in taxes—one's net loss is only $9. The costs of other inputs to on-the-job training can typically be expensed by the workers' employers and can be financed through lower wages, thereby making them tax deductible as well. The only major cost of human capital investment that is not tax deductible is college tuition and there are even more cases, discussed below, where interest on loans for tuition are deductible. Starting in 2002 and through 2005 up to $3,000 (for 2002 and 2003) or $4,000 (for 2004 or 2005) of college tuition is deductible. However, there is a means test so that filers with adjusted gross income above $130,000 do not qualify for the deduction. Although college tuition is a substantial cost ιor some, a majority of youth do not attend college, and of those who do a majority attend community colleges or state colleges where tuition costs are modest. Because most of the costs of investment are financed through foregone earnings and are tax deductible, changes in the rate of a flat tax on wages will have little effect on human capital accumulation.

In a modern society, in which human capital is a larger component of wealth than is land, a proportional tax on human capital is like a nondistorting Henry George tax as long as labor supply responses are negligible. Estimated intertemporal labor supply elasticities are small, and welfare effects from labor supply adjustment are negligible. (See the evidence summarized in Browning, Hansen, and Heckman 1999.) Taxes on human capital should be *increased*, whereas taxes on capital should be decreased, to promote wage growth and efficiency.

The current U.S. tax system, however, is not flat. The progressiveness in the tax schedule discourages human capital investment. The gain in earnings resulting from human capital investment causes some individuals to move up into a higher tax bracket. For such individuals, the returns from investment are taxed at a higher rate, but the cost is expensed at a lower rate. This discourages human capital accumulation. Consider a progressive tax system in which the only cost of investment is foregone earnings. Suppose an individual's current marginal tax rate is 10 percent. Suppose also that if he or she chooses to invest, his or her increased earnings will cause him or her to switch to a marginal tax rate of 20 percent. In this case the returns are taxed at the 20 percent level, but the costs are deducted at the 10 percent level, and progressive taxes discourage human capital investment when compared to a flat tax regime.

Taxes on physical capital are another important component of the tax system that can affect human capital investment decisions. The level of human capital investment declines when the after-tax interest rate increases, because the discounted returns to investment are then lower. Reducing the tax on interest income can have a beneficial effect both on capital accumulation and on real wages.

Heckman, Lochner, and Taber (1998b, 2000) and Heckman (2001) estimate that for the U.S. economy, a revenue-neutral move to a flat tax on consumption in the steady state would raise the wages of both skilled and unskilled workers and raise aggregate output by 5 percent (and aggregate consumption by 3.7 percent) while raising the wages of college graduates and high school graduates equally (7 percent). Such a move would barely affect overall inequality in earnings while promoting the accumulation of greater levels of both human capital and physical capital.[42] The major effect of such a reform, however, would be on physical capital and its feedback effects on wages through the increased productivity of labor. It would have only a small effect on human capital accumulation. Tilting the bias in the tax system toward capital and away from human capital would improve the earnings of both capital and labor in the long run. Low-ability and unskilled members of the current generation would not benefit from a switch to a flat tax. Most ability types would benefit from a flat consumption tax. Heckman (2001) shows that both types of reform are more popular in a period of skill-biased technical change, because tax reform facilitates transition to the new, higher-skilled equilibrium.

Reforms to tax policy on interest income are either ignored or misrepresented in popular discussions. Populists see such a move as favoring capital and hence rich people. They ignore the crucial point that higher levels of capital stocks raise the wages of all workers in a roughly uniform way.

Heckman, Lochner, and Taber (1998b, 2000) show that revenue-neutral movements to a flat income tax have more modest effects on wages than those produced by a flat consumption tax and only small effects on human capital accumulation. Based on simulations performed by these researchers, one cannot expect tax reform to substantially change human capital stocks, but a move to a flat consumption tax will improve welfare.

We next consider which individuals are encouraged to invest by the current tax system and what types of investment they are encouraged to undertake. Various features of the current tax code are biased toward more-skilled workers with higher earnings. For individuals who are employed, human capital investment costs are typically financed through foregone earnings. To the extent that formal educational expenses are not paid for in this way, they can be deducted from gross earnings provided that they are itemized and that itemizations from all sources exceed 2 percent of adjusted gross income. This feature of the tax code tends to favor high-skilled individuals, who are more likely to earn higher salaries and thus to itemize expenses.

Prior to 1987, all interest on educational loans was fully deductible as consumer interest. The consumer interest deduction was phased out by 1989. This favored children from higher-income families who were typically itemizers. Only recently the law has changed to allow deductibility of tuition in certain cases. These exclusions can have substantial disincentive effects. Whereas individuals must pay taxes on interest from savings, they cannot deduct the interest they pay on educational loans. Mortgage interest, however, is still deductible. It is possible for families with home equity to take out mortgages to finance their children's education. Again, it is the more skilled and wealthy who are most likely to own homes, so they and their children are hurt less by a tax policy that allows only mortgage interest to be deducted from taxable income.

The U.S. tax system favors public-schooling investment at the primary and secondary level over investment in private schooling and in any type of postsecondary schooling. Any student can attend public elementary and high schools free of charge, and the costs of those public schools are financed primarily through local and state taxes, which are fully deductible. Neither private school nor most college tuition (until recently) is deductible, however, so the current tax system is biased against college education and private education. Moreover, the level of tuition tends to increase with college quality, so the current tax system discourages students from attending higher-quality universities. Since private-school tuition is not tax deductible, but local taxes are, taxpayers have incentives to set up good public schools in their communities rather than send their children to private schools.

The current tax system favors human capital accumulation on the job versus full-time schooling. Human capital investments can be separated into those undertaken while working (or paid for by the employer) and those taken elsewhere (and paid for by the individual). Current tax laws favor the former over the latter, encouraging individuals to seek training on the job. Virtually all investments made through an employer can be expensed and financed through foregone wages. The employee does not need to itemize deductions to realize this tax benefit.

Educational assistance programs exempt tuition paid by employers from personal income tax, provided the schooling is job-related. Firms can sell portable vocational or employer-based training to employees and pay for it through lower wages. The foregone earnings are essentially written off on personal income taxes. The tax laws therefore encourage individuals seeking training to look to their employer for that training rather than to formal schools. In addition, firms can write off immediately up to $5,250 per year for each worker in training and schooling expenditures that are not job-related. Tuition support, however, was restricted to undergraduate level education (Joint Committee on Taxation 1992) until 2001 after which time graduate education (e.g., MBA tuition) qualifies.

Relative to investment in physical capital, some types of human capital investment are favored by the tax system, whereas others are not. To the extent that many human capital investments are immediately tax-deductible whereas physical-capital investments must be amortized, the current tax system encourages investment in human capital over investment in physical capital. In cases in which schooling or training costs cannot be deducted (primarily tuition costs for formal schooling) investment in physical capital is favored. Although which groups benefit the most from current tax provisions (the most or the least skilled) is ambiguous, employer-provided training is certainly favored over training undertaken away from the workplace. This asymmetry of the tax treatment of these two types of training is often justified by the argument that academic education has a much larger consumption value than job-specific training and that this consumption value should be taxed.[43]

Another argument for taxation and subsidy of human capital is the presence of idiosyncratic risk. Judd (2000) shows that under certain conditions on labor supply parameters, riskiness in physical assets, and levels of idiosyncratic risk, there is scope for optimal tax policy *if* idiosyncratic risk is exogenous, that is, if it cannot be affected by individual decisions. To the extent that there is moral hazard, and risk is not exogenous, the scope for optimal tax interventions is more limited. Indeed, if firms can insure workers against the idiosyncratic risk through optimal contracts, there is no scope for government tax or transfer policy, as the market provides efficient risk sharing.[44]

The Problem of the Transition

Skill-biased technical change operates to make workers trained under old regimes obsolete at prevailing wages in new regimes. This phenomenon operates with a vengeance in transition economies in Eastern Europe and Latin America that have opened up markets and now trade at world prices.

Younger workers trained under old technologies can, and have, adapted to new technologies through retraining and education. For older workers, with more limited horizons and lower levels of skill and ability, such reeducation is not always economically efficient. Displaced American workers in their forties who are offered generous retraining subsidies frequently refuse them, and the return to such training is low (see Heckman, LaLonde, and Smith 1999).

Overlapping-generations models with workers of heterogeneous ability and skill reveal that skill-biased technical change creates cohorts of workers with low earning power in the post-change economy (Heckman, Lochner, and Taber 1998b). Their children adapt to the new economy through investments in human capital. In the long run, the economy adjusts to a new, higher level of skill requirements, but the transition can last thirty years or longer, and the newly disadvantaged workers pose a serious social and economic problem. As noted above, investment in them is often not economically efficient. Based on the best available evidence, the most economically justified strategy for improving the incomes of low-ability, low-skill adults is to invest more in the highly skilled, tax them, and then redistribute the tax revenues to the poor.

Many people view the work ethic as a basic value, however, and would argue that cultivating a large class of transfer recipients would breed a culture of poverty and helplessness. If value is placed on work as an act of individual dignity, because of general benefits to families, and especially the early environments of young children and because of benefits to communities and society as a whole, then society may be prepared to subsidize inefficient jobs. Increased subsidies to employment induce people to switch out of criminal activities (Lochner 1999). Subsidies induce output that partially offsets the cost of the subsidy, and so they are a cheaper alternative than welfare (Phelps 1997). The problem with giving such subsidies to adults is that they may discourage skill formation among the young if the subsidies are extended to them (see Heckman, Lochner, and Cossa 2003). To partly alleviate these adverse incentive effects, wage subsidies should be given on a cohort-specific basis. There is evidence that the problem of rising wage inequality is cohort specific (see MaCurdy and Mroz 1995).

Job subsidies, however, are not the same as investment subsidies. The evidence points strongly to the inefficiency of subsidizing the human capital investment of low-skilled, disadvantaged workers.

Migration Policy

As noted by Borjas, Freeman, and Katz (1997) and Borjas (1999), immigration is a substantial contributor to the growth in the low-skilled workforce. Figure 2.2c reveals that in recent years close to 50 percent of all measured high school dropouts have been immigrants. In principle, one can reduce inequality by redirecting migration policy such that only skilled immigrants are permitted to enter the country. One way to do this is to sell entry visas. This would screen out the unskilled.

Given the substantial Mexican representation among the unskilled immigrants to the United States and the country's porous border with Mexico, the feasibility of such a migration policy is far from clear to us. Moreover, different groups benefit and lose from the immigration of unskilled workers. A full accounting of the winners and losers from a migration policy redirected to favor immigration of skilled workers remains to be developed, although migration policy is a potentially promising option to pursue if U.S. borders with Mexico can be secured to enforce immigration restrictions.

4. Summary and Conclusions

This chapter has presented a framework for thinking about human capital policy. It stresses the need to recognize the dynamic nature of the human capital accumulation process and the multiplicity of actors and institutions that determine human capital investments. It emphasizes heterogeneity in skills, uncertainty about returns, and the need to account for heterogeneity and uncertainty about economic returns in designing policies to foster skill. It stresses the need to conduct cost-benefit analyses to rank proposed policies rigorously.

What has been presented in this chapter is a blueprint for the life cycle analysis of human capital accumulation that requires much further elaboration. There are many gaps in the evidence on life cycle skill formation that need to be filled. A more explicit dynamic theory that accounts for uncertainty is needed to guide future empirical work. When the blueprint presented here is modified and converted into an operational empirical tool, a deeper and more comprehensive approach to the evaluation of human capital policies will be possible.

Because human capital is an investment good, it is important to account for the life cycle dynamics of learning and skill acquisition in devising effective human capital policies. Schooling is only one phase of a lifetime skill accumulation process. Families, firms, and schools all create human capital. Any comprehensive analysis of human capital policy must account for the full range of institutions that produce it.

Learning begets learning because of dynamic complementarities. The empirical evidence presented in this chapter all points in this direction. Recent research has demonstrated the importance of the early years in creating the abilities and motivations that affect learning and foster productivity. Recent research has also demonstrated the importance of both cognitive and noncognitive skills in the workplace and in the skill acquisition process. Noncognitive skills are a form of human capital and can be produced. Some of the most effective interventions operate on noncognitive skills and motivations. Evidence from dysfunctional families reveals the value of healthy ones.

This chapter has also stressed the need to understand the sources of problems in order to devise effective solutions for them. We have demonstrated the first-order importance of abilities and motivation in producing skills. Cognitive and noncognitive deficits emerge early, before schooling, and if uncorrected, create low-skilled adults. A greater emphasis needs to be placed on family policy. Studies of a limited set of small-scale, high-quality interventions reveal that early cognitive and noncognitive deficits can be partially remedied. The evidence is tantalizing but not definitive.

The traditional approach to human capital policy focuses on schools. But families are just as important as, if not more important than, schools in promoting human capital. The evidence from failed families points to possible benefits from interventions in them. This raises a new set of questions about whether or not society should respect the sanctity of the family in regard to certain dysfunctional groups.

Schools matter. The evidence shows that teachers matter, but that it is difficult to use conventional measures of teacher quality to assess who is a good teacher. Principals and parents know this. Schemes to improve productivity in schools should allow agents to use their local knowledge to create the right incentives. Movement toward choice, competition and local incentives will likely foster productivity in the classroom.

The evidence also shows that education policies based on objective quality measures (class size, teacher salaries, and the like) are unlikely to produce dramatic gains in U.S. educational achievement. At current levels of educational support, marginal changes in conventional quality measures yield only modest benefits and often fail a cost-benefit test.

The evidence on credit constraints reveals the unimportance of short-term family income constraints in accounting for the schooling differentials manifest in figures 2.4 and 2.5. Much of the evidence that is alleged to support the existence of widespread credit market problems in the financing of college education is found upon examination to be ambiguous on the importance of such problems. At the same time, we have identified a small group of high school graduates (0 to 8 percent) who are constrained and for whom a targeted transfer policy may be effective. Broadly based policies, like the HOPE Scholarship program, cut too wide a swath to work effectively. As noted in the chapter, more than 90 percent of HOPE's recipients would have gone to college without the program, so it generates massive deadweight.

We have identified heterogeneity and uncertainty of returns as pervasive features of human capital investment. Reducing uncertainty has benefits and will improve educational sorting. Targeting the persons who can benefit from interventions will improve the efficiency of those interventions. The trick is in identifying the groups for whom the interventions are likely to be effective. In many human capital programs this has proved to be an elusive goal. Although we have identified that certain types of targeted programs might be effective, much more work on efficient targeting remains to be done.

We have also stressed in this chapter the need to assess carefully the full life cycle stream of the costs and benefits of human capital interventions. Conventional methods of program evaluation frequently ignore costs altogether and are casual about the treatment of benefit duration. For many large-scale interventions, it is essential to account for general-equilibrium effects, which reverse or diminish partial-equilibrium estimates of policy impacts (see Heckman, Lochner, and Taber 1998a, 1998b, 1998c, 2000).

Tax policy is unlikely to be a strong lever to pull to foster human capital development. At the same time, effective tax policy that fosters capital accumulation can have a substantial beneficial effect on wages.

It is important to recognize that all of our discussion in this chapter has involved policies for the American economy, which has a generous subsidy structure for human capital in place. We have considered only changes in policies within the given institutional structure and have not addressed the broader question of whether there should be any subsidization of human capital at all. Many of the same basic principles established in this chapter for the American economy, however, apply more broadly, albeit with different quantitative scales.

It is also important to recognize that most of our analysis in this chapter has focused on gaps, and how to eliminate them, and not on trends. Current understanding of the trends that produce the stagnation in schooling participation rates evident in figure 2.1 is limited.[45] We have shown that migration of unskilled workers is only a minor contributing factor to this stagnation. We conjecture that the demise of the American family and the growth in single-parent families have contributed to the stagnation. Figure 2.18 shows that over time, an increasing fraction of all U.S. children are growing up in adverse environments. Our analysis in the chapter's second part has revealed the harmful consequences of bad family environments. This explanation for stagnant schooling rates is by itself, however, too

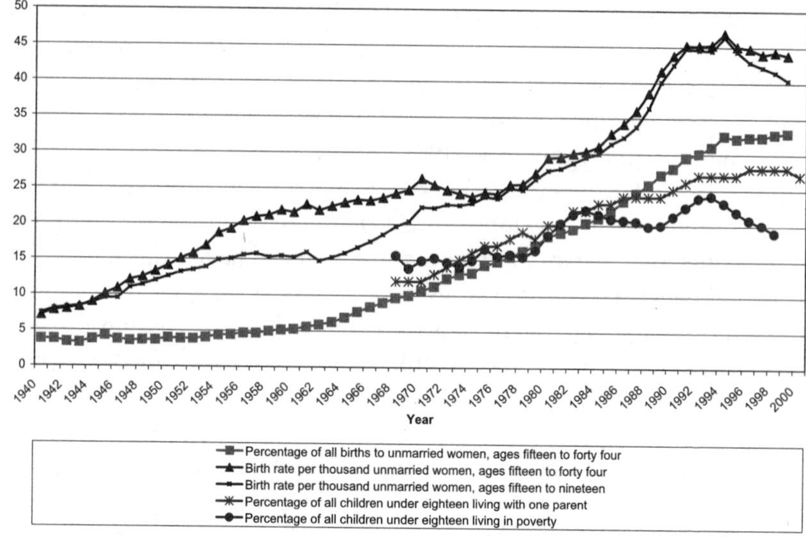

Figure 2.18
Trends in unhealthy child environments.
Notes: Data for births and birth rates are from Ventura and Bachrach 2000. Data for children living with one parent are available at the census bureau at ⟨http://www.census.gov/population/socdemo/hh-fam/tabCH-1.txt⟩. Data for children living in poverty is available at ⟨www.childtrendsdatabank.org⟩.

simplistic. The trends for failed families show continuing deterioration, whereas the trends in schooling participation are flat. Still, growth in bad family environments is a likely candidate in any scenario that explains figure 2.1. Perhaps the educational response to trends in wage differentials just offsets the educational response to trends in adverse environments. If this conjecture is verified, it reinforces the emphasis on early family policy that we have advocated in this chapter.

Appendix 2A: Rates of Return, Internal Rates of Return, and Discount Rates for Human Capital Investment Programs

Following a well-established tradition, in parts of this chapter, we use the rate of return to compare the productivity of different human capital programs.[46] Many labor economists use the terms *rate of return, internal rate of return (IRR), marginal internal rate of return,* and the coefficient on schooling from a Mincer earnings equation interchangeably, even though these are very distinct concepts. The internal rate of return is usually computed against a null project with no returns or costs. The marginal internal rate of return is computed relative to a "nearby" project using a suitable metric. Heckman, Lochner, and Todd (2003) show the conditions under which a Mincer coefficient is a marginal internal rate of return and reveal that in recent decades these conditions have not been satisfied. The required assumptions on the earnings function of separability between schooling and experience and negligible direct costs are violated in the recent data, so in recent years Mincer coefficients are not reliable estimates of marginal internal rates of return (see also Heckman, Lochner, and Taber 1998a).

It is well known that investment projects chosen according to the highest internal rate of return are not necessarily those with the highest present value. The characteristic feature of many human capital projects, however, is that costs are incurred early in the life cycle, whereas returns are incurred late. Compared to less-costly human capital projects, more-costly projects (e.g., those involving more schooling) yield higher annual returns that occur later but are characterized by a larger and longer stream of upfront costs. When a high-investment and a low-investment human capital project are compared, the differences in the cost-return age pattern are initially negative and then become positive. Payoff streams of alternative projects cross once. Comparing higher-schooling investment projects with lower-schooling investment projects, a comparison of the marginal internal rate of return with the interest rate on physical capital yields an appropriate decision rule, (i.e., it picks projects with the highest present value as long as there are no credit market imperfections). If the marginal internal rate of return that equates two human capital projects exceeds the rate of interest, the optimal present-value-maximizing policy is to pick the project that requires more human capital investment (Hirschleifer 1970). This feature of human capital investment projects justifies our use of the rate of return as a guide to comparing traditional schooling investment policies. At the same time, it is important to recognize that the returns we present apply only to marginal projects. Large scale projects that alter factor prices and returns require a full general-equilibrium analysis (Heckman, Lochner, and Taber 1998a, 1998b, 1998c, 2000).

The common practice of computing an internal rate of return to an investment (compared to no investment) and ranking projects on the basis of this computed return is known to be potentially misleading (Hirschleifer 1970). The project with the highest internal rate of return so constructed can have a lower present value than a rival project.

The case when payoff streams cross at several ages is the textbook pathological case. Although it is not empirically relevant for the classical schooling problem, it is highly relevant for comparing policies like job training and preschool policies that have payoff streams that are likely to cross more than once. It is also empirically relevant for comparing returns from human capital investment under uncertainty when there are option values (Heckman, Lochner, and Todd 2003).

As an example, consider two projects. One is a job training program in which costs are incurred at age 18 and payoffs occur after training but decay rapidly. Figure 2A.1 plots the typical shape of a job training program payoff stream. The other is an enriched preschool program that has the characteristic payoff of an early cost, a long latency period, and payoffs that begin late and persist. The payoff sequences depicted in the figure cross at multiple ages (6, 19, 25). The internal rate of return for the training program is 25 percent. For the preschool program, it is 7 percent. Yet at a 5 percent interest rate, the net present value for the training program is 13.6, whereas the net present value for the preschool program is 17.3.

This example motivates our use of present values in evaluating alternatives when it is possible to do so. A more general analysis would compute the shadow prices and returns to the full portfolio of human capital investment projects to develop an optimal human capital investment strategy. Setting up the framework to do this is beyond the scope of this chapter. The empirical evidence needed to implement this framework is not yet available.

The question of the appropriate choice of the discount rate to evaluate human capital streams is an old one. It is sometimes argued that human capital projects should be

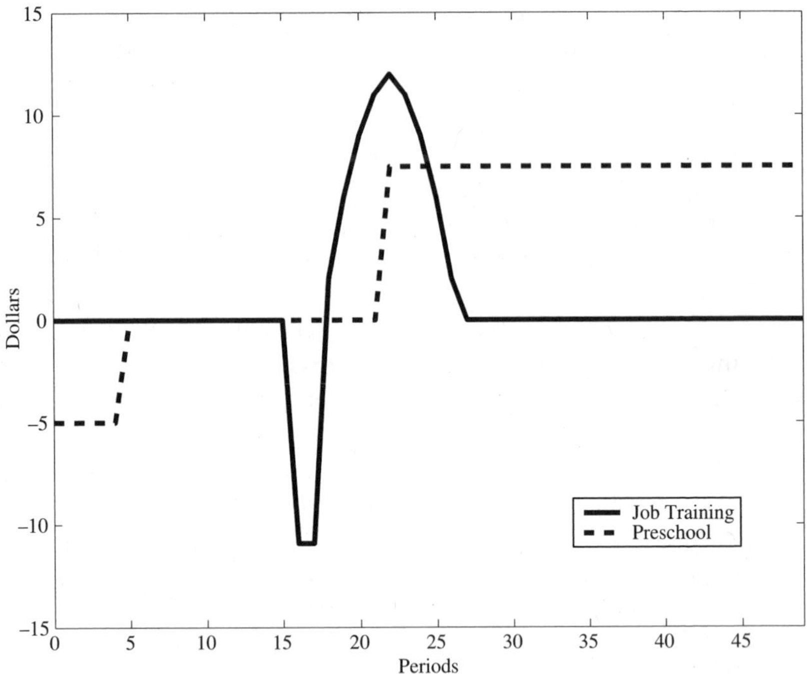

Figure 2A.1
Prototypical payoff streams

subsidized (or discounted at a rate lower than the market rate) because of idiosyncratic uncertainty that can be collectively eliminated. This argument ignores two key points. First, as noted by Judd (2000), idiosyncratic risk in human capital policy is associated with moral hazard. Private contracts between workers and firms may provide optimal insurance, so there is no role for any government tax or subsidy or for a reduction in the discount rate in evaluating human capital investment projects. Second, as noted by

Arrow and Lind (1970), a lower discount rate for government projects is warranted only if all costs and benefits of these projects accrue to the government and can be distributed without cost and without risk among taxpayers. But in the case of human capital projects, individual agents bear the risk unless the government provides full insurance against income risk, which is an infeasible policy given moral-hazard problems. For that reason, it is inappropriate to use a discount rate lower than the market rate for discounting benefits, although it may be appropriate to use a lower discount rate for costs raised from government revenue sources.

Appendix 2B: Auxiliary Tables for Credit Constraints Calculations

Table 2B.1
Family background gaps for white males, NLSY79 (measured relative to the highest family background/AFQT quartile)

	Enrollment in college			Two-year college completion		
Gap:	Coefficient	Std. err.	t-stat	Coefficient	Std. err.	t-stat
q4–q1	0.580	0.042	13.810	−0.374	0.154	−2.429
q4–q2	0.370	0.034	10.882	−0.189	0.077	−2.455
q4–q3	0.299	0.029	10.310	−0.124	−0.067	−1.851
	Four-year college completion			Proportion with no delay of entry		
q4–q1	0.615	0.108	5.694	0.499	0.159	3.138
q4–q2	0.337	0.060	5.617	0.188	0.075	2.507
q4–q3	0.137	0.043	3.186	0.099	0.056	1.768
	Enrollment in four-year versus two-year college					
q4–q1	0.040	0.084	0.476			
q4–q2	0.133	0.045	2.956			
q4–q3	0.054	0.034	1.588			

q4–q1: Gap in enrollment, completion, proportion with no delay and type of college between quartiles 4 and 1
q4–q2: Gap in enrollment, completion, proportion with no delay and type of college between quartiles 4 and 2
q4–q3: Gap in enrollment, completion, proportion with no delay and type of college between quartiles 4 and 3

Table 2B.2

Gaps in enrollment, completion, percentage with no delay, and type of college: White males, NLSY79 (measured relative to the highest family background/AFQT quartile)

Panel A—enrollment in two-year and four-year colleges

	Lowest AFQT tertile			Middle AFQT tertile			Highest AFQT tertile		
Variable:	Coefficient	Std. err.	*t*-stat	Coefficient	Std. err.	*t*-stat	Coefficient	Std. err.	*t*-stat
q4–q1	0.118	0.072	1.640	0.081	0.069	1.180	0.037	0.068	0.540
q4–q2	0.081	0.067	1.200	0.058	0.058	1.010	0.040	0.057	0.700
q4–q3	0.087	0.066	1.310	0.013	0.051	0.250	0.097	0.052	1.860
Southern residence at age 14	0.012	0.047	0.260	0.006	0.047	0.130	−0.070	0.049	−1.430
Broken home	0.076	0.051	1.500	−0.002	0.060	−0.040	0.069	0.057	1.200
Urban residence at age 14	−0.054	0.048	−1.120	−0.042	0.048	−0.870	0.013	0.047	0.280
Mother's education	−0.024	0.011	−2.310	−0.035	0.011	−3.150	−0.023	0.011	−2.100
Father's education	−0.029	0.008	−3.640	−0.042	0.008	−5.390	−0.042	0.008	−5.160
Constant	0.213	0.138	1.550	0.347	0.136	2.550	0.133	0.137	0.970

Panel B—two-year college completion rate

	Lowest AFQT tertile			Middle AFQT tertile			Highest AFQT tertile		
Variable:	Coefficient	Std. err.	*t*-stat	Coefficient	Std. err.	*t*-stat	Coefficient	Std. err.	*t*-stat
q4–q1	0.538	0.354	1.520	0.052	0.171	0.300	0.058	0.066	0.880
q4–q2	0.247	0.234	1.060	0.116	0.145	0.800	0.035	0.055	0.640

q4–q3	0.098	0.224	0.440	−0.072	0.138	−0.520	−0.040	0.053	−0.750
Southern residence at age 14	−0.010	0.204	−0.050	0.156	0.119	1.310	−0.046	0.050	−0.900
Broken home	0.188	0.268	0.700	0.057	0.154	0.370	−0.240	0.056	−4.320
Urban residence at age 14	0.084	0.182	0.460	0.247	0.139	1.770	0.036	0.045	0.790
Mother's education	0.067	0.053	1.270	−0.020	0.028	−0.720	0.012	0.012	0.990
Father's education	−0.007	0.038	−0.190	−0.012	0.021	−0.570	−0.010	0.010	−1.090
Constant	−1.510	0.618	−2.450	−0.133	0.340	−0.390	−0.040	0.136	−0.290

Panel C—four-year college completion rate

	Lowest AFQT tertile			Middle AFQT tertile			Highest AFQT tertile		
Variable:	Coefficient	Std. err.	*t*-stat	Coefficient	Std. err.	*t*-stat	Coefficient	Std. err.	*t*-stat
q4–q1	−0.281	0.144	−1.960	0.070	0.112	0.630	−0.038	0.091	−0.420
q4–q2	−0.294	0.142	−2.080	0.071	0.088	0.810	0.032	0.071	0.440
q4–q3	−0.192	0.138	−1.390	−0.066	0.072	−0.920	0.068	0.064	1.070
Southern residence at age 14	0.040	0.107	0.370	−0.008	0.074	−0.110	−0.015	0.060	−0.240
Broken home	0.186	0.120	1.550	−0.091	0.100	−0.910	−0.008	0.077	−0.110
Urban residence at age 14	−0.004	0.128	−0.030	−0.121	0.075	−1.610	−0.007	0.061	−0.120
Mother's education	−0.029	0.023	−1.230	−0.027	0.017	−1.610	−0.017	0.013	−1.320
Father's education	−0.035	0.018	−1.960	−0.026	0.012	−2.260	−0.015	0.009	−1.640
Constant	0.584	0.378	1.550	0.223	0.214	1.050	−0.338	0.169	−2.000

q4–q1: Gap in enrollment, completion, delay and type of college between quartiles 4 and 1
q4–q2: Gap in enrollment, completion, delay and type of college between quartiles 4 and 2
q4–q3: Gap in enrollment, completion, delay and type of college between quartiles 4 and 3

Table 2B.2
(continued)

Panel D—Proportion with no delay of entry

	Lowest AFQT tertile			Middle AFQT tertile			Highest AFQT tertile		
Variable:	Coeffi-cient	Std. err.	*t*-stat	Coeffi-cient	Std. err.	*t*-stat	Coeffi-cient	Std. err.	*t*-stat
q4–q1	0.164	0.211	0.780	−0.038	0.154	−0.240	−0.148	0.132	−1.130
q4–q2	0.421	0.193	2.180	0.062	0.109	0.560	0.079	0.092	0.860
q4–q3	0.372	0.191	1.950	−0.060	0.089	−0.670	0.053	0.093	0.570
Southern residence at age 14	−0.209	0.145	−1.440	−0.023	0.092	−0.250	0.090	0.086	1.040
Broken home	−0.023	0.185	−0.120	−0.117	0.119	−0.980	0.242	0.095	2.540
Urban residence at age 14	0.180	0.152	1.190	−0.142	0.096	−1.480	−0.009	0.080	−0.110
Mother's education	−0.056	0.030	−1.860	−0.022	0.024	−0.930	−0.025	0.020	−1.280
Father's education	0.028	0.027	1.030	−0.013	0.015	−0.870	−0.010	0.014	−0.680
Constant	−0.511	0.488	−1.050	−0.151	0.289	−0.520	−0.371	0.258	−1.440

Panel E—Enrollment in four-year versus two-year college

	Lowest AFQT tertile			Middle AFQT tertile			Highest AFQT tertile		
Variable:	Coeffi-cient	Std. err.	*t*-stat	Coeffi-cient	Std. err.	*t*-stat	Coeffi-cient	Std. err.	*t*-stat
q4–q1	0.040	0.126	0.320	0.009	0.081	0.110	0.110	0.076	1.440
q4–q2	0.219	0.112	1.950	0.045	0.066	0.680	0.117	0.061	1.920

q4–q3	0.270	0.107	2.520	−0.036	0.056	−0.650	0.020	0.056	0.350
Southern residence at age 14	−0.044	0.089	−0.490	0.057	0.055	1.030	−0.014	0.052	−0.260
Broken home	−0.103	0.104	−0.990	0.012	0.073	0.170	0.019	0.065	0.290
Urban residence at age 14	−0.128	0.096	−1.330	0.055	0.057	0.960	0.045	0.052	0.850
Mother's education	0.014	0.020	0.700	−0.027	0.012	−2.210	−0.025	0.011	−2.170
Father's education	0.007	0.015	0.480	−0.013	0.009	−1.550	−0.013	0.009	−1.540
Constant	−0.963	0.301	−3.200	−0.298	0.157	−1.900	−0.340	0.147	−2.320

q4–q1: Gap in enrollment, completion, percentage with no delay and type of college between quartiles 4 and 1
q4–q2: Gap in enrollment, completion, percentage with no delay and type of college between quartiles 4 and 2
q4–q3: Gap in enrollment, completion, percentage with no delay and type of college between quartiles 4 and 3

Table 2B.3
Coefficients for the construction of the family background index: Regression of college enrollment on southern and urban origin, broken home, and parental education, white males, NLSY79

Variable	Coefficient	Std. err.
Southern origin	0.0266	0.0233
Broken home	−0.0544	0.0270
Urban origin	0.0603	0.0235
Mother's education	0.0310	0.0054
Father's education	0.0400	0.0033
AFQT	0.0046	0.0006
Constant	−0.6814	0.0538

Notes

James Heckman is Henry Schultz Distinguished Service Professor at the University of Chicago and a senior fellow of the American Bar Foundation. Pedro Carneiro is a lecturer at University College London. The research reported here was supported by National Science Foundation grants SES-93-21-048, 97-30-657, and 00-99-195; NICHD grant R01-34598-03; NIH grant R01-HD32058-03; and the American Bar Foundation. Carneiro was funded by Fundacao Ciencia e Tecnologia and Fundacao Calouste Gulbenkian. We have benefited from comments received from David Bravo, Flavio Cunha, Mark Duggan, Lars Hansen, Bas Jacobs, Robert LaLonde, Steven Levitt, Dayanand Manoli, Dimitriy V. Masterov, Casey Mulligan, Derek Neal, and Jeff Smith on various aspects of this chapter. We have benefited from comments on the first draft received from George Borjas, Eric Hanushek, Larry Katz, Lance Lochner, Lisa Lynch, and Larry Summers. Flavio Cunha, Maria Isabel Larenas, Dayanand Manoli, Dimitriy V. Masterov, Maria Victoria Rodriguez and Xing Zhong provided valuable research assistance for which we are grateful. This work draws on and substantially extends Heckman (2000) and Heckman and Lochner (2000).

1. The slowdown in the growth of labor force quality has reduced productivity growth since 1980 by 0.13 percent per year (DeLong, Goldin, and Katz 2003).

2. For women, the substantial existing ethnic, racial, and family income gaps did not widen, but they did not shrink either. Secular trends dominate the female time series.

3. Write $H(a)$ as the stock of human capital at age a and $\dot{H}(a)$ as the rate of increase in the human capital stock. Generalizing the celebrated Ben-Porath (1967) model, we obtain that human capital production is governed by $\dot{H}(a)=F(H(a), I(s), a)$, where $I(a)$ is the rate of investment for each age and the stock of human capital and the production function depend on the stage of the life cycle. Dynamic complementarity arises if $\partial^2 F/(\partial H(a)\partial I(a)')$ is a positive matrix (all elements are positive).

4. The suggested market failure is somewhat whimsical, since the preferences of the child are formed, in part, by the family into which he or she is born. Ex post, the child may not wish a different family, no matter how poor his or her family of birth.

5. Evidence on educational responses to tuition subsidies is sometimes mistakenly interpreted as evidence on credit constraints. The purchase of education is governed by the same principles that govern the purchase of other goods: the lower the price, the more likely are people to buy the good. Dynarski (2000) presents recent evidence about the strength of tuition effects on college participation that is consistent with a long line of research. In addition, there is, undoubtedly, a consumption component to education. Families with higher incomes may buy more of the good for their children and may buy higher quality education as well. This will contribute to the relationship displayed in figure 2.4.

6. See BLS (2001) for a description of the NLSY data.

7. Cameron and Heckman condition on an early measure of ability in the mid-teenage years that is not contaminated by the feedback from schooling to test scores that is documented in Hansen, Heckman, and Mullen (2003).

8. Mulligan (1997) shows that, in the context of a Becker-Tomes model, tuition elasticities for human capital accumulation are greater (in absolute value) for unconstrained people. His proof easily generalizes to more-general preferences (results are available on request from the authors). We present a different argument: by a standard argument in discrete choice, Kane's claim cannot be rigorously established. Let $S=1$ if $I(t, X)\geq \epsilon$, where I is an index of net benefit from college, t is tuition, $(\partial I/\partial t)<0$ and X are other variables, including income, and ϵ is an unobservable psychic-cost's component. Then assuming that ϵ is independent of t, and X,

$$\Pr(S=1 \mid t, X)=\int_{-\infty}^{I(t, X)} f(\epsilon)\,d\epsilon,$$

where $f(\epsilon)$ is the density of psychic costs. Then

$$\frac{\partial \Pr(S=1|t,X)}{\partial t} = \left[\frac{\partial I(t,X)}{\partial t}\right] f(I(t,X)).$$

For constrained persons with very low income, $I(t, X)$ is small. Depending on the density of ϵ, the location of $I(t, X)$ in the support of the density, and the value of $(\partial I(t, X))/\partial t$, constrained persons may have larger or smaller tuition responses than unconstrained persons. Thus if ϵ is normal, and $I(t, X) \to -\infty$ for constrained people, if the derivative is bounded, the tuition response is zero for constrained people.

9. Standard errors are not presented in Cameron and Heckman's paper, but test statistics for the hypothesis of equality are.

10. See the note at the base of the table for a complete description of the method used to construct the estimates.

11. These tables have been constructed using the coefficients of the regressions in appendix table B.1. These regressions are described in the note to table 2.2.

12. Work while attending school is studied in Keane and Wolpin (2001). Delay in entry is studied in Kane (1996).

13. The graphs in figures 2.7c to 2.7f have been constructed using the coefficients of the regressions in appendix table 2B.2. These regressions are described in the caption for figure 2.7.

14. These tables are constructed using the coefficients of the regressions in appendix table 2B.2. These regressions are described in the note to table 2.2.

15. We obtain the same empirical patterns reported in the text whether or not we use per capita income measures.

16. The evidence in table 2.3 apparently runs counter to widely cited evidence reported by Duncan and Brooks-Gunn (1997, table 18.3), who show that family income at an early age has a stronger effect on child-completed schooling than family income at later ages. Duncan and Brooks-Gunn do not control for total family income (permanent income). Their evidence does not contradict our evidence. Permanent income is $P = \frac{1}{19}\sum_{t=0}^{18}(1/(1+r)^t)Y_t$. In a model in which only permanent income mattered ($S = \gamma_0 + \gamma_1 P$) the coefficient on early income entered as a separate regressor would necessarily be larger than the coefficient on later income unless $r = 0$. Controlling for permanent income P (as Duncan and Brooks-Gunn do not), there should be no effect of income receipts at any age if the permanent income model is correct. This is what we find. When we

exclude permanent income from the regression in table 2.3 we find strong effects of average income at ages 0 through 5 and weak effects of average income at ages 16 through 18. These results are available on request from the authors.

17. The take-up rate on Pell Grants and Perkins Loans targeted toward students from low-income families is low (Orfield 1992). Many more people are eligible for support than those who claim it. Binding borrowing constraints are not a plausible explanation for the lack of utilization of these potential resources. Kane (1999) suggests that nonmonetary costs of applying for financial aid may be high, especially for low-income people, because the application process is complex. He argues that decreasing these costs may be a more promising avenue for relaxing financing constraints for low-income people than expanding existing programs. He provides no evidence, however, in support of this conjecture. An alternative explanation consistent with our evidence is that many eligible persons perceive that even with a substantial tuition subsidy, the returns to college education for them are too low to pay for the foregone earnings required to attend school. Risk aversion due to the uncertainty of income flows may also reduce the returns relative to the benefits.

18. Shea splits his sample into children of educated and uneducated parents. He finds an effect of his measure of income on the schooling attainment of the children of the latter. Many interpret this as evidence for short-term credit constraints. Shea's measure of a family's income, however, is an average income over every year the family is sampled, irrespective of the age of the child. It is a long-run measure of permanent income for some families for which data are available over the life cycle of the family and the child and a short-run measure when the sampling process starts in the child's adolescent years. Shea's estimated income effect combines short-run and long-run effects in an uninterpretable fashion and is thus uninformative on the issue of the empirical importance of short-run credit constraints.

19. We first regress the test score on mother's education, mother's AFQT, and broken home at the same age the test is taken. We then rank individuals on the residuals of this regression and construct percentiles. The pictures we present show the average percentile by income group at different ages. Figure 2.10c presents gaps by race. We include family income at the age of the test (as well as the other variables mentioned above) in the regression before taking the residuals and constructing the ranks.

20. Conditioning on a family choice variable is problematic in producing causal relationships. In addition, Fryer and Levitt analyze one of many car-

dinalizations of the test score and discuss growth in levels of these arbitrary scores as if they had meaning.

21. Again, Phillips et al. choose a particular cardinalization.

22. The Anti-Social score is calculated as an aggregate of the frequency of dishonest, cruel, noncooperative, violent, or disobedient behaviors (BLS 2001). We first rank individuals by their Anti-Social scores and then construct percentiles. The figures plot average percentiles by income and race groups.

23. We first regress the Anti-Social score on mother's education, mother's AFQT, and broken home at the same age at which the score is measured. We then rank individuals on the residuals of this regression and construct percentiles. The graphs we present show the average percentile by income group at different ages. Figure 2.12c presents gaps by race. We further include family income at the age at which the score is measured in the regression as well as the other variables mentioned above before taking the residuals and constructing the ranks.

24. No meaning can be attached to the absolute levels or growth rates in levels of the test scores, since any monotonic transformation of a test score is still a valid test score. Valid observations can be made, however, about relative ranks within an overall distribution and how they change.

25. When GED holders are counted as dropouts, the U.S. high school dropout rate is found to have increased, rather than decreased, between 1975 and 1998. (See figure 2.3.)

26. For groups other than GED recipients, the rate of illegal and delinquent behavior decreases monotonically as education levels rise.

27. These authors identify counterfactuals by postulating low-dimensional factor models that generate the potential outcomes. They produce evidence that the low-dimensional models fit the data on wages. To extract estimates of uncertainty about returns to schooling, they estimate schooling-decision rules and ascertain which factors that explain future outcomes agents act on when they make their schooling decisions.

28. These gains are measured in terms of the present value of earnings over a lifetime. However, when we measure these gains in utils (assuming a log utility function in each year and no borrowing or saving), 39 percent of college graduates earn ex-post negative returns to college (55 percent of high school graduates would earn negative returns to college had they gone to college).

29. This is a partial equilibrium statement. The return to high school would rise as more people went to college. This would flatten the slope of figure 2.16 as college-going increases.

30. They also account for ceiling effects of tests. In their work, they cardinalize the test score.

31. In Hansen, Heckman, and Mullen's paper, latent ability is equated with IQ, which cannot be manipulated after age 8.

32. All dollar values presented here are in 1990 dollars.

33. These calculations were suggested to us by Sam Peltzman. Similar calculations for increasing teacher salaries by 30 percent lead to the same conclusions. The calculations presented here first appear in Heckman and Lochner (2000). Dayanand Manoli updated these estimates under our guidance.

34. Calculations employing a 3 percent productivity growth rate and a 3 percent discount rate are available on request from the authors. We thank Dayanand Manoli for his help with these calculations.

35. Prominent studies include Witte (2000), Peterson and Hassel (1998) and Rouse (1997).

36. Comparison students were matched with participants on the basis of race, gender, school attended, and ninth-grade academic performance.

37. Cameron and Heckman (1993) and Heckman (2003) have shown that a GED commands lower wages than a high school diploma in the labor market.

38. See Granger and Cytron (1998) for a summary of both.

39. See U.S. Department of Labor (1995) for a more comprehensive survey of programs aimed at increasing the skills and earnings of disadvantaged youth.

40. As noted by Kaplow (1996); Sandmo (1998); and Bovenberg and Jacobs (2001), accounting for the perceived marginal social benefit of redistribution sometimes reduces the marginal welfare cost of funds below unity. The exact figure for this marginal cost is a matter of some controversy in the literature.

41. Seven years has been selected as the measure here because Couch (1992) shows that one intensive wage subsidy program has annual benefits of that duration.

42. In order to account for the constancy of capital's share over time in the U.S. economy, they use a Cobb-Douglas (in capital and a nested labor aggregate) model, and hence assume no capital-skill complementarity. Although some others claim to find such complementarity, they are hard-pressed to explain the near constancy of the capital share over time. This absence of capital-skill complementarity is the reason for the absence of any substantial effects on earnings inequality from a revenue-neutral move to a consumption tax.

43. This account of the tax system oversimplifies many aspects of reality. A fully rigorous analysis of the bias in the tax system for or against human capital remains to be developed.

44. In his comments on this chapter, Bas Jacobs has acquainted us with his innovative research on optimal tax and subsidy policies. Bovenberg and Jacobs (2001) show that optimal taxes lead to high marginal tax rates for the poor which need to be accompanied by offsetting educational subsidies to avoid distortions in production. A more comprehensive analysis should account for the design of joint tax-subsidy policies that consider both the redistributive benefits of taxation and the productive benefits of education subsidies to offset the distortions on the production of human capital caused by progressive taxation.

45. See the analyses in Card and Lemieux (2000, 2001). Card and Lemieux's explanation of the slowdown in college participation rates and the increase in high school dropout rates using "cohort size" verges on the tautological.

46. This appendix was motivated by the comments of Lawrence Summers at the Harvard debate where this chapter was first presented.

References

Acemoglu, Daron, and Joshua Angrist. 2001. "How Large are the Social Returns to Education? Evidence from Compulsory Schooling Laws." In *NBER Macroeconomics Annual 2000*, Ben Bernanke and Kenneth Rogoff, eds. Cambridge: MIT Press.

Altonji, Joseph, and Thomas Dunn. 1996. "The Effects of Family Characteristics on the Return to Education," *Review of Economics and Statistics* 78, no. 4: 692–704.

Arrow, Kenneth, and Robert Lind. 1970. "Uncertainty and the Evaluation of Public Investment Decisions" *American Economic Review* 60, no. 3: 364–378.

Ashenfelter, Orley. 1978. "Estimating the Effect of Training Programs on Earnings," *Review of Economics and Statistics* 6, no. 1: 47–57.

Autor, David, and Lawrence Katz. 1999. "Changes in Wage Structure and Earnings Inequality." In *Handbook of Labor Economics*, vol. 3A, Orley Ashenfelter and David Card, eds. Amsterdam: Elsevier Science/North-Holland. 1463–1555.

Barnett, W. Steven. 1993. "Benefit-Cost Analysis of Preschool Education: Findings from a 25-Year Follow-Up" *American Journal of Orthopsychiatry* 63, no. 4: 500–508.

Barnett, W. Steven. 2002. Personal Communication with author, February 26.

Bartel, Ann. 1992. "Productivity Gains from the Implementation of Employee Training Programs." NBER working paper no. 3893.

Becker, Gary. 1964. *Human Capital: A Theoretical and Empirical Analysis with Special Reference to Education*. New York: Columbia University Press.

Ben-Porath, Yoram. 1967. "The Production of Human Capital and the Life Cycle Earnings," *Journal of Political Economy* 75, no. 4 (part 1): 352–365.

Bishop, John. 1994. "Formal Training and Its Impact on Productivity, Wages and Innovation" In *Training and the Private Sector: International Comparisons*, Lisa Lynch, ed. Chicago: University of Chicago Press.

Blau, Francine, and Lawrence Kahn. 2001. "Do Cognitive Test Scores Explain Higher US Wage Inequality?" NBER working paper no. 8210.

Bloom, Howard, Larry Orr, George Cave, Stephen Bell, and Fred Doolittle. 1993. *The National JTPA Study: Title II-A Impacts on Earnings and Employment at 18 Months*. Bethesda, Md: Abt Associates.

Blossfeld, Hans-Peter, and Yossi Shavit. 1993. *Persistent Inequality: Changing Educational Attainment in Thirteen Countries*. Boulder, Colo.: Westview.

Boesel, David, Nabeel Alsalam, and Thomas Smith. 1998. *Educational and Labor Market Performance of GED Recipients*. Washington, D.C.: U.S. Department of Education.

Borjas, George. 1999. *Heaven's Door*. Princeton: Princeton University Press.

Borjas, George, Richard Freeman, and Lawrence Katz. 1997. "How Much Do Immigration and Trade Affect Labor Market Outcomes?" *Brookings Papers on Economic Activity*, vol. 1, 1–67.

Bovenberg, A. Lans, and Bas Jacobs. 2001. "Redistribution and Education Subsidies are Siamese Twins." Center for Economic Policy Discussion paper 3099.

Bowles, Samuel, and Howard Gintis. 1976. *Schooling in Capitalist America.* New York: Basic.

Bowles, Samuel, Howard Gintis, and Melissa Osborne. 2001. "The Determinants of Earnings: A Behavioral Approach" *Journal of Economic Literature* 39, no. 4: 1137–1176.

Browning, Edgar. 1987. "On the Marginal Welfare Cost of Taxation." *American Economic Review* 77, no. 1: 11–23.

Browning, Martin, Lars Hansen, and James J. Heckman. 1999. "Micro Data and General Equilibrium Models." In *Handbook of Macroeconomics,* John Taylor and Michael Woodford, eds. Amsterdam: Elsevier.

Bureau of Labor Statistics (BLS). 2001. *NLS Handbook 2001.* Washington, D.C.: U.S. Department of Labor.

Burghardt, John, and Peter Schochet. 2001. *National Job Corps Study: Impacts by Center Characteristics.* Executive Summary. Princeton: Mathematica Policy Research.

Cameron, Stephen, and James J. Heckman. 1993. "The Nonequivalence of High School Equivalents." *Journal of Labor Economics* 11, no. 1 (part 1): 1–47.

Cameron, Stephen, and James J. Heckman. 1998. "Life Cycle Schooling and Dynamic Selection Bias: Models and Evidence for Five Cohorts of American Males" *Journal of Political Economy* 106, no. 2: 262–333.

Cameron, Stephen, and James J. Heckman. 1999. "Can Tuition Policy Combat Rising Wage Inequality?" In *Financing College Tuition: Government Policies and Educational Priorities,* Martin Kosters, ed. Washington, D.C.: American Enterprise Institute Press.

Cameron, Stephen, and James J. Heckman. 2001. "The Dynamics of Educational Attainment for Black, Hispanic, and White Males" *Journal of Political Economy* 109, no. 3: 455–499.

Cameron, Stephen, and Christopher Taber. 2000. "Borrowing Constraints and the Returns to Schooling." NBER working paper no. 7761.

Card, David. 1999. "The Causal Effect of Education on Earnings." In *Handbook of Labor Economics,* vol. 3A, Orley Ashenfelter, and David Card, eds. Amsterdam: Elsevier Science/North-Holland.

Card, David. 2001. "Estimating the Return to Schooling: Progress on Some Persistent Econometric Problems." *Econometrica* 69, no. 5: 1127–1160.

Card, David, and Alan Krueger. 1992. "Does School Quality Matter? Returns to Education and the Characteristics of Public Schools in the United States." *Journal of Political Economy* 100, no. 1: 1–40.

Card, David, and Alan Krueger. 1997. "Comment on 'Class Size and Earnings'." *Journal of Economic Perspectives* 11, no. 4: 226–227.

Card, David, and Thomas Lemieux. 2000. "Dropout and Enrollment Trends in the Post-war Period: What Went Wrong in the 1970s?" In *An Economic Analysis of Risky Behavior among Youth*, J. Gruber, ed. Chicago: University of Chicago Press.

Card, David., and Thomas Lemieux. 2001. "Can Falling Supply Explain the Rising Return to College for Younger Men? A Cohort-Based Analysis." *Quarterly Journal of Economics* 116, no. 2: 705–746.

Carneiro, Pedro. 2002. "Heterogeneity in the Returns to Schooling: Implications for Policy Evaluation." Ph.D. diss., University of Chicago.

Carneiro, Pedro, Karsten Hansen, and James J. Heckman. 2001. "Removing the Veil of Ignorance in Assessing the Distributional Impacts of Social Policies." *Swedish Economic Policy Review* 8: 273–301.

Carneiro, Pedro, Karsten Hansen, and James J. Heckman. 2003. "Estimating Distributions of Treatment Effects with an Application to the Returns to Schooling." *International Economic Review* 44, no. 2: 361–422.

Carneiro, Pedro, and James J. Heckman. 2002. "The Evidence on Credit Constraints in Post-secondary Schooling." *Economic Journal* 112, no. 482: 705–734.

Carneiro, Pedro, James J. Heckman, and Edward Vytlacil. 2003. "Understanding What Instrumental Variables Estimate: Estimating Marginal and Average Returns to Education." University of Chicago working paper (revised from 2001 version).

Carnevale, Anthony, and Richard Fry. 2000. "Crossing the Great Divide: Can We Achieve Equity When Generation Y Goes to College?" Educational Testing Service Leadership 2000 Series, Princeton, N.J.

Cawley, John, James J. Heckman, Lance Lochner, and Edward Vytlacil. 2000. "Understanding the Role of Cognitive Ability in Accounting for the Recent Rise in the Return to Education." In *Meritocracy and Economic Inequality*, Kenneth Arrow, Samuel Bowles, and Steven Durlauf, eds. Princeton: Princeton University Press.

Cawley, John, James J. Heckman, and Edward Vytlacil. 1999. "On Policiesto Reward the Value Added by Educators." *Review of Economics and Statistics* 81, no. 4: 720–727.

Coleman, James, and Thomas Hoffer. 1983. *Public and Private High Schools.* New York: Basic.

Cossa, Richard. 2000. "Determinants of School Attainment in Argentina: An Empirical Analysis with Extensions to Policy Evaluation." Ph.D. diss., University of Chicago.

Couch, Kenneth. 1992. "New Evidence on the Long-Term Effects of Employment Training Programs," *Journal of Labor Economics* 10, no. 4: 380–388.

Cullen, Julie, Brian Jacob, and Steven Levitt. 2000. "The Impact of School Choice on Student Outcomes: An Analysis of the Chicago Public Schools." NBER working paper no. 7888.

Currie, Janet, and Duncan Thomas. 1995. "Does Head Start Make a Difference?" *American Economic Review* 85, no. 3: 341–364.

DeLong, J. Bradford, Claudia Goldin, and Lawrence Katz. 2003. "Sustaining U.S. Economic Growth." In *Agenda for the Nation*, Henry Aaron, James Lindsay, and Pietro Nivola, eds. Washington, D.C.: Brookings Institution Press.

Donohue, John, and Peter Siegelman. 1998. "Allocating Resources among Prisons and Social Programs in the Battle against Crime." *Journal of Legal Studies* 27, no. 1: 1–43.

Duncan, Greg, and Jeanne Brooks-Gunn. 1997. "Income Effects Across the Life Span: Integration and Interpretation." In *Consequences of Growing Up Poor*, Greg Duncan and Jeanne Brooks-Gunn, eds. New York: Russell Sage.

Dynarski, Susan. 2000. "Hope for Whom? Financial Aid for the Middle Class and Its Impact on College Attendance," *National Tax Journal* 53, no. 3 (part 2): 629–662.

Dynarski, Susan. 2001. "Does Aid Matter? Measuring the Effects of Student Aid on College Attendance and Completion." Harvard University working paper.

Edwards, Richard. 1976. "Individual Traits and Organizational Incentives: What Makes a Good Worker?" *Journal of Human Resources* 11, no. 1: 51–68.

Ellwood, David. 2001. "The Sputtering Labor Force of the 21st Century: Can Social Policy Help?" Harvard University working paper.

Ellwood, David, and Thomas Kane. 2000. "Who is Getting a College Education?: Family Background and the Growing Gaps in Enrollment." In *Securing the Future: Investing in Children from Birth to College*, Sheldon Danziger and Jane Waldfogel, eds. New York: Russell Sage.

Fryer, Roland, and Steven Levitt. 2002. "Understanding the Black-White Test Score Gap in the First Two Years of School," NBER working paper no. 8975.

Garber, Howard. 1988. *The Milwaukee Project: Preventing Mental Retardation in Children at Risk*. Washington, D.C.: American Association of Mental Retardation.

Garces, Eliana, Duncan Thomas, and Janet Currie. 2002. "Longer-Term Effects of Head Start." *American Economic Review* 92, no. 4: 999–1012.

Glazerman, Steven, Peter Z. Schochet, and John Burghardt. 2001. *National Job Corps Study: The Impacts of Job Corps on Participants' Literacy Skills*. Washington, D.C.: U.S. Department of Labor.

Granger, Robert, and Rachel Cytron. 1998. "Teenage Parent Programs: A Synthesis of the Long-Term Effects of the New Chance Demonstration, Ohio's Learning, Earning, and Parent (LEAP) Program, and the Teenage Parent Demonstration (TPD)." MDRC working paper.

Gray, Susan, Barbara Ramey, and Rupert Klaus. 1982. *From Three to Twenty: The Early Training Project*. Baltimore: University Park.

Griliches, Zvi. 1977. "Estimating the Returns to Schooling: Some Econometric Problems," *Econometrica* 45, no. 1: 1–22.

Grogger, Jeffrey, and Derek Neal. 2000. "Further Evidence on the Effects of Secondary Schooling." *Brookings-Wharton Papers on Urban Affairs*, Washington, D.C.: Brookings Institution Press: 151–193.

Hansen, Karsten, James J. Heckman, and Kathleen Mullen. 2002. "The Effect of Schooling and Ability on Achievement Test Scores." NBER Working Paper W9881. Forthcoming in *Journal of Econometrics*.

Hanushek, Eric. 1971. "Teacher Characteristics and Gains in Student Achievement: Estimation Using Micro-data." *American Economic Review* 61, no. 2: 280–288.

Hanushek, Eric. 1997. "Budgets, Priorities, and Investment in Human Capital," In *Financing College Tuition: Government Policies and Social Priorities*, Michael Kosters, ed. Washington, D.C.: American Enterprise Institute Press.

Hanushek, Eric. 1998. "The Evidence on Class Size," In *Earning and Learning: How Schools Matter*, Susan E. Mayer and Paul Peterson, eds. Washington, D.C.: Brookings Institution Press.

Hanushek, Eric. 2000. "Further Evidence of the Effects of Catholic Secondary Schooling: Comment." *Brookings-Wharton Papers on Urban Affairs*, Washington, D.C.: Brookings Institution Press: 194–197.

Hanushek, Eric. 2002. "Publicly Provided Education." NBER Working Paper W8799.

Hanushek, Eric. 2003. "The Failure of Input Based Schooling Policies." *Economic Journal* 113, no. 485: F64–F98.

Hanushek, Eric, and Javier Luque. 2000. "Smaller Classes, Lower Salaries? The Effects of Class Size on Teacher Labor Markets." In *Using What We Know: A Review of the Research on Implementing Class-Size Reduction Initiatives for State and Local Policymakers*, Sabrina Laine and James Ward, eds. Oak Brook, Ill.: North Central Regional Educational Laboratory.

Hauser, Robert. 1993. "Trends in College Attendance Among Blacks, Whites, and Hispanics." In *Studies of Supply and Demand in Higher Education*, Charles Clotfelter and Michael Rothschild, eds. Chicago: University of Chicago Press.

Heckman, James J. 1995. "Lessons from *The Bell Curve*." *Journal of Political Economy* 103, no. 5: 1091–1120.

Heckman, James J. 1999. "Education and Job Training: Doing It Right" *Public Interest*, no. 135: 86–107.

Heckman, James J. 2000. "Policies to Foster Human Capital." *Research in Economics* 54, no. 1: 3–56.

Heckman, James J. 2001. "Micro Data, Heterogeneity, and the Evaluation of Public Policy: Nobel Lecture" *Journal of Political Economy* 109, no. 4: 673–748.

Heckman, James J., ed. 2003. *The GED*. Unpublished manuscript, University of Chicago.

Heckman, James J., Carolyn Heinrich, and Jeffrey Smith. 2002. "The Performance of Performance Standards." *Journal of Human Resources* 37, no. 4: 778–811.

Heckman, James J., Neil Hohmann, Michael Khoo, and Jeffrey Smith. 2000. "Substitution and Dropout Bias in Social Experiments: A Study of an

Influential Social Experiment." *Quarterly Journal of Economics* 115, no. 2: 651–694.

Heckman, James J., Jingjing Hsee, and Yona Rubinstein. 2001. "The GED is a 'Mixed Signal': The Effect of Cognitive and Noncognitive Skills on Human Capital and Labor Market Outcomes." University of Chicago working paper.

Heckman, James J., and Peter Klenow. 1998. "Human Capital Policy" In *Policies to Promote Capital Formation*, Michael Boskin, ed. Stanford, Calif.: Hoover Institution.

Heckman, James J., Robert LaLonde, and Jeffrey Smith. 1999. "The Economics and Econometrics of Active Labor Market Programs." In *Handbook of Labor Economics*, vol. 3A, Orley Ashenfelter and David Card, eds. Amsterdam: Elsevier.

Heckman, James J., Anne Layne-Farrar, and Petra Todd. 1996. "Human Capital Pricing Equations with an Application to Estimating the Effect of Schooling Quality on Earnings." *Review of Economics and Statistics* 78, no. 6: 562–610.

Heckman, James J., and Lance Lochner. 2000. "Rethinking Myths about Education and Training: Understanding the Sources of Skill Formation in a Modern Economy." In *Securing the Future: Investing in Children from Birth to College*, Sidney Danziger and Jane Waldfogel, eds. New York: Russell Sage.

Heckman, James J., Lance Lochner, and Ricardo Cossa. 2003. "Understanding the Incentive Effects of the EITC on Skill Formation." In *Designing Inclusion*, Edmund Phelps, ed. Cambridge: Cambridge University Press.

Heckman, James J., Lance Lochner, Jeffrey Smith, and Christopher Taber. 1997. "The Effects of Government Policy on Human Capital Investment and Wage Inequality." *Chicago Policy Review* 1, no. 2: 1–40.

Heckman, James J., Lance Lochner, and Christopher Taber. 1998a. "Explaining Rising Wage Inequality: Explorations with a Dynamic General Equilibrium Model of Earnings with Heterogeneous Agents." *Review of Economic Dynamics* 1, no. 1: 1–58.

Heckman, James J., Lance Lochner, and Christopher Taber. 1998b. "General Equilibrium Treatment Effects: A Study of Tuition Policy" *American Economic Review*, 88, no. 2: 381–386.

Heckman, James J., Lance Lochner, and Christopher Taber. 1998c. "Tax Policy and Human Capital Formation," *American Economic Review* 88, no. 2: 293–297.

Heckman, James J., Lance Lochner, and Christopher Taber. 2000. "General Equilibrium Cost Benefit Analysis of Education and Tax Policies." In *Trade, Growth and Development: Essays in Honor of T. N. Srinivasan*, Gustav Ranis and Lakshmi K. Raut, eds. Amsterdam: Elsevier Science.

Heckman, James J., Lance Lochner, and Petra Todd. 2003. "Fifty Years of Mincer Regressions." NBER Working Paper W9732.

Heckman, James J., and Yona Rubinstein. 2001. "The Importance of Noncognitive Skills: Lessons from the GED Testing Program." *American Economic Review* 91, no. 2: 145–149.

Heckman, James J., and Jeffrey Smith. 1998. "Evaluating the Welfare State." In *Econometrics and Economic Theory in the 20th Century: The Ragnar Frisch Centennial Symposium*, S. Strøm, ed. Cambridge: Cambridge University Press.

Heckman, James J., Jeffrey Smith, and Nancy Clements. 1997. "Making the Most out of Social Experiments: The Intrinsic Uncertainty in Evidence from Randomized Trials with an application to the National JTPA Experiment." *Review of Economic Studies* 64, no. 4: 487–535.

Heckman, James J., and Edward Vytlacil. 2001. "Identifying the Role of Cognitive Ability in Explaining the Level of and Change in the Return to Schooling" *Review of Economics and Statistics* 83, no. 1: 1–12.

Herrera, Carla, Cynthia Sipe, Wendy McClanahan, Amy Arbreton, and Sarah Pepper. 2000. *Mentoring School-Age Children: Relationship Development in Community-Based and School-Based Programs*. Philadelphia: Public/Private Ventures.

Herrnstein, Richard, and Charles Murray. 1994. *The Bell Curve*. New York: Free Press.

Hill, Martha. 1992. *The Panel Study of Income Dynamics: A User's Guide*. Newbury Park, Calif.: Sage.

Hirschleifer, Jack. 1970. *Investment, Interest and Capital*. Englewood Cliffs, N.J.: Prentice Hall.

Hoxby, Caroline. 2000. "Does Competition among Public Schools Benefit Students and Taxpayers?" *American Economic Review* 90, no. 5: 1209–1238.

Johnson, Amy. 1996. *An Evaluation of the Long-Term Impacts of the Sponsor-a-Scholar Program on Student Performance*. Princeton: Mathematica Policy Research.

Johnson, Dale. 1988. "Primary Prevention of Behavior Problems in Young Children: The Houston Parent-Child Development Center." In *14 Ounces of Prevention: A Casebook for Practitioners*, Richard Price, Emory Cowen, Raymond Lorion, and Julia Ramos-McKay, eds. Washington, D.C.: American Psychological Association.

Joint Committee on Taxation, United States Congress. 1992. *Description and Analysis of Tax Provisions Expiring in 1992: Scheduled for Hearings before the House Committee on Ways and Means on January 28–29 and February 26, 1992*. Washington, D.C.: U.S. Government Printing Office.

Jorgenson, Dale, and Mun Ho. 1999. "The Quality of the U.S. Work Force, 1948 to 95." Harvard University working paper.

Judd, Kenneth. 2000. "Is Education as Good as Gold? A Portfolio Analysis of Human Capital Investment," Stanford University working paper.

Kane, Thomas. 1994. "College Entry by Blacks since 1970: The Role of College Costs, Family Background, and the Returns to Education." *Journal of Political Economy* 102, no. 5: 878–911.

Kane, Thomas. 1996. "College Costs, Borrowing Constraints and the Timing of College Entry," *Eastern Economic Journal* 22, no. 2: 181–194.

Kane, Thomas. 1999. *The Price of Admission: Rethinking How Americans Pay for College*. Washington, D.C.: Brookings Institution.

Kane, Thomas. 2001. "College Going and Inequality: A Literature Review." Russell Sage Foundation working paper.

Kaplow, Louis. 1996. "The Optimal Supply of Public Goods and the Distortionary Cost of Taxation." *National Tax Journal* 49, no. 4: 513–533.

Karoly, Lynn. 2001. "Investing in the Future: Reducing Poverty through Human Capital Investments." In *Understanding Poverty*, S. Danzinger and R. Haveman, eds. New York: Russell Sage.

Karoly, Lynn, Peter Greenwood, Susan Everingham, Jill Hube, M. Rebecca Kilburn, C. Peter Rydell, Matthew Sanders, and James Chiesa. 1998. "Investing in Our Children: What We Know and Don't Know About the Cost and Benefits of Early Childhood Interventions." ED 419 621. Santa Monica, Calif.: RAND.

Keane, Michael, and Kenneth Wolpin. 2001. "The Effect of Parental Transfers and Borrowing Constraints on Educational Attainment." *International Economic Review* 42, no. 4: 1051–1103.

Klein, Roger, Richard Spady, and Andrew Weiss. 1991. "Factors Affecting the Output and Quit Propensities of Production Workers." *Review of Economic Studies* 58, no. 2: 929–954.

Krueger, Alan. 1999. "Experimental Estimates of Education Production Functions," *Quarterly Journal of Economics* 114, no. 2: 497–532.

Krueger, Alan. 2000. "Economic Scene: A Study Backs Up What George Foreman Already Said," *New York Times*, 30 March.

Lally, J. Ronald, Peter Mangione, and Alice Honig. 1988. "The Syracuse University Family Development Research Program: Long-Range Impact on an Early Intervention with Low-Income Children and Their Families," In *Parent Education as Early Childhood Intervention*, Douglas Powell, ed. Norwood, N.J.: Ablex.

Laurence, Janice. 2000. "The Military Performance of GED Holders." In *The GED*, James J. Heckman, ed., Unpublished manuscript. University of Chicago. Department of Economics.

Levenstein, Phyllis, John O'Hara, and John Madden. 1983. "The Mother-Child Program of the Verbal Interaction Project." In *As the Twig is Bent: Lasting Effects of Pre-school Programs*. Consortium for Longitudinal Studies, Hillsdale, N.J.: Erlbaum.

Lillard, Lee, and Hong Tan. 1986. "Private Sector Training: Who Gets It and What Are Its Effects?" R-3331-DOL/RC. Santa Monica, Calif.: RAND.

Lochner, Lance. 1999. "Education, Work, and Crime: Theory and Evidence." University of Rochester working paper.

Long, David, Charles Mallar, and Craig Thornton. 1981. "Evaluating the Benefits and Costs of the Job Corps." *Journal of Policy Analysis and Management* 81: 55–76.

Lynch, Lisa. 1992. "Private-Sector Training and the Earnings of Young Workers." *American Economic Review* 82, no. 1: 299–312.

Lynch, Lisa. 1993. *Training and the Private Sector: International Comparison*. Chicago: University of Chicago Press.

MaCurdy, Thomas, and Thomas Mroz. 1995. "Estimating Macro Effects from Repeated Cross-Sections." Stanford University discussion paper.

Martin, John, and David Grubb. 2001. "What Works and for Whom: A Review of OECD Countries' Experience with Active Labour Market Policies." *Swedish Economic Policy Review* 8, no. 2: 9–56.

Meghir, Costas, and Marten Palme. 1999. "Assessing the Effect of Schooling on Earnings Using a Social Experiment." IFS working paper no. W99/10.

Mincer, Jacob. 1974. *Schoolings, Experience, and Earnings*. Cambridge, Mass.: NBER, distributed by Columbia University Press, New York.

Mincer, Jacob. 1993. "Investment in U.S. Education and Training." Columbia University discussion paper no. 671.

Monroe, Eliza, and Morris, S. McDonald. 1981. "Follow up Study of the 1966 Head Start Program, Rome City Schools, Rome, Georgia." Unpublished manuscript.

Mulligan, Casey. 1997. Notes on Credit Constraints. Unpublished manuscript. University of Chicago, Department of Economics.

Murnane, Richard. 1975. *The Impact of School Resources on the Learning of Inner-City Children*. Cambridge, Mass: Ballinger.

National Center for Education Statistics (NCES). 1997. *The 1997 Digest of Education Statistics*. Washington, D.C.: NCES.

Neal, Derek. 1997. "The Effects of Catholic Secondary Schooling on Educational Achievement." *Journal of Labor Economics* 15, no. 1: 98–123.

Orfield, Gary. 1992. "Money, Equity, and College Access." *Harvard Educational Review* 2, no. 3: 337–372.

Organization for Economic Cooperation and Development (OECD) and Statistics Canada. 1995. *Literacy, Economy and Society: Results of the First International Adult Literacy Survey*. Toronto: Federal Publications, Inc.

Palmer, Francis. 1983. "The Harlem Study: Effects by Type of Training, Age of Training and Social Class." In *As the Twig is Bent: Lasting Effects of Pre-school Programs*, Consortium for Longitudinal Studies. Hillsdale, N.J.: Erlbaum.

Peterson, Paul, and Bryan Hassel. 1998. *Learning from School Choice*. Washington, D.C.: Brookings Institution Press.

Phelps, Edmund. 1997. *Rewarding Work: How to Restore Participation and to Self-Support Free Enterprise*. Cambridge: Harvard University Press.

Phillips, Meredith, Jeanne Brooks-Gunn, Greg Duncan, Pamela Klebanov, and Jonathan Crane. 1998. "Family Background, Parenting Practices, and the Black-White Test Score Gap." In *The Black-White Test Score Gap*, Christopher Jencks and Meredith Phillips, eds. Washington, D.C.: Brookings Institution Press.

Quigley, John, and Eugene Smolensky. 1990. "Improving Efficiency in the Tax Treatment of Training and Educational Expenditures." In *Labor Economics and Public Policy: Research in Labor Economics*, vol. 11, Lauri Bassi, and David Crawford, eds. Greenwich, Conn.: JAI Press.

Ramey, Craig, Donna Bryant, Frances Campbell, Joseph Sparling, and Barbara Wasik. 1988. "Early Intervention for High-Risk Children: The Carolina Early Intervention Program." In *14 Ounces of Prevention: A Casebook for Practitioners*, Richard Price, Emory Cowen, Raymond Lorion, and Julia. Ramos-McKay, eds. Washington, D.C.: American Psychological Association.

Rouse, Cecilia. 1997. "Private School Vouchers and Student Achievement: An Evaluation of the Milwaukee Parental Choice Program." NBER working paper no. 5964.

Sandmo, Agnar. 1998. "Redistribution and the Marginal Cost of Public Funds." *Journal of Public Economics* 70, no. 2: 365–382.

Schochet, Peter, John Burghardt, and Steven Glazerman. 2001. *National Job Corps Study: The Impact of Job Corps on Participants' Employment and Related Outcomes*. Washington, D.C.: U.S. Government Printing Office.

Schweinhart, Lawrence, Helen Barnes, and David Weikart. 1993. *Significant Benefits: The High-Scope Perry Pre-school Study through Age 27*. Ypsilanti, Mich.: High Scope Press.

Seitz, Victoria. 1990. "Intervention Programs for Impoverished Children: A Comparison of Educational and Family Support Models." In *Annals of Child Development: A Research Annual*, vol. 7, Ross Vasta, ed. London: Kingsley.

Shea, John. 2000. "Does Parents' Money Matter?" *Journal of Public Economics* 77, no. 2: 155–184.

Shonkoff, Jack, and Deborah Phillips, eds. 2000. *From Neurons to Neighborhoods: The Science of Early Childhood Development*. Washington, D.C.: National Academy Press.

Spence, A. Michael. 1974. *Market Signaling: Informational Transfer in Hiring and Related Screening Processes*. Cambridge: Harvard University Press.

Stanley, Marcus. 1999. "Education, Opportunity, and the Mid-Century G.I. Bills." Harvard University working paper.

Sternberg, Robert. 1985. *Beyond IQ: A Triarchic Theory of Human Intelligence*. Cambridge: Cambridge University Press.

Taber, Christopher. 2001. "The Rising College Premium in the Eighties: Return to College or Return to Unobserved Ability?" *Review of Economic Studies* 68, no. 3: 665–691.

Taggart, Robert. 1995. *Quantum Opportunity Program Opportunities*. Philadelphia: Industrialization Center of America.

Tierney, Joseph, and Jean Grossman. 1995. *Making a Difference: An Impact Study of Big Brothers/Big Sisters*. Philadelphia: Public/Private Ventures.

United States Department of Labor. 1995. *What's Working (and What's Not): A Summary of Research on the Economic Impacts of Employment and Training Programs*. Washington, D.C.: U.S. Department of Labor.

United States General Accounting Office. 1996. *Job Training Partnership Act: Long-Term Earnings and Employment Outcomes*. Report no. GAO/HEHE 96-40. Washington, D.C.: U.S. General Accounting Office.

Urquiola, Miguel, and Chang-Tai Hsieh. 2002. "When Schools Compete, How Do They Compete? An Assessment of Chile's Nationwide School Voucher Program," Cornell University working paper.

Ventura, Stephanie J., and Christine A. Bachrach. 2000. "Nonmarital Childbearing in the United States, 1940–99." *National Vital Statistics Reports*, 48(16). Hyattsville, Md.: National Center for Health Statistics.

Walker, Gary, and Frances Viella-Velez. 1992. *Anatomy of a Demonstration*. Philadelphia: Public/Private Ventures.

Willis, Robert. 1986. "Wage Determinants: A Survey and Reinterpretation of Human Capital Earnings Functions." In *Handbook of Labor Economics*, vol. 1, Orley Ashenfelter and David Card, eds. New York: North-Holland.

Willis, Robert, and Sherwin Rosen. 1979. "Education and Self-Selection." *Journal of Political Economy* 87, no. 5: S7–S36.

Winship, Christopher, and Sanders Korenman. 1997. "Does Staying in School Make You Smarter? The Effect of Education on IQ in *The Bell Curve*," In *Intelligence, Genes, and Success: Scientists Respond to* The Bell Curve, Bernie Devlin, Stephen Feinberg, Daniel Resnick, and Kathryn Roeder, eds. New York: Springer and Copernicus.

Witte, John. 2000. *The Market Approach to Education: An Analysis of America's First Voucher System*. Princeton: Princeton University Press.

3 Comments

GEORGE J. BORJAS

The papers by Pedro Carneiro and James Heckman and Alan Krueger provide state-of-the-art surveys of what we know about the link between wage inequality and human capital policy. Both papers use the theoretical framework of human capital theory and the voluminous empirical evidence to present a focused discussion of how particular policies can be used to alter both the skill endowment of the workforce and the shape of the wage distribution, and to offer some informed opinions about whether such policies are likely to be effective.

In my view, there is a remarkable degree of agreement between the two papers on the larger issues in the debate. For example, both Carneiro and Heckman and Krueger conclude that some low-income persons are indeed credit-constrained and obtain less schooling than would be socially desirable. The two papers disagree on what empirical evidence one should trust to reach this conclusion, with Krueger putting far more emphasis on the validity of instrumental-variables estimates than Carneiro and

Heckman (or I) believe is warranted. Similarly, both papers conclude that long-term factors, such as a person's ability and the permanent level of economic resources in his or her family, are important determinants of human capital investments, and that there is relatively little that government policies can do to alter these endowments. Finally, both papers suggest that noncognitive skills—persistence, motivation, drive—are key determinants of economic success, even though they are seldom explicitly analyzed in the human capital literature. In an important sense, the surveys of Carneiro and Heckman and Krueger show the promise as well as the limits of pursuing human capital policies to improve the skill endowment of less-advantaged workers.

Krueger goes a step further than Carneiro and Heckman and concludes that current inequality is, as the title of his paper suggests, "too much of a good thing." I personally do not believe that such a conclusion is warranted either by the theoretical discussion or by the empirical evidence summarized in either paper. Put more bluntly, the available evidence suggests that there should still be a question mark at the end of the title of Krueger's paper.

Although there is far greater inequality now than there was thirty years ago, an important question remains unanswered: So what? It is far from clear that current levels of inequality are above what would be socially optimal. After all, the "natural" level of inequality need not be a constant. The natural level could well have been lower in the 1950s and 1960s but have increased as a result of structural changes in the U.S. and global economies. Furthermore, even if there were widespread agreement that there is now "too much" inequality, it is far from clear that spending more on human capital policies to equalize incomes across workers would be socially desirable. There are thousands of programs that compete for the government's scarce financial resources. One could plausibly argue that the returns to other forms of investments, such as space exploration or better intelligence regarding the political turmoil in the Middle East, yield far higher returns than additional subsidies to college education or cutting class size and would lead to larger improvements in the well-being of *all* Americans, including the low-income population.

In the original drafts of the papers presented at the symposium, both Carneiro and Heckman and Krueger discussed the "usual list of suspects" in the long list of human capital policies but ignored the role played by immigration. The large-scale resurgence of immigration to the United States since the mid-1960s drastically altered the skill endowment of the U.S. workforce in the past three decades. As I will show below, the immigration policy pursued by the United States in recent years has dramatically increased the number of workers with very low levels of skills, making it increasingly more difficult and increasingly more expensive to pursue the kinds of equalizing human capital policies that Carneiro and Heckman and Krueger discuss.

The major impetus for the resurgence of large-scale immigration to the United States came from the 1965 Amendments to the Immigration and Nationality Act. Before 1965, immigration to the United States was guided by the national-origins quota system, which greatly restricted the size of the immigrant flow and imposed quotas to allocate visas across countries. The number of visas given to each country was based on the representation of that country in the ethnic composition of the U.S. population in 1890. As a result, 60 percent of all available visas were awarded to applicants from only two countries, Germany and the United Kingdom.

The 1965 Amendments repealed the national-origins quota system. Along with subsequent minor legislation, the amendments set a higher worldwide numerical limit for immigration and enshrined a new objective for allocating entry visas among the many applicants: the reunification of families. The 1965 shift in immigration policy had a historic impact on the number of immigrants admitted to the United States. Even though only 250,000 legal immigrants entered the country annually during the 1950s, almost one million were entering each year by the 1990s. In 1970, 4.8 percent of the population was foreign-born; by 2000, 11.1 percent was foreign-born. In fact, immigration now accounts for over half of the growth in population in the United States.

There has also been a substantial increase in illegal immigration. The latest wave of illegal immigration began in the late 1960s after the end of the *bracero* program, an agricultural guest worker program for Mexicans that was discontinued because of its perceived harm to the economic opportunities of competing native workers. In its most recent published estimate (in October 1996), the Immigration and Naturalization Service (INS) reported that five million illegal aliens resided in the United States. The population counts from the 2000 Census suggest, however, that the INS may have greatly underestimated the number of illegal aliens; there may be as many as ten million illegal aliens now living in the United States.

The impact of the large-scale resurgence of immigration on the skill composition of immigrants has been studied extensively in the literature (see the summary of the evidence in Borjas 1999). A key finding in this literature is that there has been a substantial decline in the relative economic status of immigrants over the past few decades. In 1960, for example, the typical immigrant man earned 4 percent more than the typical native worker. By 1980, immigrants earned 8 percent less than natives. And by 2000, the wage disadvantage suffered by immigrants had increased to 20 percent. There is a great deal of evidence suggesting that much of this increase in the wage gap between the two populations can be attributed to declining human capital among immigrants relative to that among natives.

Figure 3.1 shows the differences in the cumulative distributions of educational attainment for both immigrants and natives in 2000.[1] The figure reveals two important findings. First, immigrants are much more likely than natives to lack a high school diploma. In particular, 32 percent of the immigrant population had not completed 12 years of schooling, as compared to only 11 percent of the native population. Second, the label *high school dropout* means very different things in the two populations. In particular, only 3 percent of native workers have fewer than ten years of schooling. In

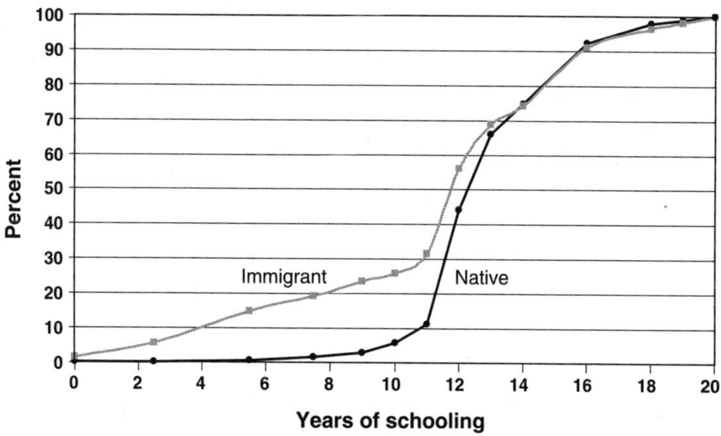

Figure 3.1
Cumulative distributions of educational attainment, 2000

contrast, 24 percent of immigrants have fewer than ten years of schooling, and 19 percent have fewer than eight years of schooling. In short, not only are high school dropouts relatively more numerous among immigrants, but there is also a huge skill gap between immigrants and natives even *within* the high school dropout population.

Figure 3.2 provides an alternative way of describing the distribution of educational attainment of immigrants and natives, and also shows how this distribution shifted between 1970 and 2000.[2] In 1970, the share of foreign-born workers in each schooling group hovered between 5 and 15 percent. For example, about 15 percent of workers with six years of schooling were foreign-born, and around 5 percent of workers with twelve years of schooling were foreign-born. The resurgence of large-scale immigration obviously

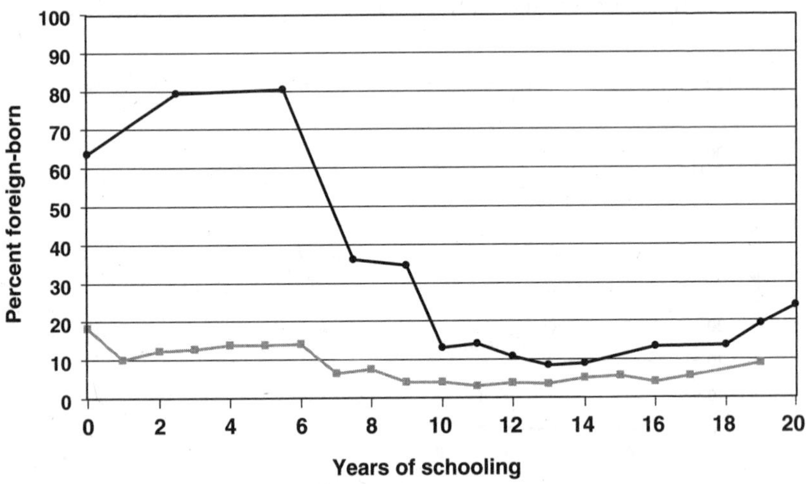

Figure 3.2
Immigrant educational attainment, 1970 and 2000

shifted the curve indicating the foreign-born share upward for each level of educational attainment. More interestingly, the immigration of large numbers of low-skilled workers, combined with the decline in the number of native workers who do not complete high school, dramatically shifted the shape of the foreign-born share curve, giving it a much more pronounced mode at the bottom of the skill distribution. By 2000, around 80 percent of persons with eight or fewer years of schooling were foreign-born, and only around 10 percent of workers with twelve years of schooling were foreign-born.

As the Carneiro and Heckman and Krueger surveys suggest, there are hundreds of programs that are designed to improve the educational attainment of disadvantaged populations. The large-scale immigration of low-skilled workers has obviously increased the magnitude of the problem that these programs are trying to address, and it has significantly increased the cost of pursuing such policies.

To illustrate, suppose the United States adopted a policy that attempted to improve the skills of immigrants at the very bottom of the educational-attainment distribution. In particular, this policy would undertake the investments necessary to raise the skills of the average immigrant who is a high school dropout to the level of the typical native who is also a high school dropout. In other words, if this policy were successful, the mean educational attainment of high school dropouts would be the same for the two groups. In 2000, the typical native-born high school dropout had 9.7 years of schooling, as compared to only 6.9 years for immigrants. Each of the 7.5 million immigrant high school dropouts would therefore have to be "injected" with 2.8 years of schooling to bring them up to the same level of educational attainment as native-born dropouts. Hoxby (2002) has estimated that each grade-year costs around $8,100. The total cost of the policy would then be around $170 billion. In short, even a policy with a very limited objective—making low-skill immigrants comparable to low-skill natives—carries a cost that far exceeds the cost of most of the human capital policies that are seriously discussed in the public debate. As an example, consider the Clinton administration's highly publicized (and ill-fated) 1993 initiative to "invest in workers." This major policy proposal was budgeted at $16.5 billion annually. To raise the skills of low-skilled immigrants—so that they would be just as skilled as low-skilled natives—would require that this program be entirely targeted to the immigrant population for nearly a decade.

Not surprisingly, the entry of large numbers of low-skilled immigrants had a substantial compositional impact on the wage distribution. Figure 3.3 shows the fraction of

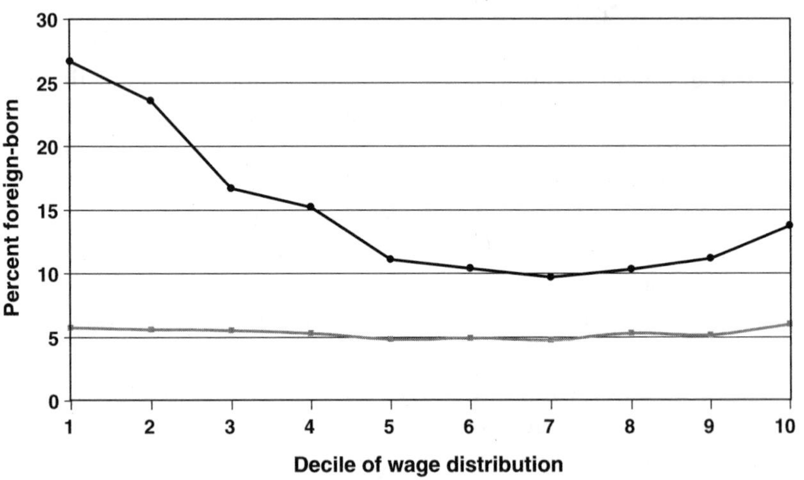

Figure 3.3
Immigrant male wage distributions, 1970 and 2000

foreign-born workers in each decile of the wage distribution both in 1970 and in 2000. In 1970, the representation of the foreign-born in each decile of the wage distribution was remarkably uniform, with roughly 10 percent of the workers in each decile being foreign-born. By 2000, the figure illustrating the immigrant share in each decile of the distribution took an unmistakable U shape, with immigrants being somewhat overrepresented at the upper end of the distribution and extremely overrepresented at the lower end. Even though slightly over 10 percent of the workforce was foreign-born in 2000, immigrants comprised nearly 14 percent of the workers in the top decile and around 25 percent of the workers in each of the bottom two deciles. Put differently, the entry of large numbers of low-skilled immigrants has effectively led to a "foreignization" of the low-income workforce in the United States.

Moreover, the impact illustrated in figure 3.3 is purely compositional: It ignores the fact that the supply shock resulting from the entry of large numbers of low-skilled immigrants will itself alter the wages of low-skilled workers (and of high-skilled workers as well). Although there is a great deal of debate in the literature about the magnitude of this effect on the value of marginal product of different skill groups, it is likely that the type of immigration experienced by the United States in the past few decades has increased the wage gap between high-skilled and low-skilled workers.

It is also worth noting that the adoption of an immigration policy that would restrict the entry of some low-skilled workers would have a substantial impact on the wage distribution, even putting aside the potential impact of low-skilled immigration on the relative wage of low-skilled workers. Consider, for example, how the wage distribution would shift if the United States banned the entry of persons who have fewer than ten years of schooling. Note that this policy would not deny entry to all high school dropouts; it would simply deny entry to workers who have a level of educational attainment that is substantially below that of the least-skilled native-born workers.

Figure 3.4 shows how the adoption of this immigration policy would change the share of foreign-born workers in each decile of the wage distribution. In 2000, about 27 percent of workers in the bottom decile of the wage distribution were foreign-born. If the United States prohibited the entry of workers with fewer than ten years of schooling, only 17 percent of workers in the bottom decile of the wage distribution would be foreign-born. Similarly, 24 percent of workers in the second decile of the wage distribution are now foreign-born, and this statistic would also drop to around 17 percent if the policy proposal were adopted. Put

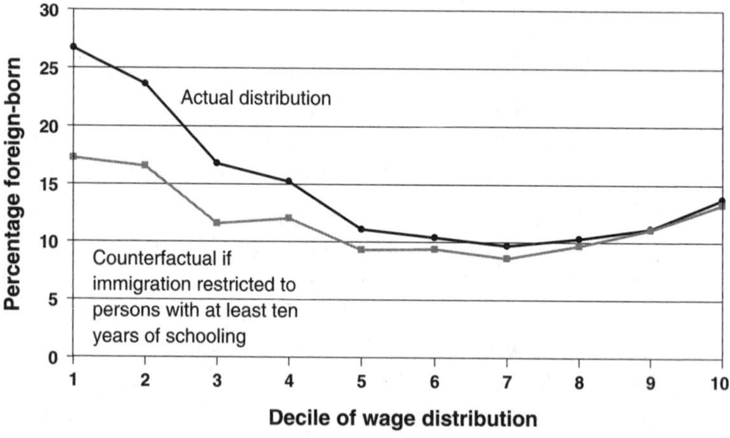

Figure 3.4
Impact of immigration policy restrictions on immigrant male wage distribution

differently, the adoption of this particular immigration policy would drastically cut the number of low-income persons in the population.

The main insight of the evidence on the skill composition of the immigrant population is straightforward: Immigration policy is an important item on the menu available to policymakers who wish to influence the human capital endowment of the country's workforce. The type of immigration policy that the United States pursues—namely, how many and which types of persons are allowed to enter the country—has important consequences both for the human capital endowment of the country's workforce, and for the cost and effectiveness of policies designed to improve the human capital endowment in the economy as well. In particular, the resurgence of large-scale immigration in the past few decades has led to a substantial increase in the number of low-skilled workers in the population and to an equally substantial increase in the cost of pursuing policies designed to improve the skills of disadvantaged workers.

Notes

1. The data discussed are drawn from the March 2001 Supplement of the Current Population Survey. I restrict the analysis to salaried workers aged 25–64.

2. The data for 1970 are drawn from a 1 percent random sample of the U.S. Decennial Census. As before, the analysis is restricted to salaried workers aged 25–64.

References

Borjas, George J. 1999. *Heaven's Door: Immigration Policy and the American Economy*. Princeton: Princeton University Press.

Hoxby, Caroline. 2002. "The Cost of Accountability." Unpublished paper. Harvard University.

ERIC A. HANUSHEK

The 2002 Alvin Hansen Symposium addressed what I believe to be one of the most critical issues of the day: What public policies should be pursued toward investments in human capital? The authors of the symposium's papers, Pedro Carneiro and James Heckman and Alan Krueger, are also ideal people to set out the options and to highlight the difficulties and dilemmas facing policymakers.

The common ground between the two papers is truly important to note. First, each is based firmly in the belief that human capital investments are important and that they should not be neglected. Second, each advocates thinking very broadly about policy options, including attempting to influence or supplant families in the education of children. Third, each asserts that government has a legitimate and important role in fostering human capital investment. And, fourth, each argues that we could do better than we currently are doing.

The agreement represented by this common ground is important. There is not currently unanimity on any of these points among policymakers or among scholars. Therefore, when the respected authors of two such carefully constructed papers review the extant evidence and underlying conceptual ideas and come to agreement on such central conclusions, people should take notice.

Almost as impressively, having agreed on fundamental issues of perspective and direction, the two papers provide what I believe to be dramatically different prescriptions for policies to be pursued within these areas of agreement. The contrasting positions indeed lay out paths that would lead, at least by existing evidence, to very different outcomes for the nation.

The Differences in Policy Perspectives

To frame the discussion, I want to highlight the key points of difference between the two papers. Table 3.1 provides the contrasting views and recommendations of each paper. Krueger would build on and expand the existing investment programs that span preschool to job training. Carneiro and Heckman, on the other hand, would target investment more toward the young and worry about improving the quality of existing programs. These differences suggest, as discussed below, quite a different array of policies. And which path the country takes is likely to have important ramifications for the future.

Background of Current School Performance

One perspective on these contrasting views comes from the aggregate data on U.S. school performance. Before

Table 3.1
Summary of key policy recommendations by Krueger and Carneiro and Heckman

	Krueger	Carneiro and Heckman
Preschool	Expand the current programs, including full funding of Head Start	Target largest investments on early age groups with focus on high-quality programs
K–12 schooling	Expand the current programs and organization with more time and smaller classes	Alter the incentives in schools to improve quality
Age focus	Invest across a broad spectrum ranging from preschool to job training	Target investments early in individual life cycle

considering the policy proposals the two papers advance, it is useful to understand what the history of investment policy has been and where U.S. schools stand.

Perhaps the most misunderstood element of the current schooling discussions is the pattern and scope of investment in schooling in the United States over the past decades. Many popular discussions of policies toward schooling would suggest that we have been scrimping on our schools, and that version of reality provides an obvious explanation for our current dissatisfaction with results.

Table 3.2 displays the pattern of resources supplied to public schools in the United States between 1960 and 2000. Several things are obvious from this table. First, the United States has been running a class size "experiment" for forty years. Between 1960 and 2000, the pupil-teacher ratio in U.S. schools fell by more than a third. Second, there has also been an expansion over the same period in the conventional measures of teacher quality: graduate education and experience. The percentage of teachers with a master's degree or higher more than doubled over the period, with the typical teacher now having an advanced degree. The median

Table 3.2
Public-school resources in the United States, 1960–2000

	1960	1980	2000
Pupil-teacher ratio	25.8	18.7	16.0
Percentage of teachers with master's degree or higher	23.5	49.6	56.2[a]
Median years teacher experience	11	12	15[a]
Real expenditure/average daily attendance (2000–01 dollars)	$2,235	$5,124	$7,591

Source: U.S. Department of Education 2002.
a. Data for 1996.

number of years of teacher experience also reached new heights.

An obvious implication of these changes in the real resources of schools is that spending on schools has risen dramatically over the last forty years. Teacher education and experience are prime determinants of teacher salaries, and the pupil-teacher ratio determines across how many students the salaries are spread. Thus, as the last line of the table indicates, real spending per pupil in schools was *240 percent higher* in 2000 than in 1960. That is, after the figures are adjusted for inflation, we have had truly dramatic increases in our school spending over the past four decades, increases that appear to exceed public perceptions by a wide margin.

The contrast of resource increases with what has happened to student performance is equally startling. Figure 3.5 displays the pattern of performance of U.S. seventeen-year-olds from the National Assessment of Educational Progress

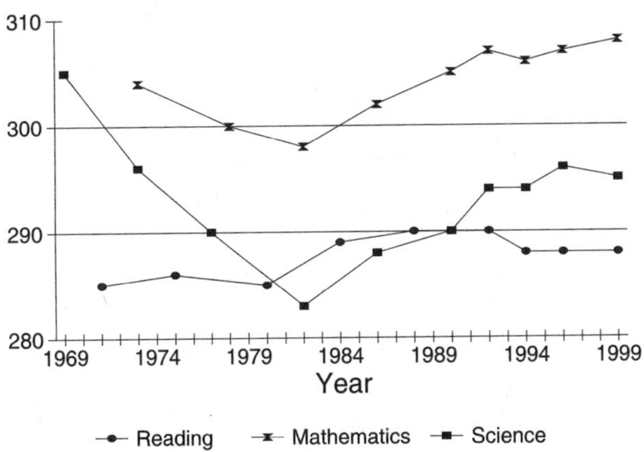

Figure 3.5
National Assessment of Educational Progress: Seventeen-year-olds

(NAEP) over a thirty-year period from 1969 to 1999. The NAEP provides a consistent measure of performance over time for a random selection of students. As the figure shows, mathematics and reading performance are slightly up over the period, whereas science performance is down.[1] A simple summary of performance over this period is that it was flat. School resources more than tripled, but there has been no discernible effect on performance.

Of course the overall trends could be misleading, particularly if there were significant changes in the student population or in the institutional structure of schools over the period. For example, it is frequently cited that families are now less stable than they were three or four decades ago or that there are more difficult-to-educate immigrants in the schools now than there were then. Table 3.3 highlights some of the significant changes in families that have occurred over the time period. Indeed, until the 1990s, the proportion of children in poverty in the United States had been rising. Relatedly, the proportion of children in single-parent families has risen throughout. Finally, in terms of factors adversely affecting achievement, families not speaking English at home are now more prevalent.

But these adverse changes have coincided with other changes that would generally be viewed as favorable for children and learning. As shown in the bottom panel of table 3.3, parents are now more educated than they were thirty years ago, and families are smaller. Additionally, greater percentages of children ages 4 and 5 are attending preschool programs.

It is difficult to determine precisely the net overall effect of these factors on students. The best estimates available, though surrounded by uncertainty, suggest that it is, if anything, positive (Grissmer et al. 1994). Without taking a stand

Table 3.3
Changes in family characteristics, 1970–2000

	1970	1980	1990	2000
Changes less favorable to achievement				
Percentage of children in poverty	15	18	20	16
Percentage of children under age 18 not living with both parents	15	23	27	31
Percentage of population ages 5 to 17 not speaking English at home	N/A	9	13	17
Changes more favorable to achievement				
Percentage of high school graduates or higher, population ages 25 to 29	74	85	86	88
Percentage of families with children that have three or more children	36	23	20	15
Preschool enrollment rate, five-year-olds	69	85	89	89
Preschool enrollment rate, four-year-olds	28	46	56	69

Source: U.S. Bureau of the Census, *Current Population Reports*, various issues.

stronger than that justified by the evidence, it is sufficient to conclude that the evidence does not show an overwhelming decline in "student input quality."

In addition to changes in the composition of the student population, a further factor on the cost side is that federal legislation now requires that children with specific disabilities be provided with special services to meet their educational needs. The increases in the numbers of special-education students have been large, resulting in an increase in their representation in the student population from 8 percent at the time of the legislation in 1977 to more than 13 percent in 2000. Because programs for these students are significantly more expensive than those for most other students, and because these students often are excluded or exempted from the testing programs in which other students participate, expenditures on schools can increase without a commensurate improvement in measured performance. Direct analysis, however, suggests that the increase in expenditure on programs to meet the needs of special-education students, although significant, still explains only a limited portion of the overall spending increases for education (Hanushek and Rivkin 1997).

In sum, the aggregate data do not suggest that the existing schooling system in the United States has been performing very well, even though resources have been provided at sharply increasing levels over the past several decades.

Nonetheless, a different perspective is possible. If U.S. performance has been high and has exceeded that of other nations, the fact that it is flat over time might not be such a concern. In that case, the main issue to be considered here would be the continual pressures to increase expenditure (with the implication that inefficiency in government provision of schooling has been increasing). Unfortunately, such an interpretation does not hold up under examination of the evidence. Table 3.4 shows the U.S. ranking on international math and science examinations given in 1995. The results of the Third International Mathematics and Science Study (TIMSS) show that particularly by the twelfth grade, U.S. students are simply not competitive with those from other countries, ranking nineteenth and sixteenth out of the participating twenty-one countries in mathematics and science, respectively.

Table 3.4
U.S. rank on the Third International Mathematics and Science Study, 1995

	Fourth grade	Eighth grade	Twelfth grade
Mathematics	12 out of 26	28 out of 41	19 out of 21
Science	3 out of 26	17 out of 41	16 out of 21

Krueger and Carneiro and Heckman Policy Recommendations

The overview of U.S. schools provided in the previous section is important for putting the policy proposals of the Krueger and Carneiro and Heckman papers into perspective. Each of the papers takes the research evidence and current state of the educational system as providing a different basic thrust for policy. Because other commentators concentrate on the job training aspects of the two programs, the discussion here looks entirely at the policies for younger people: preschool and K–12 education.

The Krueger Program

The heart of Alan Krueger's policy program, when viewed across the different potential areas of investment he identifies, is simply expanding the scale of current programs while maintaining the existing structure and incentives. As such, it takes the position that the current government provision is satisfactory. There is just not enough of it.

In terms of equity and distributional aspects, he also believes that disadvantaged children and workers respond as much or more to governmental programs than the more advantaged. Therefore, an element of his proposed program is that the expansion of existing programs should be compensatory, focusing importantly on improving programs for the disadvantaged.

The elements of Krueger's program start with fully funding Head Start, the federal preschool program designed for low-income children largely aged 3 and 4. Currently, the program serves 900,000 children, an estimated 60 percent of those eligible. With annual appropriations of $6 billion, the average expenditure in 2000 was approximately $6,600 per enrollee, an amount close to the per pupil spending on K–12 education.

In addition to giving Head Start full funding, Krueger would lengthen the school day and the school year in the United States. Other nations around the world typically have longer school years, some by as much as 30 percent. They often also have longer school days. These two factors combined ensure that the typical U.S. primary- or secondary-school student gets noticeably less instruction each academic year than his or her counterparts around the globe. Krueger would modify both of these aspects of time spent in school, particularly for disadvantaged students.

Additionally, he would increase the intensity of schooling through reductions in class size. The reductions he proposes would follow on those that have occurred already, including the recent wave of reductions following the California class size reduction of 1997 (Stecher and Bohrnstedt 1999).

Finally, Krueger would also increase the salaries of teachers as a way of improving teacher quality. Although his proposal in this area is not specific, the increases would appear to be partly geographically targeted toward low-income areas but would also involve across-the-board raises for teachers in all areas.

Krueger's proposed program is close to the one that has been more or less continuously implemented over the past three decades (with the exception of the component for lengthening the amount of school time). Why would one expect any different results in the future than in the past? On this score, Krueger does not address the policies that have been pursued but instead calls on evidence of a selective few existing studies that investigate aspects of the current system. To judge Krueger's program, then, it is useful to consider the pieces of evidence that he emphasizes.

First, he notes that the Tennessee class size experiment in the mid-1980s (Project STAR) indicated positive gains if large class size reductions were implemented in early grades. His essential argument here is that of all evidence on class size available, only the STAR evidence is relevant, because this evidence comes from a random-assignment experiment.

Although it has become common among those who want to see class size reduction to invoke Project STAR as the justification, the evidence and policy conclusions are not as straightforward or obvious as we are led to believe. Two issues arise: quality of randomization, and strength and import of the results. STAR was a random-assignment program that divided a group of kindergarteners between small classes (fifteen students/class) and regular-sized classes (twenty-three students/class). Achievement was measured annually, and students were to be kept in the assigned class sizes through third grade. By the end of four years, less than half of the original sample remained in the experiment, with greater attrition from the group in regular-sized classes; significant proportions of students crossed treatment groups, with noticeably larger proportions making the transition to small classes; up to 12 percent of students in any year failed to take the achievement tests; and questions remain about the randomization of teachers across groups. Although the sources are difficult to assess precisely, there is evidence that the combination of these factors biased the results toward showing greater impact of small classes (Hanushek 1999).

But even if the STAR results are accepted at face value, the policy implications are far from obvious. The experiment suggests that the effects of small classes accrue almost entirely during the first year in a small class: kindergarten or possibly first grade.[2] Further, the experiment indicates the effect only for a very large reduction down to 15 students per class and provides no information about other, smaller reductions in class size. And the resultant effects are very small, particularly when compared to the large cost of such reductions. Krueger's back-of-the-envelope estimates of the benefits of class size reduction rely on heroic assumptions, little data, and optimistic projections—and even then cannot marshal very strong support for class size reduction policies.

The key to Krueger's interpretation of class size results is that he places weight only on the random-assignment results of the Tennessee experiment. He ignores or at least disregards the prior evidence, gathered over the past four decades, about the results of actually changing class sizes. Nor does he give any attention to the econometric evidence (which provides no support for the kinds of class size reductions that he advocates).

In addition to evidence on the effect of class size, Krueger refers to econometric studies of depreciation in learning over summers ("summer fallback"). The studies he cites suggest that counteracting summer fallback is more important for children from disadvantaged backgrounds, leading him to advocate longer school years and new summer learning programs, particularly for children from low-income families. Interestingly, Krueger fails to even note the existence of the STEP program, which involved a random-assignment experiment for which the evidence runs counter to his preferred policy (but provides part of the evidentiary base for Heckman's analysis).

Third, to support his policy proposal to fund Head Start fully, he brings in evidence on the Perry Preschool program, a small-scale experiment in intensive preschool: extensive home visits by teachers with master's degrees in child development who taught in very small classes. He uses the positive results from later outcomes for the fifty-eight children who participated in the program to justify expansion of Head Start. But Head Start is far removed from the Perry Preschool program. To begin with, evaluations of Head Start have quite uniformly suggested that it achieves at most only modest educational gains for its participants. This is not overly surprising, since Head Start has been conducted during most of its existence as a health and nutrition endeavor staffed more as a community development program than as an educational program. (For example, program reauthorization recently established the goal of having half of the program's teachers hold an associate's degree, compared to the requirement in the Perry program that all of its teachers have a master's degree in child development). The Perry Preschool program thus offers little, if any, relevant evidence to support expansion of Head Start.

Finally, Krueger advocates a program of raising teacher salaries to increase teacher quality. On this matter, although he does not present the evidence, there is somewhat stronger support. Teacher salaries have gone up in real terms over the past decades, but as figure 3.6 shows, salaries in teaching have not kept up with salaries elsewhere. Teachers, particularly female teachers, have been drawn from

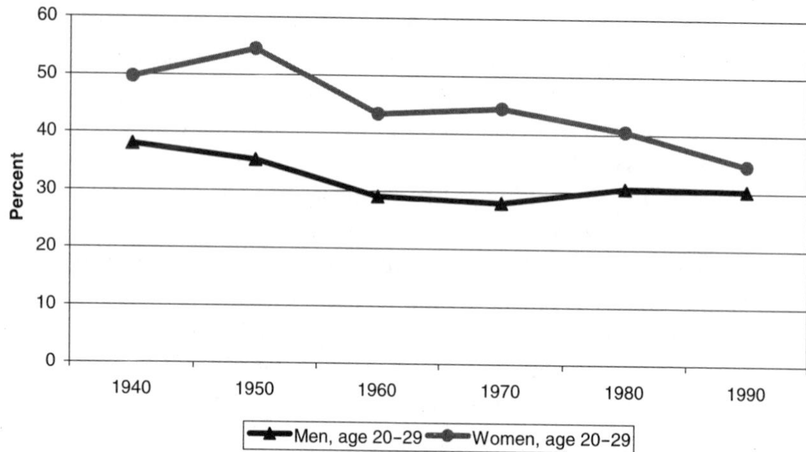

Figure 3.6
Percentage of teachers with salary greater than average salary of nonteaching workers with bachelor's degree or more, by gender

deeper down in the distribution of college graduates than previously was the case. It is interesting that this policy change—moving to smaller classes while letting teacher salaries decline—has been the choice of schools. Nonetheless, given the decline in salaries that has occurred, it remains unclear what policies should be pursued. It is well-documented that there are shortages of high-quality teachers as well as of teachers in some specialties, such as math and science. Krueger's proposed approach is to raise all salaries in hopes that future career decisions will lead different people to enter teaching—and that these new people will be high-quality teachers in the fields in which such teachers are most needed. We have no evidence, however, that this will happen with sufficient responsiveness to gain noticeable improvements in student outcomes.

In short, the combination of policies Krueger advocates looks much more like labor and employment policies for existing workers than like policies to improve the human capital of our youth. They do not relate closely to the evidence that exists either from the results of past educational policy or from a reading of the full research record.

The Carneiro and Heckman Program

Having gone through the Krueger program and the related evidence, it is easy and straightforward to go through the Carneiro and Heckman analysis and policy. Their basic position has three central elements. First, investments in human capital early in life (preschool and early elementary school) have noticeably higher payoffs that investments made later (high school and job training). Second, the important focus throughout should be on quality of programs. The heterogeneity of existing public programs is an important feature that must enter into policy deliberations and choices. And third, the existing institutional structure has not shown a capacity to achieve good results. Therefore, alternative devices are needed, such as changes in school decision making or expanded choice of schools by parents.

In developing this program and their broader critique of human capital investment programs, Carneiro and Heckman make careful use of the available evidence. A significant portion of this evidence, particularly in the area of job training, has of course been developed by Heckman, so it is not surprising that use of appropriate evidence figures importantly in that realm. They do not stop there, however, as they carry the same thoroughness into assessments of the other areas of human capital investment.

Some uncertainty about what policies are appropriate to implement still remains, however. For example, their proposals for strengthening the breadth and quality of preschool programs must rely on the analysis of the Perry Preschool program and a few other small-scale preschool experiences. Similarly, assessments of how to adjust hiring practices to improve the quality of teachers must rely on just a few studies, because they represent the universe of existing studies on the matter.

Carneiro and Heckman provide a thoughtful and thorough walk through the existing evidence on these and other questions, and the policy conclusions that follow from that evidence. They also acknowledge the uncertainty of those conclusions even as they makes their best guesses about policies that we should pursue. Nonetheless, they provide an overarching set of conclusions and recommendations that deserve serious attention by policymakers.

Finally, it is easy to get blinded by the trees and not see the whole forest. Carneiro and Heckman provide an underlying conceptual and empirical framework for thinking about human capital policies. A subtext to their analysis is that we should not simply focus on individual areas of research and of investment but should put it all together in a unified structure. Once this has been done, ideas about the timing of investment and the kinds of policies to pursue become much clearer. Specifically, both research and policy tend to look at individual areas in isolation, not seeing how they interact with one another. Carneiro and Heckman suggest large gains from making more-strategic choices about where to invest, and they particularly point to investment at earlier ages than found implicitly in the range of current policies.

In summary, Carneiro and Heckman provide a program that looks more like an education and development program for improving the human capital stock than does

Krueger's. As such, even though they have similar goals and desires, Carneiro and Heckman's views of appropriate policies diverge significantly from those of Krueger. In my opinion, they diverge for the better.

A Final Word

One aspect of the entire discussion deserves special attention. The authors were asked to provide their understanding of the best kinds of policies to pursue in the area of human capital. Both sides of the debate took on this task with the energy and skill that has been characteristic of Heckman's and Krueger's past work. And both sides came up with a set of policy recommendations based on their best reading of the available evidence.

The available evidence in many cases is quite weak: a handful of students in a specific program, a single flawed random-assignment experiment, and so forth. Where econometric evidence exists, it has been subject to a variety of concerns. One strategy that both sides of the debate failed to include was an aggressive program to expand on our knowledge base in this important area of economic and public-policy referring. From a larger perspective, policies currently arrive and are implemented at a very rapid pace relative to the accumulation of knowledge about the impacts of incentives, programs, and resources.

At least a portion of any human capital investment program should emphasize research into human capital investments. It is typical to call for more research at the end of any policy discussion. This is natural, and it is generally automatic. But in the area of human capital investment, it takes little to demonstrate how thin the existing evidence is, particularly when compared to the magnitude of decisions that are being made. For example, K–12 education is currently a $350 billion per year industry, yet investment decisions hinge on interpretation of evidence developed through programs implemented fifteen to thirty years ago. These choices come not so much because the research evidence was conclusive, but more because any analysis that has done in relevant areas has not been replicated.

If I had to bet on whether we would be better off (i.e., have a higher human capital stock) in fifty years by either investing significant resources in today's best guesses of programs or investing the same amount in developing new knowledge, I would bet on the latter. A concerted program of social experimentation, akin to that of the 1970s, seems to me more productive than putting money into new programs, given the uncertainties that surround the best ways to produce higher-quality outcomes.

Notes

1. Writing performance, not shown, was assessed between 1984 and 1996 and was significantly down over that period, although there are questions about the reliability of the scoring of the writing examinations. Longer time series evidence on performance comes from the SAT test, scores on which have shown declines since the mid-1960s. This trend toward declining scores is difficult to interpret, however, because the SAT is a voluntary test, participation rates on which have increased significantly over time. Nonetheless, analyses of these score changes, particularly the earlier ones, suggests that the downward movement has resulted from a combination of decreased selectivity in test taking and of real changes in skills and performance (Congressional Budget Office 1986, 1987).

2. This pattern of impact is of course inconsistent with the common arguments that smaller classes are better because they allow more individualized instruction, permit more and better interaction with the teacher, lead to less disruption, and so forth. If these arguments held, the smaller classes in later grades of the experiment should have expanded the achievement differential of being in a small class.

References

Congressional Budget Office. 1986. *Trends in Educational Achievement.* Washington, D.C.: Congressional Budget Office.

Congressional Budget Office. 1987. *Educational Achievement: Explanations and Implications of Recent Trends.* Washington, D.C.: Congressional Budget Office.

Grissmer, David W., Sheila Nataraj Kirby, Mark Berends, and Stephanie Williamson. 1994. *Student Achievement and the Changing American Family.* Santa Monica, Calif.: RAND.

Hanushek, Eric A. 1999. "Some findings from an independent investigation of the Tennessee STAR experiment and from other investigations of class size effects." *Educational Evaluation and Policy Analysis* 21, no. 2 (Summer): 143–163.

Hanushek, Eric A., and Steven G. Rivkin. 1997. "Understanding the Twentieth-Century Growth in U.S. School Spending." *Journal of Human Resources* 32, no. 1 (winter): 35–68.

Stecher, Brian M., and George W. Bohrnstedt. 1999. *Class Size Reduction in California: Early Evaluation Findings, 1996–98.* Palo Alto, Calif.: American Institutes for Research.

U.S. Department of Education. 2002. *Digest of Education Statistics, 2001.* Washington, D.C.: National Center for Education Statistics.

LAWRENCE F. KATZ

Alan B. Krueger and the team of Pedro Carneiro and James J. Heckman have produced superb papers on recent U.S. trends in inequality and the conceptual issues and evidence related to the design and evaluation of appropriate human capital policies. The Heckman team and Krueger both emphasize the significant rise in disparities in the economic fortunes of American families over the past twenty-five years. Economic inequality in terms of wages, family income, and wealth reached higher levels in the mid-1990s than at any time in the past sixty years, although some reductions in wage inequality are apparent (at least in the bottom half of the distribution) in the late 1990s. Labor market changes that have greatly increased overall wage dispersion and shifted wage and employment opportunities in favor of the more educated and more skilled have played an integral role in this process.

I would like to use my brief discussion to put the recent period and issues related to human capital policy into a longer-term historical perspective. I would also like to mention some crucial issues for current U.S. human capital policies that were relatively neglected in the analyses of the Heckman team and of Krueger: the impact of criminal-justice policies and dramatic increases in incarceration rates on the economic and social situations of low-income and minority families, and the rising geographic concentration of poverty and growing residential segregation of U.S. families by economic status.

Historical Perspective: The Human Capital Century

The rising inequality and educational wage differentials of the last twenty-five years represent a break from the pattern of most of the twentieth century. Most of the century was a "human capital century" in which the United States moved ahead of the world in educational attainment, first through the "high school" movement of the first half of the twentieth century, and then with the expansion of college education following World War II (Goldin 2001). The country's rapid expansion of educational attainment was associated with great technological dynamism, rapid economic growth, and declining or stable wage inequality and educational wage differentials, as rapid skill supply growth kept pace with rapid skill demand growth from skill-biased technological change (Goldin and Katz 2001). But educational wage differentials and overall wage inequality increased sharply in the 1980s through the early 1990s, with some slowing, as noted above, in the second half of the 1990s.

A simple labor market framework emphasizing the role of supply factors, demand factors, and labor market institutions goes reasonably far toward explaining the historical evolution of U.S. educational wage differentials (Katz and Autor 1999). New technologies and shifts in the industrial and occupational composition of employment have been skill-biased (education-biased) throughout the twentieth century. But this growth in the relative demand for skill was more than matched by rapid growth in the relative supply of skills (educational upgrading) throughout most of the century. Something changed with a sharp slowdown in the growth of educational attainment for U.S. cohorts starting with the baby boom cohorts of the late 1940s and early 1950s. The combination of the slowdown of educational progress across successive cohorts of labor market entrants and of shifting demographics (e.g., the aging of the baby boom cohorts and the labor market entrance of smaller baby bust cohorts) has meant a sharp reduction in the growth rate of the relative supply of skills (the relative supply of "college-equivalent" workers) in the last two decades relative to previous decades.

Figure 3.7 illustrates the slowdown of the rate of increase of educational attainment of U.S. birth cohorts starting with cohorts born around 1950. Average educational attainment increased by 0.08 years per birth cohort (or two full years of schooling for every twenty-five successive cohorts) for the

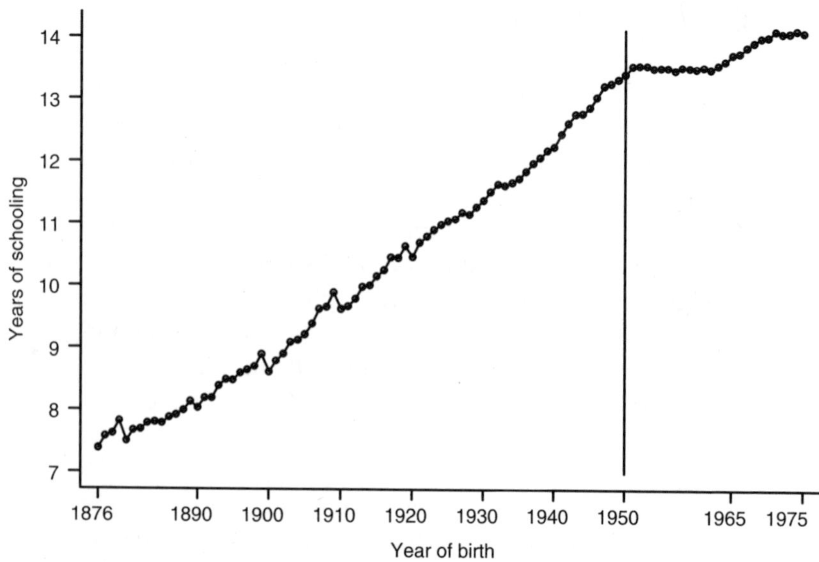

Figure 3.7
Years of schooling by birth cohort, U.S. natives, normed at age 35
Sources: U.S. Census of Population, Integrated Public Use Microsamples (IPUMS), 1940, 1950, 1960, 1970, and 1990; Current Population Surveys, Merged Outgoing Rotation Groups, 1999 and 2000. Years of schooling for each birth cohort for age 35 or the year closest to age 35 in the utilized Census samples. See DeLong, Goldin, and Katz 2002 for details.

birth cohorts from 1876 to 1950. But over the last twenty-five years (the 1950 to 1975 birth cohorts), the educational attainment of young cohorts increased by only 0.68 years (or 0.027 years per cohort). Similar patterns of slowdown hold for the share of workers going to college or graduating from college starting in the 1970s (the birth cohorts around 1950), with a renewed increase in the rate of growth of college attendance and completion for the most recent cohorts over the last decade. The consequence has been that the expansion in educational productivity of the U.S. workforce (measured by educational attainment weighted by educational wage differentials), which was 0.55 percent per year from 1940 to 1980 (and over 0.6 percent per year in the 1960s and 1970s), slowed down to only 0.35 percent per year for 1980 to 2000 (DeLong, Goldin, and Katz 2003). Slower growth of the educational attainment of the workforce directly reduces economic growth by slowing growth in labor force "quality" and may have an adverse impact on the rate of technological advance. And changes in the growth of the relative supply of skills have a major impact on wage inequality.

In particular, a slowdown in educational expansion associated with even stable trend relative labor demand growth favoring more-educated workers can generate an increase in educational wage differentials and overall wage inequality. In the United States, growth in the relative supply of college-equivalent workers slowed from a rate of 3.8 percent per year from 1960 to 1980 to below 2.5 percent per year in the 1980s and 1990s (Katz and Autor 1999). Countries with decelerations in the rate of educational advance in recent cohorts (the United States, United Kingdom, and Canada) have all experienced substantial increases in educational wage differentials, especially for younger cohorts (Card and Lemieux 2001).

The slowdown in the growth of U.S. college enrollment and completion rates has been concentrated among individuals from lower-income and minority families. Much of the early slowdown might have reflected strained schooling resources from the large baby boom cohorts born in the 1950 and early 1960s, reduction in male college-going rates from the "abnormally" high levels associated with Vietnam draft avoidance behavior in the late 1960s, and a response to the decline in the college wage premium observed during the 1970s. As emphasized by Carneiro and Heckman, the large and growing college wage premium of the 1980s and 1990s led to a substantial increase in college-going rates for middle-class youth but not much increase for lower-income youth.

A key question for policy is what accounts for the large and growing gaps in college enrollment and completion rates for youths according to parental income, race, and ethnicity? Carneiro and Heckman argue that differences in college going by family income are driven by differences in academic investments earlier in the life cycle that arise from family inputs, neighborhood influences, and the quality of preschools and primary and secondary schools. This perspective suggests that changes in household composition in recent decades, such as the decline in the share of children growing up in two-parent households, might reinforce these factors. Although Krueger does not disagree with this assessment, he also points out that financing constraints may remain a significant barrier to college going for many low- and moderate-income youths.

Recent estimates of the rates of return to schooling using "quasi-experimental" variation in access to college and college costs systematically generate high rates of return to schooling to the marginal (typically low-income) families affected by these kinds of policy interventions (Card 1999). This evidence suggests that financing and information barriers to college attendance remain for some families and that improved college financial aid, earlier mentoring policies, and a more transparent financial-aid application and information system could have substantial positive payoffs for disadvantaged youth and could feed back into secondary-school performance by creating better incentives for high academic achievement.

Crime, Incarceration, and Human Capital Policy

U.S. human capital policies for those from disadvantaged backgrounds need to take into account the large and growing impact of criminal activity, criminal labor market opportunities, and the criminal-justice system on poor families and their communities. The U.S. incarceration rate has increased at around 8 percent per year over the last thirty years from around 1 in 1,000 adults in prison or jail in 1970 to 9 per 1,000 incarcerated by 1998. The proportion of the population in prison or jail has doubled since the mid-1980s. Currently approximately two million American adults are incarcerated and around seven million are under the control of the criminal-justice system (in prison or jail or on probation or parole). The vast majority of those incarcerated are less-educated males, especially African American males from poor neighborhoods. The criminal-justice-control rate is higher than the college completion rate for young African American males. The growth in resources allocated to the criminal-justice system has far outstripped those going to further education and training for young male dropouts from disadvantaged backgrounds.

The role of human capital policies as crime prevention policies needs to be further emphasized and studied. The social returns to human capital investments for those from disadvantaged backgrounds may be much greater than the private returns through the impacts on criminal activities and criminal-justice system and victimization costs (Lochner and Moretti 2001). We also need to understand better the long-run impacts on labor market earnings of the stigma and loss of human capital associated with arrests and incarceration. These impacts need to be properly weighed against the crime reduction effects of such policies through deterrence and incapacitation effects.

Growing Residential Segregation by Economic Status

Poverty in the United States has become increasingly concentrated in central cities and high-poverty neighborhoods. Table 3.5 shows that poverty rates in suburban and nonmetropolitan areas of the United States have declined substantially over the past forty years, but poverty has persisted in central city areas. The share of the poor in central cities increased from 27 percent in 1959 to 42 percent in 2000 despite a large growth in suburbanization that reduced the share of the population in central cities. A broader pattern of growing residential segregation by economic status (family income) is also apparent in U.S. Census data since 1970 (Watson 2002). The growth of income inequality itself

Table 3.5
The growing concentration of U.S. poverty in central cities, 1959–2000

Panel A. Poverty rates (in percent) by residence				
Year	Overall	Central City	Suburbs	Nonmetro
1959	22.4	18.3	12.2	33.2
1973	11.1	14.0	6.4	14.0
1994	14.5	20.9	10.3	16.0
2000	11.3	16.1	7.8	13.4
Panel B. Percentage of total population and of poor in central cities				
Year	All	Poor		
1959	32.2	26.9		
1973	29.6	37.4		
1994	29.4	42.2		
2000	29.1	41.6		

Source: U.S. Bureau of the Census 2002, tables 2 and 8.

plays an important role in increasing residential segregation by economic status, as wealthier families increasingly can outbid poorer families for neighborhood amenities.

The growing concentration of poverty in inner cities has potentially disturbing implications, because residential neighborhoods are associated with both the current well-being and future opportunities of residents. Children who grow up in poor neighborhoods fare worse on many socio-economic outcomes than those who grow up with more affluent neighbors. One interpretation of these findings is that residential location greatly affects access to opportunity through peer influences on youth behavior and through substantial observed differences according to neighborhood wealth—such as school quality, safety from crime, and supervised after-school activities. Although attempts to sort out the true causal impacts of neighborhoods from other (difficult to observe) family background factors are fraught with difficulties, recent work on the quasi-experimental Gautreaux and random-assignment Moving to Opportunity housing mobility programs indicates that moves from high-poverty inner-city areas to lower-poverty areas can have large positive impacts on children's human capital development (Katz, Kling, and Liebman 2001; Ludwig, Ladd, and Duncan 2001; Rosenbaum 1995).

Changes in the residential concentration of poverty may greatly affect the ability of schools to deal with social problems and disadvantages. School policies need to be understood in this context. And housing mobility policies (housing vouchers) may be an important complementary policy to educational policies in improving human capital development.

Furthermore, as Krueger points out, the success of residential-based job training programs for disadvantaged youths (the Job Corps) relative to similar training programs without a residential component is further evidence of the need for taking peer and neighborhood interactions into account in the design of education and training programs.

References

Card, David. 1999. "The Causal Effect of Education on Earnings." In *Handbook of Labor Economics*, vol. 3A. O. Ashenfelter and D. Card, eds. Amsterdam: Elsevier.

Card, David, and Thomas Lemieux. 2001. "Can Falling Supply Explain the Rising Return to College for Younger Men? A Cohort-Based Analysis." *Quarterly Journal of Economics* 116, no. 2: 705–746.

DeLong, J. Bradford, Claudia Goldin, and Lawrence F. Katz. 2003. "Sustaining U.S. Economic Growth." In *Agenda for the Nation*, H. Aaron, J. Lindsay, and P. Nivola, eds. Washington, D.C.: Brookings Institution Press, forthcoming.

Goldin, Claudia. 2001. "The Human Capital Century and American Economic Leadership: Virtues of the Past." *Journal of Economic History* 61, no. 2: 263–291.

Goldin, Claudia, and Lawrence F. Katz. 2001. "Decreasing (and Then Increasing) Inequality in America: A Tale of Two Half Centuries." In *The Causes and Consequences of Increasing Income Inequality*, F. Welch, ed. Chicago: University of Chicago Press.

Katz, Lawrence F., and David H. Autor. 1999. "Changes in the Wage Structure and Earnings Inequality." In *Handbook of Labor Economics*, vol. 3A. O. Ashenfelter and D. Card, eds. Amsterdam: Elsevier.

Katz, Lawrence F., Jeffrey R. Kling, and Jeffrey B. Liebman. 2001. "Moving to Opportunity in Boston: Early Results of a Randomized Mobility Experiment." *Quarterly Journal of Economics* 116, no. 2: 607–654.

Lochner, Lance, and Enrico Moretti. 2001. "The Effect of Education on Crime: Evidence from Prison Inmates, Arrests, and Self-Reports." NBER working paper no. 8605.

Ludwig, Jens, Helen F. Ladd, and Gregory J. Duncan. 2001. "The Effects of Urban Poverty on Educational Outcomes." *Brookings-Wharton Papers on Urban Affairs 2001*, 147–201.

Rosenbaum, James E. 1995. "Changing the Geography of Opportunity by Expanding Residential Choice: Lessons from the Gautreaux Program." *Housing Policy Debate*, VI, 231–269.

U.S. Bureau of the Census. 2002. "Historical Poverty Tables—People." Available online at ⟨www.census.gov/hhes/poverty/histpov/hstpov2.html and www.census.far/hhes/poverty/histpov/hstpov8.html⟩.

Watson, Tara. 2002. "Inequality and the Rising Income Segregation of American Neighborhoods." Unpublished manuscript. Harvard University.

LISA M. LYNCH

As we assess the potential role of human capital policies in addressing growing inequality in America, there are many points on which there is no disagreement in the papers presented by Pedro Carneiro and James Heckman and Alan Krueger. These authors agree that those with a college education have done substantially better in terms of earned income over the last two decades than those with a high school degree or less. In addition, interventions that affect the cognitive ability of the very young appear to be cost effective and provide a solid foundation upon which to build. Human capital begets human capital, creating a virtuous circle for those who get on the right investment track. Finally, a major determinant of successful school outcomes is having successful parents (in terms of their income, education, and family environment), and this intergenerational transmission of well-being affects both the cognitive abilities and attitudes of children.

The authors also agree that in spite of the evidence of the rising importance in the labor market of more schooling, we see that the college enrollment response to this rising demand for education has been greatest for children from high-income families. Even more depressingly we see, as Carneiro and Heckman write, that the United States is now producing a greater fraction of low-skilled dropout youth than it was thirty years ago. As a result, America has an underclass of unskilled and illiterate persons with no counterpart in northern Europe. As shown in figure 3.8, in a survey of adult literacy undertaken by the OECD in the mid-1990s slightly more than 25 percent of young people aged 16 to 25 in the United States could not do simple addition or subtraction, whereas this percentage in northern European countries was in the range of 5–8 percent.

But although the two papers presented have many areas of agreement, there are three important issues on which the authors disagree that are of particular concern for policymakers today: the impact of short-term credit constraints of parents on the schooling decisions of their children, the returns to school quality measures such as smaller class size,

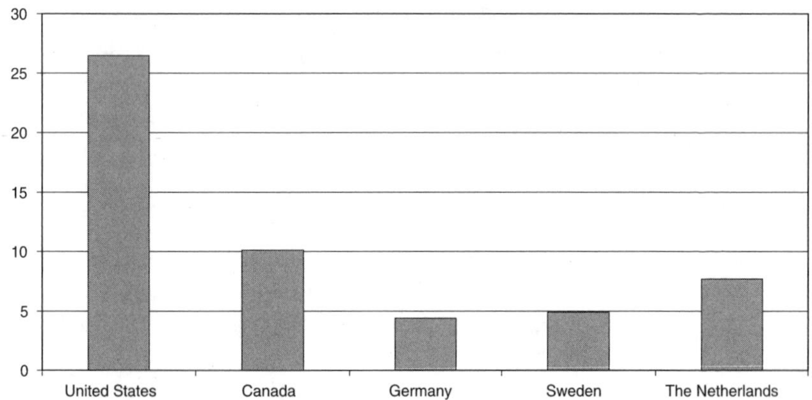

Figure 3.8
Proportion of sixteen- to twenty-five-year-olds with minimal quantitative skills, by country
Source: OECD International Adult Literacy Survey, minimal quantitative score for 1994.

and the effectiveness of second-chance programs for older youth and adults. Other discussants have spoken to the issue of short-run credit constraints and class size, so I will focus my comments on the role of second-chance programs in addressing inequality.

Let me use an analogy to make thinking about this issue easier. Imagine you are trying to change the temperature of bath water than has become tepid. One solution is to turn on the hot water and add it to the bath. But it will take time for this to change the overall temperature of the water. A second solution might be to find some method to heat up the existing water—some sort of heat immersion device. One solution addresses the flow, the other the stock. The same is true here in terms of the focus of the two papers on how to direct human capital policy. The Carneiro and Heckman paper focuses on raising the quality of the inflow into the labor market, whereas the Krueger paper makes a case for also trying to fix the existing stock. This is not to say that the Carneiro and Heckman paper does not make any recommendations about those workers who find that their skills are in low demand in the labor market. It proposes that these workers should receive a wage subsidy (on a cohort-specific basis) rather than having any money spent on remediation programs for them.

Now where a policymaker may finally choose to allocate scarce funding—wage subsidies versus remediation—will very much depend on whether or not we believe that there are cost-effective measures for raising the skill level of the stock of workers already in the labor market. In spite of the well-documented failures of some government training programs, there is a fair amount of agreement that returns to classroom education are relatively high and that there are some extremely successful public training programs for disadvantaged workers. As both papers discuss, successful government training programs such as the Center for Employment Training in San Jose that provide very high returns to participants. But what makes programs like CET work so well seems in part to be the close ties they have with local private employers.

This brings me to my next observation. Anyone reading this volume might look at the breadth and depth of the two main papers and decide that anything that could be studied in human capital has been. But take heart: Not all has been researched in human capital. Carneiro and Heckman's paper has pointed to an important issue that needs further research: noncognitive-skills development. But there is a second area that needs further study, and that is the role of the private sector in skill development. As Carneiro and Heckman state, on-the-job training accounts for about one-third to one-half of human capital accumulation after entry into school. Recent research suggests that rates of return to private-sector training are very high, although it is clear that this may reflect in part unobserved selection in terms of who gets employer-provided training. Research such as Lynch 1992 suggests that a half year of employer-provided training for a non-college-bound youth can provide earnings returns that are equal to an additional year of schooling. So there is evidence that the training of even low-skilled workers, when it is linked to the private sector, seems to work.

As both papers note, however, low-skilled workers are less likely to receive private-sector training than higher-skilled workers. What is not discussed in these papers, though, is that firm size also seems to matter a great deal in terms of the probability of a worker's receiving training. Workers in smaller firms are much less likely to get private-sector training, even when education is controlled for, than those in larger firms (see, for example, Lynch and Black 1998).

So how do we get more of the training of low-skilled workers done in the private sector? First we need to recognize that low-wage workers suffer from two deficiencies: skills and time. As low-skilled workers saw their hourly wages fall over the past twenty years, many increased the number of hours they worked to try to make up for the gap, especially in the late 1990s. This time constraint (which may go some way toward explaining why take-up rates by adults of government programs aimed at increasing their human capital accumulation are so low) reduces the amount of discretionary time available to acquire skills. It also reduces the amount of time that low-skilled workers who are parents can spend with their children, which is a double blow, since we know that this time is critical for children's cognitive and noncognitive development. This mixture of time and skill deficits is why some of the current policy discussion has focused on trying to stimulate more private-sector training that occurs during the working day.

The second item we must address is the way in which we fund national government-supported training. Krueger argues that the Workforce Investment Act can be used to address the skills gap of workers currently in the workforce, but I do not see how this is possible under the current system of allocating more funds for national government-supported training programs when the economy slows and less when the economy is growing. This has meant that resources for national government-supported training programs fell sharply during the booming 1990s, even as employers were complaining of large skill shortages and low-skilled workers saw their wages fall. Many states tried to fill the gap through state-financed employer-provided training programs. But their ability to do this in a sustained fashion is currently being challenged as tax revenues fall.

How successful these newly launched state-financed employer-provided training programs were over the past ten years is hard to evaluate, given the appalling lack of data on private-sector training. As a result, the public-policy debate on human capital has been hindered by lack of the quality data on education and national government-sponsored training programs. This deficiency needs to be addressed if we hope to develop better programs going forward.

Let me conclude by saying that as we get better data on training and conduct further cost-benefit analyses of public and private training programs, we need to account for the fact that the benefits of training may have an additional channel that researchers have ignored. This is the impact that human capital accumulation has on workers' children. We all recognize that parents as teachers have much to contribute to the cognitive and noncognitive development of their children. So interventions such as job training (especially programs such as those promoting literacy, numeracy, problem solving, computer, and communication skills) may also help parents become better teachers to their children. This in turn will bring its rewards in future generations and help warm up that tub of water a bit faster by changing both the stock and the flow.

References

Lynch, Lisa M. 1992. "Private Sector Training and the Earnings of Young Workers." *American Economic Review* 82 (March): 299–312.

Lynch, Lisa M., and Sandra E. Black. 1998. "Determinants of Employer-Provided Training." *Industrial and Labor Relations Review* 52 (October): 64–81.

LAWRENCE H. SUMMERS

First, I would like to make the case that public-expenditure analysis is too important to be left to labor economists. I will raise some concerns about the approach to expenditure-plus-benefit analysis used in the paper by Alan Krueger, many of the papers he cites, and, implicitly, the comments by Pedro Carneiro and James Heckman. Second, I would like to offer some broad reflections on human capital and inequality.

The Correct Approach to Public-Expenditure Analysis

One of the first lessons we teach in public finance is that you should not rank a set of projects on the basis of their internal rate of return; it is wrong to think that pursuing the projects with the highest internal rate of return represents an efficient allocation of resources. The scale of each project matters, and hence projects should be compared based on their discounted net benefits. Moreover, in projects that are subject to the "reswitching" phenomenon (that is, projects that involve spending money, getting benefits, and then spending more money), allocating resources based on the rate-of-return criterion can be very misleading. Consider the example of Head Start, one of the expected benefits of which is that participants will be more likely to attend college—a benefit that first requires making a further investment. In such a scenario, whether the Head Start program is desirable is not necessarily even a monotonic function of the interest rate. Thus it is very important to qualify policy recommendations based on rate-of-return calculations with the caution that this is not the right way to judge investments.

A second concern is the benchmark rate of return that Krueger suggests we use when deciding whether to pursue human capital programs. He offers the 6.3 percent average return on the stock market as an appropriate benchmark. At a minimum, however, one would want to look at the social return of capital investment that includes the portion taken by the government in the form of corporate taxation. Estimates of the social return to capital investment, as measured from profit rates, are in the 10 to 11 percent range. Moreover, even this benchmark is questionable, given the choices made by the individuals who would be affected by the proposed human capital interventions. Many poor families in America have debt outstanding at rates of interest close to 18 percent, or they make choices to rent rather than buy housing, furniture, or automobiles, choices that imply that their discount rates are substantially in excess of 11 percent. There may be broad social benefits to education—and I suspect that there are—but arguing that there is an 8 percent rate of return to further education initiatives does not establish a compelling case for the government to support an investment in them.

In addition, the estimated benefits of a publicly funded program must be discounted to account for the fact that all public expenditures are financed by taxation, which is distortionary, so raising a dollar of public revenue involves some deadweight loss. Estimates vary on the amount of deadweight loss involved. Conservatives think it costs $1.50 to $2.00 to raise a dollar of revenue; liberals think it costs $1.20 to raise a dollar of revenue, but even this lower bound can substantially affect the implied rate of return. If a public investment is financed as a consol, one must scale the rate of return by a factor of $1.00 divided by $1.20. If, instead, the investment involves spending $1.00 today and earning $1.10 next year, then the fact that the $1.00 one is investing really costs one $1.20 changes the rate of return from positive 10 percent to negative 10 percent. The education investments we are discussing probably have time horizons between those in those two cases, but the important point is that distortionary taxation would substantially reduce the rate of return to the investments.

Finally, when we use evidence from small interventions to advocate significantly greater public expenditure, we must recognize that we will run into some combination of diminishing returns and higher prices as we scale up programs. It is difficult to quantify this decrease in benefits and increase in costs, but almost certainly, large-scale programs will have lower rates of return than those measured for small-scale programs. Imagine that the state of Tennessee decided to implement the STAR program's recommendation of smaller class size. Tennessee would need to hire more teachers, which presumably would involve both hiring teachers of lower average quality than the existing teachers and paying higher wages to teachers. Similar general-equilibrium effects hold for other programs. Experience suggests that it is very difficult for the government to generate more of any activity without rewarding a significant part of activity that is underway. Extra Job Corps training would come, to some extent, at the expense of existing employer-provided on-the-job training. Similarly, if federal money were allocated to the states for job training, it would displace some of the training the states would have done anyway out of their existing budgets, since funds are at least partly fungible. Thus, I would caution that, even if one can demonstrate rates of return in the 10 percent range for the interventions discussed here, the case for our getting an enormous benefit from putting significantly more money into similar human capital programs is a little weaker than any of us would like it to be.

Labor economists have provided us with very valuable analyses of education and training programs, but as we assess which human capital policies will have benefits that outweigh their costs—which policies to pursue as a society—I think we also need the input of public economists.

General Observations on Human Capital and Inequality

First, I would like to reinforce the point made by Carneiro and Heckman that it is extremely important that we learn more and think more about how to make the process of human capital production more efficient. For example, whether vouchers are terribly unjust and perpetuate inequality or will reduce *x*-inefficiency in the educational system is not something on which I have a definite opinion—except that it is ludicrous as a society to spend $600 billion a year on education without systematically trying to answer that question. Determining how to make the education system more efficient requires great study.

Second, there is a lot of evidence that children's peer groups have an enormous impact on how they grow up and what their lives are like (Harris 1998). Interventions that create better mixing of children have potentially large benefits, and these types of programs need to be explored in the same rate-of-return context as that used for exploring the alternatives involving human capital that have been suggested here.

I appreciate the sensitivity of this third remark I will make. Carneiro and Heckman argued very strongly, and Krueger took a quite close position, that Head Start, an intervention that is half a day, five days a week, eight months a year, has profound impacts on children's lives going forward twenty-five years. It seems to me that if there is such plasticity before the age of four, then one has to believe that how children are cared for—whether their parents are at home with them, or the nature of their child care arrangements—must have enormous implications for children's futures. Following the logic of the plasticity argument leads us in important, and very complicated, directions. It pushes us toward having stronger policies to improve the quality of day care. It also raises questions about what our policy should be toward parents' working versus parents' staying at home to care for their children. What the right conclusions are, I have no idea. But I think we have to face the fact that it is difficult to believe there is as much plasticity in young children as evidenced by Head Start and also to believe that an enormous range of child care arrangements work out equally well for children. Yet this tends to be a prevailing belief.

Fourth, nobody has touched on something that I suspect is very important for issues of inequality, namely, the demand side of the labor market. In particular, it is striking that when market competition is less than perfect, employers choose to compress wages very substantially relative to true productivity. Thus the degree of wage inequality that we observe is a reflection of two things, how much inequality in productivity there is and also the extent to which the underlying inequality of productivity is translated into inequality of wages. And the extent to which productivity differences are translated into wage differences seems to have become much more pronounced over time. Anecdotally, it appears that wage compression was much more prevalent in American academia twenty-five years ago than it is today. I think that most people would say that wage compression in other spheres of the economy have followed a similar pattern. Productivity has a greater impact on wages than used to be the case, so some of the recent changes in wage inequality stem not from changes in the inequality of human capital (or more generally productivity), but from changing wage policies or norms.

Finally, David Ellwood (2001) has recently estimated that the portion of the labor force that graduated from college increased by nearly 50 percent over the last twenty years, and that the fraction of people between the ages of twenty-five and fifty-four increased very substantially over the same period (Ellwood 2001). Over the next twenty years the increase in the fraction of the labor force that attends college will increase only negligibly, and the fraction aged twenty-five to fifty-four will decline quite substantially. And so to an extent that we have not fully appreciated, we have had rising human capital as a wind behind our backs in improving the performance of the economy over the last twenty years, and we will not have a similarly large thrust from increasing levels of human capital in the future. Essentially, the retirement of those born early in the century proved to be a boon to average human capital, but those individuals have all retired now, and a major source of productivity growth has dried up. Since we can expect smaller gains in the future from an increased quantity of human capital, it seems we must turn to improving the quality of human capital, both to address the issues of inequality that we have discussed in this symposium and also to fuel growth.

Note

I make these remarks not in my capacity as president of Harvard University, but in my capacity as professor of economics.

References

Ellwood, David T. 2001. "The Sputtering Labor Force of the 21st Century: Can Social Policy Help?" In *The Roaring Nineties: Can Full Employment Be Sustained?* A. Krueger and R. Solow, eds. New York: Russell Sage.

Harris, Judith Rich. 1998. *The Nurture Assumption: Why Children Turn Out the Way They Do*. New York: Free Press.

4 Responses

ALAN B. KRUEGER

I want to thank Pedro Carneiro and Jim Heckman and all five discussants for sharing their thoughtful comments on this important subject. There are a number of points on which Carneiro and Heckman and I are in agreement, and some on which we respectfully disagree. It is worth highlighting the following seven general areas of agreement before responding to the key areas of disagreement:

• All of the participants agree that rising income inequality has been a real phenomenon in the United States over the last twenty years and, to varying degrees, agree that it is undesirable. Also, there is agreement that the rise in the payoff to skill is an important part of the reason for the rise in inequality.

• There is agreement that there has been a slowdown in the *growth* of supply of relatively well-trained workers. This point was made most clearly by Lawrence Katz in his comments, and is carefully documented in Ellwood 2001. Autor, Katz, and Krueger (1998) emphasize the slower growth in the supply of skilled workers, and the smaller size of entering cohorts of workers, as a major factor behind the rise in the return to schooling. Although the educational attainment of the workforce has been rising, it has been rising more slowly over the last two decades than earlier in the last century.

• Children from lower-income families are less likely to graduate from high school and less likely to attend college than are children from wealthy families. In general, children from poor families receive less investment in their human capital than do children from middle- or upper-income families.

• Investments in the human capital of young children, such as those generated by preschool programs, have been found to have an impact on economic, cognitive, and social outcomes, especially when such programs are targeted to children from low-income families.

• The skills that are relevant for economic outcomes are broader than the types of cognitive ability measured by standardized tests and likely involve attributes such as comportment, ambition, and stamina.

• Individuals who spend more time in school tend to earn more when they enter the labor market, and this earnings differential appears to be mainly a causal result of their extra schooling rather than a confounding effect of some other uncontrolled factor or set of factors.

• Carneiro, Heckman, and I agree that the empirical support for externalities from education that raise the growth rate is rather weak. This does not mean, though, that other forms of externalities from education, such as reduced crime or increased civic participation, are insignificant.

In the remainder of this response I will focus on the areas where there is disagreement. Most importantly, I think the evidence is too tenuous and premature for the relationship depicted in figure 2.6a, which displays a downward-sloping relationship between the return to investment in human capital and the age of the recipient, to play a central role in human capital policy. In essence, Carneiro and Heckman are saying that after age 5 (i.e., after preschool age) it is either too late or too expensive to improve the human capital of most children from disadvantaged families with education and training programs. This conclusion strikes me as too pessimistic and inconsistent with the evidence. I suspect skill acquisition involves more of a cumulative process that can begin at a wider range of ages.

From my perspective, I think the horizontal axis of figure 2.6a is mislabeled. Instead of the age of the recipient, I think family income should be a key dimension of interest for human capital policy. In my view, theory and evidence suggest that the social returns to education and training are at least as great for those at the bottom of the income distribution as they are at the top, irrespective of the age of the recipient. This is why carefully targeted human capital policy can be used as an effective instrument to help reverse the trend toward rising levels of inequality in America. But I do not want to oversell this conclusion: Education and training programs cannot produce miracles. They can have reasonable rates of return, but neglected children who grow up in poverty have multiple disadvantages, and human capital policy can go only so far in improving their life chances. There is no free lunch.

Evidence reviewed in my paper suggests that, on the margin, the rate of return to investment in human capital tends to either fall or remain constant with the recipient's family income. For example, Dale and Krueger (2002) find that attending a more expensive (or more highly ranked) college has a higher payoff for children from low-income families than for children from high-income families. In addition, the rate of return from many preschool programs and the Job Corps program, which focus on disadvantaged youth at two ends of the age spectrum, exceed the commonly estimated Mincerian rate of return to schooling for the population at large (e.g., Jaeger 2002), and the conventional Mincerian return is an overestimate because it ignores the direct monetary costs of schooling. Furthermore, the gain in test scores from attending a smaller class is greater for students on free lunch than for those not on free lunch. The evidence thus suggests to me that there are *declining returns* to investment in human capital, just as there are declining returns to investment in many other domains. It would make sense for individuals to learn first the most valuable skills, such as basic literacy and basic math, and then learn the less valuable skills. Because children from lower-income families receive less investment in their human capital, on the margin they probably benefit most from additional human capital investment. And I suspect that the likely negative externalities from a low-educated, indigent population strengthen this effect.

Heckman and Carneiro instead argue that the returns to human capital investments are much greater for the young and for those in whom much human capital has already been invested. They support this by referring to theories of brain development and by arguing that job training programs for disadvantaged teenagers, such as JTPA, have low or nil rates of return. They do not address the serious reservations involving the "myth of the early years" espoused by respected neuroscientists (e.g., Bruer 1999). Nor do they raise compelling objections to the National Job Corps Study (see below), which concluded that the Job Corps program had an internal rate of return of 10.5 percent, in the same ballpark as the most successful preschool programs. In my view, although there are differences across programs, a reasonable approximation is that the return to investment in training from most programs targeted at disadvantaged youth is about 10 percent per annum, regardless of whether the program is targeted for preschool children, high school dropouts, or young adults. This null hypothesis is certainly hard to reject with available evidence.

Carneiro and Heckman question whether pooling outcomes for male and female subjects who were part of the JTPA study is appropriate. Instead, they defend the General Accounting Office's approach of splitting the sample up by gender. The power of the estimates, however, is increased if the data are pooled. One can always generate an insignificant effect by dividing the sample into ever smaller subsamples. There is no evidence that the effects differ by gender, and even if they did, the pooled sample still provides an interpretable estimate for the population of youth as a whole, which is most relevant for policy considerations and for determining whether it is too late to help disadvantaged teenagers with government job training.

Likewise, Carneiro and Heckman criticize the National Job Corps Study because the large positive gain found in earnings for youth who participated in the program primarily was due to white sixteen- to seventeen-year-olds. But why does an experiment need to document that there are gains for every subgroup of youths to justify the point that the Job Corps program seems to produce positive earnings gains for *teenagers as a whole*. Is the theory of critical periods of brain development race, gender, and age specific? The average impact for teenagers as a whole is relevant for a cost-benefit study of the program and for drawing an inference concerning whether it is too late to improve life outcomes for disadvantaged teenagers through intensive training programs like the Job Corps.

Carneiro and Heckman do acknowledge that among white and black twenty- to twenty-four-year-old males the annual earnings gains from Job Corps were also substantial. But this would seem to weigh against the view that, once the window of opportunity for learning closes, it is too late to remediate disadvantaged young adults. Why does this suddenly fail to hold for the twenty- to twenty-four-year-olds? I would be tempted to interpret the statistically insignificant (but positive) earnings effect of the Job Corps found for sixteen- to seventeen-year-old blacks as noise that is reduced in the full sample of sixteen- to seventeen-year-olds.

Carneiro and Heckman further seek to dismiss evidence on the Job Corps program by arguing that it is "a GED factory" (p. 191). This criticism ignores the fact that Job Corps does more than produce GED holders. Participants in the program also undergo classroom and hands-on training for specific vocations. In addition, it disregards the serious criticisms that have been raised concerning the conclusion that the GED is a worthless certification; no mention is made of the careful studies by Tyler, Murnane, and Willett (2000) and Clark and Jaeger (2002), for example. And even if the GED were not valuable, that fact would not contradict one of the central themes of my paper: *time on task* is critical. In fact, it would strengthen it. Holding a GED is not a reflection of time devoted to acquiring skills, so if obtaining a GED certification yielded no benefit, one would be more justified in concluding that something that goes on in the process of acquiring cognitive and noncognitive skills in school over time is what is relevant for producing human capital, not the fact that one has a paper graduation certificate. The Job Corps probably produced positive results because it increased time devoted to learning worthwhile general and vocational skills. Fortunately, the United States has a long track record of increasing years of schooling through universal public high schools, compulsory schooling, longer school years (until the 1950s), community colleges, and expanded college enrollment, so increasing time on task is not beyond the reach of human capital policy.

Carneiro and Heckman are right to point out that earnings gains for Job Corps participants in the fourth year after random assignment were extrapolated into the future by Mathematica to estimate the total discounted benefits of the Job Corps program. Such extrapolation is necessary, because data are not available beyond the fourth year. This limitation creates inherent and unavoidable uncertainty in the cost-benefit estimates. I am sure we agree that more follow-up research of such experiments over the longer term is desirable. Nevertheless, there are good reasons to think the extrapolation Mathematica used is conservative. First, there is no evidence that the earnings gain attributable to formal years of education depreciates over time. Indeed, it appears to grow, as on-the-job training is a complement to human capital. The earnings gain from Job Corps participation showed no indication of eroding during the four-year follow-up period. So standard human capital theory and available evidence would suggest that the earnings gain would persist or grow.

Second, the Job Corps study was conducted during an extraordinarily tight labor market, and there are reasons to believe the tight labor market benefited the controls more than program participants. In a more normal labor market, the gains are likely to be larger.

Third, Carneiro and Heckman's reliance on Couch (1992) to argue that the earnings gain from job training is unlikely to persist beyond seven years (see their note 39) is inconsistent with Couch's findings. Couch, who examined eight years of posttraining earnings from the National Supported Work (NSW) experiment, reported that "[t]hese results for the AFDC [Aid to Families with Dependent Children] treatment group provide evidence that the initial positive earnings effect observed in prior evaluations of the NSW is maintained 8 years after treatments exited the program" (p. 384). Whereas the effect in the eighth year after training was positive and statistically significant, it was insignificantly different from the effect in the earlier years. Thus, Couch concluded, "[t]he information presented in table 1 shows that the earnings effect for the AFDC treatments does not decay over the first 8 posttraining years."[1] And Carneiro and Heckman's claim that "Ashenfelter (1978) estimated a 25 percent annual depreciation rate" (386) in the gain from job training is inconsistent with Ashenfelter's stated conclusion, which was that for males, the gain from training "is between $150 and $500 per year in the period immediately following training, but declining to perhaps half this figure after five years." For females, he found that the gain is "between $300 and $600 in the period immediately after training and does not seem to decline in the succeeding years."[2] Moreover, Ashenfelter concludes that the Manpower Development and Training Act (MDTA) training program he studied likely had a positive net benefit using a 10 percent discount rate for both men and women.

Even if the scientific evidence suggested that stages of brain development were such that the law of decreasing returns did not apply to human capital investments, the unavoidable economic fact is nevertheless that investments in young children take a longer time to gestate because it takes a while before young children will enter the labor market, or reach an age where they produce social externalities. (In the context of the hypothetical lottery that Carneiro and Heckman describe, the cost of giving money to lottery winners when they are young is greater than the cost of giving money to lottery winners when they are older, so the benefits should be compared to the differential costs.) Thus even if in a cognitive sense there is less of a gain from investment in older children or young adults, there is a faster payoff that can compensate for this deficit.

Two other reasons why the payoff to human capital investment is likely to decrease with family income are worth considering. The first is that low-income families have low levels of wealth and face credit constraints. The second is that many children from low-income families tend to find school particularly unpleasant, which raises the total (psychic and financial) marginal cost of devoting more time to investing in human capital. Carneiro and Heckman criticize David Card and me for suggesting that credit constraints are part of this story. But they take a very narrow view on our work and our interpretation. My paper in this symposium explicitly states that, instead of credit constraints, "the convex supply-of-funds curves could be interpreted as reflecting an increasing marginal distaste for school that varies [inversely] with family income" (pp. 55–57). In his Fisher-Schultz lecture, Card (2001) presents a life cycle model of schooling in which the relative disutility of school versus work is a convex function that varies across individuals. Moreover, given the evidence from behavioral economics that low-educated individuals are more likely than better-educated individuals to make myopic financial decisions (e.g., Warner and Pleeter 2001), it would not be surprising if poor families irrationally apply a very high discount rate to human capital investments. Indeed, Carneiro and Heckman themselves acknowledge that "[c]hildren's tastes for education and their expectations about their life chances are shaped by those of their parents" (p. 100). Assuming families are utility maximizers and not at a corner solution, this implies that the payoff to investment in human capital would be *higher* for children from low-income families than for children from high-income families, because the total marginal cost of additional investment should be equated to the marginal benefit. The marginal cost includes the psychic as well as the financial costs, so even if credit constraints were unimportant, the marginal cost of education would nonetheless be higher for those from low-income families because of their higher marginal distaste for school, and therefore the marginal benefit would be higher as well.

Carneiro and Heckman argue that "[t]here is no evidence that rates of return to schooling are higher for children from low-income families than for children from high-income families" (p. 125) and cite Altonji and Dunn (1996), who study the impact of parental education on siblings' earnings, to bolster their point. Altonji and Dunn themselves, however, are rather circumspect about their conclusion. They note that "the evidence is not compelling if one places much weight on the specifications without fixed effects or the NLS pooled sample [of men and women], particularly when one considers the fact that the estimates are likely to be biased upward" (p. 702). Also particularly relevant are the findings of Ashenfelter and Rouse (1998), who estimate similar models for identical twins. Ashenfelter and Rouse conclude that "the estimates suggest that individuals from families with higher levels of ability receive lower returns to their schooling investment. In addition, this difference is generally statistically significant" (p. 269). Carneiro and Heckman also cite Meghir and Palme 2001 as evidence that the return to schooling is higher for high-ability people than for low-ability people, but they neglect to mention that Meghir and Palme's study considered the impact of an intervention that varied compulsory schooling levels, and that in Meghir and Palme's study, compulsory schooling led to "significant increases in the educational attainment of individuals from poorer backgrounds," (p. 1) and that schooling and earnings rose for people from poor families as a whole as a result of higher compulsory-schooling requirements. The fact that, among those from poor families, earnings gains were tilted toward those with more ability does not negate Meghir and Palme's findings that earnings and education rose significantly as a result of the education reform for children with unskilled fathers.

Similarly, Carneiro and Heckman argue that there is no effect of JTPA training at the bottom of the distribution. But most of those in JTPA were probably in the bottom half of the overall income distribution to begin with. Even if the top half of earners in JTPA benefited most from the training, overall income inequality would likely still be reduced by participation in the program. Moreover, Abadie, Angrist, and Imbens (2002) find that the proportionate effect of JTPA participation on earnings was largest (although not always significant) in the middle quantiles of participants for adult men and largest in the lower quantiles for adult women.

Carneiro and Heckman question the instruments that have been used to identify the return to years of schooling in the natural-experiments literature, yet they uncritically accept the heroic and often hidden identifying assumptions that underlie many dynamic models of education with heterogeneous returns. I will leave it to the reader to decide whether the estimates of the payoff to education in the papers surveyed by Card (2001) are more or less credible than the identifying assumptions underlying econometric estimates of the full distributions of returns and the returns to marginal entrants induced to complete more schooling.

Carneiro and Heckman, citing Hanushek (2000) for support, claim that there has been "a decline in the academic performance of American students" (p. 86) over the past thirty years. Although it is popular to criticize public schooling, this alleged decline is inconsistent with most of the available evidence. According to the National Center for Education Statistics (2000, 26), average math and reading scores on the National Assessment for Educational Progress (NAEP) tests—the most comparable, representative data available—have trended significantly upward since the early 1970s for five of the six age groups tested, and are flat for the sixth.[3] Berliner and Biddle (1995) summarize additional evidence that shows an upward trend in the California Achievement Test, Stanford Achievement Test, Comprehensive Test of Basic Skills, and other commercial tests in the 1980s. Given the "growth in bad family environments" (p. 208) that Carneiro and Heckman allude to, this progress with regard to test scores is all the more a remarkable achievement and probably a reflection of the ability of public schools to help overcome growing disadvantages faced by their students. This is one reason why I disagree with Eric Hanushek's argument that past increases in school resources have been ineffective. The correlation between school spending and NAEP scores over time is positive, and about in line with what one would expect from the Tennessee STAR experiment (see Krueger 1998).

Carneiro and Heckman also dismiss evidence from the Tennessee STAR experiment on the effect of lowering class sizes, claiming that "kindergarten students in smaller classes initially have higher test scores than those in larger classes, but in later grades, treated and the untreated students' tests scores become virtually indistinguishable" (p. 156). This is not accurate. In eighth grade, attending a small class in the early grades raised test scores by 0.17 standard deviations for black students and by 0.13 standard deviations for students on free lunch. By the end of high school, black students from small classes were 20 percent more likely to take the ACT or SAT college entrance exam as a result of being in a small class in the early grades, and those who took one of the exams scored 0.24 standard deviations higher on the exam; students on free lunch were 11 percent more likely to take a college entrance exam as a result of early-grade small class size, and those who took a college entrance exam scored 0.13 standard deviations higher on it.

Carneiro and Heckman also casually dismiss the evidence from the STAR experiment, writing, "Like those in the Tennessee STAR program, teachers in the early-intervention programs studied may have been motivated more than would be possible in a permanent large-scale program" (p. 174). There is, in fact, no evidence that teachers assigned to teach small classes in the STAR experiment were more highly motivated than teachers in large classes or that the random assignment of teachers and students in the experiment was somehow flawed; indeed, one could just as convincingly argue that the teachers in the larger classes were more motivated to help their students overcome the disadvantage of being assigned to a large class. Most importantly, the examination of the effect of class size on performance for control group members in Krueger 1999 suggests that neither Hawthorne nor John Henry effects were at work in the STAR experiment.

Carneiro and Heckman have a much more optimistic view of the effect of private-school attendance on student achievement than I think is warranted by available evidence. First, the private-school scholarship experiments in New York City, Dayton, and Washington find no significant effect of private-school attendance on student test performance for low-income students or for Hispanic students (see Howell and Peterson 2002). Second, evidence in Krueger and Zhu 2002 suggests that the statistically significant effect that has been found for black students (or, more precisely, students with a non-Hispanic black mother) in the New York City experiment is not robust when students with missing baseline test data are included in the analysis. Nevertheless, I would favor more experimentation with school choice.

Larry Summers is technically correct, of course, to point out that the preferred method of ranking various interventions is by computing the present value (PV) of cost-benefit differences, not internal rates of return (IRR). Theoretically, the two can give different rankings of programs. As a practical matter, however, I doubt this critique has nearly as much force as Summers attributes to it.

First, the nature of human capital investment in general, and of virtually all the programs that Carneiro and Heckman and I considered, is that investment is made up front and then returns are garnered later on. Descartes' conditions for multiple internal rates of return to equate benefits and costs are therefore very unlikely to hold. Moreover, because in most educational and training programs the income gain is, I suspect, persistent and constant after the participant leaves the program, it is unlikely that the IRR and the PV of net benefits will yield different rankings.

I was therefore surprised to see Carneiro and Heckman's claim that the hypothetical example they present in figure

2A.1 shows that the training program has a higher IRR but lower PV of net benefits than the preschool program. Although their example is extreme—assuming that the gain from training is totally dissipated in seven years—I was still surprised to see such a reversal of rankings. To check this conclusion, I therefore entered numbers corresponding to the training and preschool programs from their figure as closely as I could into an Excel spreadsheet. The only way I could come close to replicating their results was to discount benefits to year 0 in *both* cases, even though the training program does not start until year 18, whereas the preschool program starts in year 0. That is, for preschool it appears they discounted benefits and costs to the start of the program, but for the training program they discounted benefits and costs to a point eighteen years prior to when the program began. This is equivalent to saying that at birth we will set aside money under a mattress to fund a training program that will not commence until eighteen years later, and we will not receive any return on this money in these intervening eighteen years. If the programs were discounted to the year when they commenced, as I believe is conventional, the IRR and net PV would give the exact same rankings in this hypothetical example.[4]

Second, as a practical matter, published studies use different discount rates to compute the present value of benefits and costs. It is not uncommon for some studies to use a discount rate of 3 percent and others to use a discount rate of 7 percent. Comparing benefits and costs that were discounted with different discount rates is like comparing apples and oranges. The IRR puts all the comparisons on the same footing.

Third, from the standpoint of market failure in the market for human capital, and from the standpoint of the theories of brain development that Heckman and Caneiro emphasize, the IRR is relevant. I emphasized the IRR to draw general inferences about investment in human capital for children at different ages and from different family backgrounds. To quote one of Robert Summers's favorite aphorisms: A difference that makes no difference is no difference. In this case, I think we can be reasonably confident that the difference-cubed principle applies.

I do agree with Jim Heckman and Larry Summers that the cost of tax revenues should be taken into account in computing the costs of funding human capital investments. This is not an easy task, as there is not uniform agreement on the distortionary effects of taxes, but I accept the criticism that the rates of returns that I summarized do not make any attempt to compute the distortion costs of taxes. In my defense, however, I would point out that because people can privately make investments in human capital, to understand whether the private market for human capital has failed, one might want to ignore the tax distortion. But for policy purposes, I quite agree that the tax costs of financing are relevant and ought to be taken into account.

Larry Summers also questions my use of the historical stock market return as a rough point of comparison for the rate of return on human capital investments. His suggestion of using the profit rate as a benchmark is interesting. But using the profit rate implicitly assumes that the incidence of the corporate tax falls entirely on capital, which may or may not be the case. One could argue that my use of the stock market return was conservative, as I could have used a long-term government interest rate, which is a lower return, as a point of comparison. And in any case, my reading of the evidence is that the return to investment in human capital is around 10 percent, which is close to the figure Summers uses for the profit rate.

Although there is much in Eric Hanushek's comment that I agree with, there is one characterization of my position with which I disagree. I am not necessarily in favor of "maintaining the existing structure and incentives" (p. 259). I would like to see more experimentation with alternative incentive systems. I would like to do it carefully, though, because we should be careful not to throw out the baby with the bathwater in education. For this reason, I have favored a program of vouchers for summer school. This will give experience with voucher programs in grades K through 12 and expand the amount of time children spend in school. I would also favor experimentation with teacher incentives, if we can devise an adequate system of accountability and evaluation.

I also think Hanushek misreads my paper if he thinks it "calls on evidence of a selective few existing studies that investigate aspects of the current system" (p. 261). Indeed, figure 1.7 draws on the entire literature that Hanushek assembled and has been examining to draw inferences about the effect of class size on student achievement. The reason why we draw a different conclusion is that I give each study an equal weight, rather than place disproportionately more weight on the studies from which Hanushek has selected more estimates. I place weight on the entire literature as well as on the STAR experiment; they are not inconsistent. I would also add that the issue of attrition that he raises concerning the STAR experiment has been addressed in previous work (e.g., by looking at ACT and SAT data, which are not subject to attrition, and by estimating selection-adjusted models) and has been found not to be a problem. And his point that the benefit of smaller class size accrued only in kindergarten is simply incorrect: Students who entered small classes in first or second grade displayed a large gain in achievement as well, and it is possible the benefit for others would have dissipated over time had class size not been reduced for all four years. The STAR experiment was simply not designed to answer the question of how *varying* lengths of time in a small class would affect student achievement. I am sure we would all agree that conducting more randomized experiments would be a desirable way to answer this question. Indeed, I share Eric and Larry's desire for more scientific research on human capital and suspect that investment in research in this field probably has the highest return of all.

Notes

1. Couch found no discernable earnings effect of NSW for youth, and this null finding was persistent throughout the eight years as well.

2. If the gain for men had fallen by 50 percent after five years, the depreciation rate would be 15 percent per year. The implied depreciation rate for women would be zero.

3. Trends in scores on the science test are more ambiguous than those in scores on the other tests, but there have been large changes in the subject matter taught in U.S. science classes since the early 1970s, so one could question how comparable the results of this test are across time.

4. As mentioned, the exact figures to perform this calculation were not reported, so I have done my best to reconstruct the hypothetical example by entering the figures graphed in figure 2A.1 in an Excel spreadsheet. My conclusion must therefore be considered approximate. But suffice it to say that in the data that seem to me to be presented in figure 2A.1, the ranking of the two programs based on IRR and PV would be no different if the present value were discounted to the start of the program in both cases.

References

Abadie, Alberto, Joshua Angrist, and Guido Imbens. 2002. "Instrumental Variables Estimates of the Effect of Subsideized Training on the Quantiles of Trainee Earnings." *Econometrica* 70, no. 1 (March): 91–117.

Altonji, Joseph, and Thomas Dunn. 1996. "The Effects of Family Characteristics on the Return to Education." *Review of Economics and Statistics* 78, no. 4: 692–704.

Ashenfelter, Orley, and Cecilia Rouse. 1998. "Income, Schooling, and Ability: Evidence from a New Sample of Identical Twins." *Quarterly Journal of Economics* 113, no. 1 (February): 253–284.

Autor, David, Lawrence F. Katz, and Alan B. Krueger. 1998. "Computing Inequality: Have Computers Changed the Labor Market?" *Quarterly Journal of Economics* 113, no. 4 (November): 1169–1213.

Berliner, David C., and Bruce J. Biddle. 1995. *The Manufactured Crisis: Myths, Fraud, and The Attack on America's Public Schools*. Reading, Mass.: Addison-Wesley.

Bruer, John. 1999. *The Myth of the First Three Years*. New York: Free Press.

Card, David. 2001. "Estimating the Return to Schooling: Progress on Some Persistent Econometric Problems." *Econometrica* 69, no. 5 (September): 1127–1160.

Clark, Melissa, and David Jaeger. 2002. "Natives, the Foreign-Born and High School Equivalents: New Evidence on the Returns to the GED." IZA working paper no. 477.

Couch, K. 1992. "New Evidence on the Long-Term Effects of Employment Training Programs." *Journal of Labor Economics* 10, no. 4: 380–388.

Dale, Stacy, and Alan Krueger. 2002. "Estimating the Payoff to Attending a More Selective College: An Application of Selection on Observables and Unobservables." *Quarterly Journal of Economics* 117, no. 4 (November): 1491–1527.

Ellwood, David. 2001. "The Sputtering Labor Force of the Twenty-First Century: Can Social Policy Help?" *The Roaring Nineties: Can Full Employment Be Sustained?* Alan B. Krueger and Robert Solow, eds. New York: Russell Sage.

Hanushek, Eric. 2000. "Further Evidence of the Effects of Catholic Secondary Schooling: Comment." *Brookings-Wharton Papers on Urban Affairs*, 194–197.

Howell, William G., and Paul E. Peterson. 2002. *The Education Gap: Vouchers and Urban Schools*. Washington, D.C.: Brookings Institution Press.

Jaeger, David. 2002. "Estimating the Returns to Education Using the Newest Current Population Survey Education Questions." IZA working paper no. 500.

Krueger, Alan B. 1998. "Reassessing the View that American Schools Are Broken." *Economic Policy Review* (Federal Reserve Bank of New York) 4, no. 1 (March): 29–46.

Krueger, Alan B. 1999. "Experimental Estimates of Education Production Functions." *Quarterly Journal of Economics* 114, no. 2 (May): 497–532.

Krueger, Alan B., and Pei Zhu. 2002. "Another Look at the New York City School Voucher Experiment." Paper presented at Conference on Randomized Experimentation in the Social Sciences, Yale University, August 20.

Meghir, Costas, and Marten Palme. 2001. "The Effect of a Social Experiment in Education." Stockholm School of Economics, mimeo.

National Center for Education Statistics. *NAEP 1999: Trends in Academic Progress*. NCES 2000-469. Washington, D.C.: U.S. Department of Education, Office of Educational Research and Improvement.

Tyler, John H., Richard J. Murnane, and John B. Willett. 2000. "Estimating the Labor Market Signaling Value of the GED." *Quarterly Journal of Economics* 115, no. 2 (May): 431–468.

Warner, John, and Saul Pleeter. 2001. "The Personal Discount Rate: Evidence from Military Downsizing." *American Economic Review* 91 (March): 33–53.

PEDRO CARNEIRO AND JAMES J. HECKMAN

It is surprising to us that most of the discussants see so little difference between our chapter and the Krueger chapter in terms of the nature of the argument presented and treat the two as equals. In our chapter, we present a comprehensive, empirically documented analysis of a variety of human capital policies. We outline a framework that provides a basis for comparing alternative policies through understanding the sources of the problems that the policies are designed to address. Instead of presenting what is arguably selective evidence on whether certain programs "work" or "do not work", we report exhaustive evidence on the sources of the problems that the programs are designed to address in an effort to develop an informed basis for human capital policy. The differences between our chapter and Krueger's are not small. The approach Krueger takes is to advocate cures without understanding the problems being cured, and to evaluate programs without properly accounting for costs.

Figure 2.6a is a crucial part of our argument. Throughout our chapter, we present evidence that skill begets skill: that the highest returns to schooling and training are for the more able. We recognize a multiplicity of abilities.

Our chapter makes the following main points that are neglected by most of our discussants and by Krueger:

- Human capital accumulation is a dynamic life cycle process. Skill begets skill in a synergistic way. Evaluating human capital investment programs requires that analysts account for the dynamic nature of human capital accumulation.
- Many factors contribute to the formation of human capital. Early family factors play a crucial role that current discussions of human capital policy ignore. Schools work with what families give them. Job training programs work with what schools and families give them. Understanding these multiple channels of influence and their dynamic interrelationship is critical to understanding disparities in human capital formation across socioeconomic groups and how they might be remedied. Current policy discussions treat job training, schooling, and early-childhood programs as unrelated activities. This myopia in academic thinking gives rise to the current division of human capital policy among three cabinet level agencies that rarely coordinate their skill investment strategies. Our chapter breaks from this myopic tradition by developing an understanding of the fundamentals of life cycle skill acquisition before advocating specific policies. Decades of treatment effect analyses of social programs have produced many failed policies.

• Our analysis points to the importance of the family in creating differences in cognitive and noncognitive abilities that shape success in life. Differences in these abilities across children from different families appear early and persist. There is some evidence that they widen with age, that cognitive abilities are fairly stable after age 8, and that noncognitive abilities can be improved until the late teenage years.

• Both cognitive and noncognitive skills matter, although most of the discussion of human capital policy focuses on cognitive skills. Krueger presents no evidence on the importance of noncognitive skills, whereas we present original research. We show that early-interventions have the greatest impact on noncognitive skills. Our discussion refocuses the policy analysis of skill formation on an important and neglected dimension. Test scores, as used by Krueger and others to evaluate the effectiveness of educational policies, measure only a small part of the output of the skill formation process.

• The new evidence we present on the importance of noncognitive skills, coupled with our evidence that noncognitive skills can be improved, suggests that defective early environments can partially be remedied, but at a high cost. Full remediation may be possible, but there is no evidence that it is feasible.

• The evidence that family income affects schooling is intrinsically ambiguous. Any effect found for family influence on schooling can be due to short-run credit constraints or to long-run family factors. This issue is very important. Current policy on educational shortfalls is guided by a short-run credit constraint point of view that attributes shortfalls in education to shortfalls in family resources during the child's late adolescent years. This point of view focuses attention on tuition subsidies and family income subsidies as vehicles for eliminating educational deficits. We show that most of the shortfall in educational attainment is properly attributed to long-term family influences that cannot be rectified by tuition and family income policy focused on a child's adolescent years. To substantially eliminate educational gaps, we have to remedy the early cognitive and noncognitive skill deficits. That said, we present original evidence that suggests that up to 8 percent of American youth may be constrained in the short-run sense just defined. Blacks are among the least constrained group. Although targeted tuition and aid policies are cost effective, they will not substantially reduce gaps in college enrollment or attainment.

- Public-sector job training programs are not generally effective, although a few components of these programs, such as classroom training, are. The returns to public-sector job training are sufficiently low that it cannot be counted on to reverse years of neglect by parents and schools. Krueger disregards a large body of empirical evidence that supports this point of view (see Heckman, LaLonde, and Smith 1999).
- Tax policy is unlikely to be an effective way to boost skills, although it can raise wages.

We now turn to a point-by-point response to the main points of our discussants. We conclude with additional comments on Krueger.

Hanushek

We thank Hanushek for reading our chapter carefully and noting the differences between our chapter and Krueger's.

We agree with him that pursuing the Krueger approach of "more of everything" without any structural reform in education or job training is unlikely to be fruitful.

Hanushek's discussion of schooling quality is insightful. It usefully frames the discussion. Expenditure and schooling quality have increased over time, but measures of achievement have not. Table 2.5 supports Hanushek's contention that more of the same type of policies advocated by Krueger will not solve Americans' skill formation problems. Indeed, that table shows that the quality improvement policies advocated by Krueger do not pass a cost-benefit test. We would amend Hanushek's brief by noting that family quality has declined in the recent decades, and this likely contributes to the poor performance of public schooling (see figure 2.18).

Our evidence shows that family quality substantially contributes to the formation in children of the cognitive and noncognitive skills that determine success in school. The precise mechanisms through which families contribute to the formation of these skills need much further exploration. We urge Hanushek and other researchers to use both cognitive and noncognitive measures to evaluate the performance of public education.

Borjas

Borjas makes the point that migration policy could boost the wages of native-born Americans. Partly in response to his remarks at the debate, we consider how much of the slowdown in the growth of the educational attainment rates of recent cohorts can be explained by migrants. Figure 2.2c demonstrates that immigrants are major contributors to the growth in the effective high school dropout rate. The slowdown in college participation in American society, however, cannot be attributed to immigrants (figure 2.2a), as this slowdown occurs among native-born Americans.

Borjas's proposal to limit migration of the unskilled is potentially promising. If implemented, it would boost the wages of low-skilled, native-born Americans. Given, however, that Mexicans are the major source of unskilled migrant labor in the United States and that the U.S. border with Mexico is porous, we doubt the practicality of Borjas's suggestion.

Lynch

Lynch finds numerous points in common between the two chapters. Many of the points she attributes to both chapters are, however, systematically developed only in our chapter.

We reject her bathtub comparison. Our chapter is about both stocks and flows. We evaluate policies to improve the quality of the intake and to remediate the skills of neglected persons. We point out that, on cost-benefit grounds, many adult remediation programs are ineffective. This is especially true for those aimed at older workers and the less able.

We welcome her attempt to broaden the analysis of human capital policies. Part of the cost of a mother working may be the developmental time she does not spend with her child. This suggests that a neglected cost of the two-decade-long decline in male real wages for the unskilled that drove many women into the workforce may be a decline in the quality of their offspring. However, the evidence on this point is far from clear.

We agree with Lynch that Krueger's evidence on the effectiveness of public training is flimsy and selective. He systematically ignores a large body of empirical evidence that shows the ineffectiveness of public training. Public training programs cannot remedy early skill gaps.

We also agree with her that much more work needs to be done to evaluate private-sector programs, although she is unduly modest about her own contributions. Note, however, that the evidence presented in table 2.12 shows that private training is a disequalizing institution. More-able people get more of it. Skill begets skill.

Katz

His figure 3.7 is important. It stimulated us to revise our chapter. We agree with Katz that explaining the slowdown in college attendance is an important unsolved problem. To this point we add evidence on the growth in the effective supply of dropouts.

Katz does not discuss our substantial treatment of the evidence against the importance of short-run credit constraints in accounting for schooling gaps. He chooses to interpret Card's evidence that IV estimates of the returns to schooling exceed OLS estimates as proof that short-run credit constraints are operative. As we summarize in our chapter and develop in Carneiro and Heckman (2002), such evidence has no bearing on this question. Card's argument confuses the OLS estimate of the return to schooling with return earned by people who go to school. In addition, the instruments used in the literature are systematically biased toward finding IV > OLS, even though there are no credit constraints; comparative advantage in the labor market can produce this result; and the argument neglects the choice of schooling quality. Krueger suggests that comparative advantage in the labor market is a contrived explanation, contrary to a large body of evidence summarized in Sattinger (1993). We do not deny the existence of short-term credit constraints. We deny their quantitative importance, although we show that policies targeted toward the truly constrained are likely to be cost effective.

We like Katz's point that the criminal-justice system is a major factor in producing educational disparity (especially the disparity between blacks and whites) and that investments in education may reduce crime. A major point we make in our chapter is that early childhood and young-adult mentoring programs have large effects in reducing crime through fostering noncognitive skills. Donohue and Siegelman (1998) show that high-quality preschool programs targeted toward disadvantaged black males would more than pay for their cost in reduced incarceration expenses. The analyses reported by Lochner and Moretti (2001) demonstrate the importance of education in reducing crime. Data limitations prevent them from studying the impacts of cognitive and noncognitive skills that have been found to have an important influence on crime. As our chapter shows, these abilities are fostered by families and emerge early. They can also be produced by high-quality interventions.

Katz's discussion of residential segregation is interesting but incomplete. He does not specify particular causal mechanisms through which neighborhood and peer effects are supposed to operate. He proposes no specific intervention except locating children from bad neighborhoods in better neighborhoods with better peers. There is no discussion of how many disadvantaged persons can be moved to more advantaged neighborhoods without diluting the beneficial peer effects. No cost-benefit or social-welfare analysis is conducted, so it is difficult to gauge the overall benefits of his proposal. Thirty-five years ago, busing programs were proposed to enable poor people to benefit from better peers. No tangible benefit of these programs was ever documented, although disruptions to communities were documented. Perhaps Katz is right. But before the social engineering he advocates is implemented, we hope that his evidentiary base is substantially strengthened.

Summers

Summers does not give us credit for making many of the points that he faults Krueger for not making. We show the importance of accounting for the social opportunity cost of funds in evaluating job training programs (see table 2.13), but the point is not as simple as he states it (see Bovenberg and Jacobs 2001). In addition, we show how alternative treatment of the duration of program benefits critically affects cost-benefit calculations.

We agree with Summers that general-equilibrium effects are potentially very important. Heckman, Lochner, and Taber (1998a, 1998b, 1998c, 1999) and Heckman (2001) demonstrate how accounting for general-equilibrium effects greatly affects the cost-benefit ratios computed for various policies. As we discuss in our chapter, and as is noted in the papers we cited, a partial-equilibrium treatment effect framework can be highly misleading in evaluating policies applied at a national level.

We also agree with him that recognizing the synergistic nature of human capital investment vitally affects the way we think about human capital policy. Recognizing that skill begets skill causes us to suggest redirection of investment to younger ages, especially for children from disadvantaged environments. We further agree with him that the slowdown in college participation rates across cohorts (see figure 2.1) is a problem of great concern for the growth of productivity and output in the American economy in the coming decades.

Summers reminds us of the well-known and valuable point that the rate of return can be a misleading guide for evaluating human capital. As we note in appendix 2A, for many human capital projects with payoff streams that cross once, use of the rate of return to rank projects is appropriate. Schooling payoffs fall into this category as long as we ignore option values in sequential investment programs (Heckman, Lochner, and Todd 2003). As is well known, if payoff streams cross more than once, the internal rate of return is often an inappropriate criterion. We offer an example in that appendix of a preschool program with a 7 percent internal rate of return and a job training program with a 25 percent rate of return in which the preschool program has the higher present value of net benefits and so should be preferred. To avoid problems arising from the use of rate of return, we use present values wherever possible to evaluate alternative projects.

Krueger

The evidence that Krueger presents is very selective. We offer two examples.

Krueger's discussion of the evidence from the JTPA study ignores the evidence documented in a U.S. General Accounting Office (1996) report in a five-year follow-up study of that program. He claims that a reanalysis of the JTPA study shows that it had substantial positive effects on youth wages and income. We question his use of the underlying JTPA data. The GAO data that Krueger combines to produce an

Table 4.1
Annual earnings before and after JTPA assignment

Time period	Treatment group	Control group	Difference	Difference statistically significant at 5% Level
Adult males				
Three years before	$5,883	$5,924	−$41	no
Two years before	5,680	5,894	−214	no
One year before	5,106	5,246	−140	no
Assignment	4,439	4,242	197	no
One year after	6,901	6,410	491	yes
Two years after	7,792	7,254	538	yes
Three years after	7,936	7,363	573	yes
Four years after	8,282	7,725	557	no
Five years after	8,651	8,326	325	no
Adult females				
Three years before	$3,262	$3,020	$242	no
Two years before	3,377	3,215	162	no
One year before	3,230	3,048	182	no
Assignment	2,823	2,703	120	no
One year after	4,702	4,323	379	yes
Two years after	5,705	5,047	658	yes
Three years after	5,902	5,319	583	yes
Four years after	6,367	5,811	556	yes
Five years after	6,556	6,154	402	no
Male youths				
Three years before	$860	$828	$32	no
Two years before	1,456	1,575	−119	no
One year before	2,179	2,303	−124	no
Assignment	2,894	3,014	−120	no
One year after	4,612	4,792	−180	no
Two years after	5,620	5,963	−343	no
Three years after	6,130	6,497	−367	no
Four years after	6,687	6,425	262	no
Five years after	7,554	6,778	776	no

Table 4.1
(continued)

Time period	Treatment group	Control group	Difference	Difference statistically significant at 5% Level
Female youths				
Three years before	$629	$663	–$34	no
Two years before	1,069	1,090	–21	no
One year before	1,529	1,707	–178	no
Assignment	1,974	2,098	–124	no
One year after	3,339	3,389	–50	no
Two years after	4,045	4,125	–80	no
Three years after	4,393	4,383	10	no
Four years after	4,934	4,610	324	no
Five years after	5,433	5,209	224	no

Source: General Accounting Office, 1996, 22–23.

overall positive effect for youth show no statistically significant treatment effects for either subgroup (male youth or female youth) five years after participating in the program (see table 4.1). The only positive news from the GAO study is that the large negative effects found for the male youth in the early years of the study seem to vanish five years after training is completed. Otherwise, the long-term follow-up tells the same dreary story of general ineffectiveness that has been found in the job training literature around the world.

Krueger's enthusiastic endorsement of the Job Corps is also based on a selective reading of the evidence. Job Corps is a GED factory. As quoted in our chapter, the official report on the Job Corps evaluation indicated that there was no statistically significant effect on participant earnings over a four-year period. All of the large effects that Krueger finds come from extrapolating four-year impacts indefinitely, ignoring the high rates of depreciation reported in the literature on job training. As Cameron and Heckman (1993) show, the receipt of GED is not the same as completing schooling, and treating GED certification like schooling (with no depreciation) ignores the negligible long-term effects on wages and employment found for GED certification.

References

Bovenberg, Lans, and Bas Jacobs. 2001. "Redistribution and Education Subsidies are Siamese Twins." Center for Economic Performance Discussion Paper 3099.

Cameron, Stephen, and James Heckman. 1993. "The Nonequivalence of High School Equivalents." *Journal of Labor Economics* 11, no. 1: 1–47.

Carneiro, Pedro, and James Heckman. 2002. "The Evidence on Credit Constraints in Post-Secondary Schooling." *Economic Journal* 112, no. 482: 705–734.

Donohue, John, and Peter Siegelman. 1998. "Allocating Resources Among Prisons and Social Programs in the Battle Against Crime." *Journal of Legal Studies* 27, no. 1: 1–43.

Heckman, James. 2001. "Micro Data, Heterogeneity, and the Evaluation of Public Policy: Nobel Lecture." *Journal of Political Economy* 109, no. 4: 673–748.

Heckman, James, Robert LaLonde, and Jeffrey Smith. 1999. "The Economics and Econometrics of Active Labor Market Programs." In *Handbook of Labor Economics*, vol. 3, Orley Ashenfelter and David Card, eds. Amsterdam: Elsevier.

Heckman, James, Lance Lochner, and Christopher Taber. 1998a. "Explaining Rising Wage Inequality: Explorations With A Dynamic General Equilibrium Model of Earnings With Heterogeneous Agents." *Review of Economic Dynamics* 1, no. 1: 1–58.

Heckman, James, Lance Lochner, and Christopher Taber. 1998b. "General Equilibrium Treatment Effects: A Study of Tuition Policy." *American Economic Review* 88, no. 2: 381–386.

Heckman, James, Lance Lochner, and Christopher Taber. 1998c. "Tax Policy and Human Capital Formation." *American Economic Review* 88, no. 2: 293–297.

Heckman, James, Lance Lochner, and Christopher Taber. 1999. "Human Capital Formation and General Equilibrium Treatment Effects: A Study of Tax and Tuition Policy." *Fiscal Studies* 20, no. 1: 25–40.

Heckman, James, Lance Lochner, and Petra Todd. 2003. "Fifty Years of Mincer Regression." NBER Working Paper W9732.

Lochner, Lance, and Enrico Moretti. 2001. "The Effect of Education on Crime: Evidence from Prison Inmates, Arrests, and Self-Reports." NBER working paper no. 8605, revised December, 2001.

Sattinger, Michael. 1993. "Assignment Models of the Distribution of Earnings." *Journal of Economic Literature* 31, no. 2: 831–880.

United States General Accounting Office. 1996. *Job Training Partnership Act: Long-Term Earnings and Employment Outcomes*. Report No. GAO/HEHE 96-40. Washington, D.C.: General Accounting Office.

5 Rejoinders

ALAN B. KRUEGER

Carneiro and Heckman lament that the discussants see little difference between their paper and mine. They reiterate their central theme that returns to schooling and training are highest for the most able and virtually nonexistent for disadvantaged children after preschool. I suspect the reason the discussants see little difference is that they find Carneiro and Heckman's argument that it is impossible or excessively expensive to improve the human capital prospects of poor children after they leave preschool to be unpersuasive, or at least speculative. The theoretical framework that I present, which suggests "that the *social return* from investment in education and training for poor children, from infancy through early adulthood, is at least as great as the social return from investments in education and training in the general public" (p. 23), is much simpler and consistent with most of the evidence. If one modifies figure 2.6a to put family income instead of age on the horizontal axis, then there is much in common between our papers.

Carneiro and Heckman further accuse me of "presenting what is arguably selective evidence" (p. 312). They make two arguments to back up this accusation, which I address seriatim.

First, they claim that my "discussion of the evidence from the JTPA study ignores the evidence documented in a U.S. General Accounting Office (1996) report in a five-year follow-up study of that program" (p. 321). This claim is misleading. My paper clearly makes the point: "The GAO reported the difference in average earnings between the treatment and control groups separately for male youth and female youth, as well as for adults. Separating the sample by gender reduces the precision of the estimates, and the GAO found insignificant effects for male youths and female youths each year" (p. 51). Carneiro and Heckman's reproduction of the GAO data by sex in their comment adds nothing new. They provide no argument for why the samples of males and females should *not* be combined. Yes, the GAO found that the effects are insignificant if one looks separately by gender. But why does one want to look separately by gender? Splitting the samples only serves to increase the standard errors. Carneiro and Heckman provide no economic rationale or statistical argument for splitting the samples. The effects are statistically significant if the youth are pooled. One cannot reject from these data that male and female youth receive the same benefit. For policy analysis of the benefit of training—as well as for Carneiro and Heckman's argument that it is virtually impossible to increase the human capital of disadvantaged youth—the full sample of youth, and not a gender-separate sample, is the relevant sample.

And in any event, my argument was not that the longer-term follow-up *proves* that JTPA was successful for youth, but rather that it demonstrates that the argument that it is impossible to improve the job prospects of disadvantaged youth is on shaky grounds if it rests largely on the results of the JTPA experiment. Indeed, commenting on a paper of mine in another conference volume, Heckman (2000, 336) argued that the evidence that JTPA was ineffective for youth is unpersuasive because Heckman, Hohmann, and Smith (2000) "document how access to good substitutes for a program being evaluated by a social experiment [JTPA] led to its demise—even though it was an effective program.... An experimental evaluation showing 'no treatment effect' emerged because both treatments and controls took essentially the *same* training, which turns out on closer scrutiny to be quite effective, compared to no training at all" (336). The likelihood of this type of substitution is the reason that I focused on the Job Corps program, a more intensive program for which there are few substitutes.

Far from being a selective use of evidence, considering JTPA—the program that many believe (myself included) generates the lowest return to training for youth—is an instance of bending over backward to address evidence from a program that is unlikely to be supportive of my theoretical interpretation. Moreover, there is much evidence that I did not consider that suggests that people of low ability receive a high return from training. For example, Bangser (1985) finds positive returns from the Structured Training and Employment Transitional Services intervention for mentally retarded young adults aged 18–24, which challenges Carneiro and Heckman's notion that it does not pay to invest in training of low-ability young adults. Indeed, the employment effects Bangser found were much bigger for those with more-severe forms of mental retardation. And Decker and Thornton (1995) find that the significant employment and earnings gains from transitional employment services provided to the mentally retarded persisted throughout the entire six-year follow-up period they examined.

Second, Carneiro and Heckman claim that my "enthusiastic endorsement of the Job Corps is also based on a selective reading of the evidence. Job Corps is a GED factory" (p. 323). Although it is true that Job Corps raises the likelihood that participants earn a GED, it also provides a great deal of other training. Moreover, a body of literature that Carneiro and Heckman ignore (e.g., Tyler, Murnane, and Willett 2000 and Clark and Jaeger 2002) finds that receipt of a GED can have a lasting beneficial effect on recipients' job prospects. But it is unnecessary to take a stand on whether Job Corps works or doesn't work on the basis of whether many of its participants receive GEDs: One can look directly at labor market outcomes. Here, Carneiro and Heckman agree that the program raised earnings three to four years after training, but they question whether the gains will persist, arguing that I ignore "the high rates of depreciation reported in the literature on job training" (p. 324). As I explain in my response, however, the evidence they cite on depreciation frankly does not support the high rates of depreciation that they posit. Carneiro and Heckman claim, for example, that Couch (1992) finds that posttraining benefits persisted for seven years only, but Couch did not have data beyond eight years, and he concluded that "the earnings effect for the AFDC treatments does not decay over the first 8 posttraining years." Human capital theory—as well as evidence on the returns to schooling—would suggest that the gain from training would grow over time, so I suspect Mathematica was conservative in assuming a constant-dollar gain (declining proportional gain, because earnings rise with age) over time.

Nevertheless, I think we would all agree that more long-term follow-ups of programs like the Job Corps are desirable. Moreover, in view of the money and effort having already been invested in conducting the initial short-term randomized evaluation, it is relatively easy and cost-effective to collect long-term follow-up data, especially if administrative records are available. I am very supportive of conducting more long-term follow-ups, even of programs that are now defunct. But I do not think society should have to wait another twenty years until long-term data have been collected to act on the skills gap for teenagers.

Carneiro and Heckman criticize me for focusing on internal-rate-of-return calculations. I chose this focus in part because Carneiro and Heckman focus on the rate of return by age in figure 2.6a (see the *y*-axis), which they consider the core of their paper. If their argument is that it is not worth investing in poor, low-ability children because they get a low return from such investments, I fail to see why internal rates of return are the wrong concept. For ranking policy proposals, however, I agree with Larry Summers that present values are more appropriate if the government can implement only a limited number of proposals. As a practical matter, however, I doubt the difference matters very much, despite Carneiro and Heckman's highly stylized example (see my response).

I do not disagree with Carneiro and Heckman that noncognitive skills are important. In fact, that is why I have focused on labor market outcomes as the main outcome of interest in most of my research (e.g., Card and Krueger 1992, on school quality) and in the work I surveyed. This is also why I would not simply dismiss the evidence on Job Corps by deriding it as a GED factory; one should want to look at actual labor market outcomes.

In the end, I suspect the biggest difference between Carneiro and Heckman and me involves methodology. I prefer simple models, both simple theoretical models and simple econometric models, in which the assumptions used to identify key parameters are clear, plausible, and testable.

Occam's razor and available evidence lead me to favor an economic model in which the return to investment in education and training from most programs targeted at disadvantaged youth is about 10 percent per annum, regardless of whether the program is targeted for preschool children, high school dropouts, or young adults. One does not need either credit constraints or irremediable long-run family factors to explain such a result, as Carneiro and Heckman assert; if poor children and their families have high discount rates because they find human capital acquisition unpleasant or unfamiliar, then programs designed to increase the time poor children spend in school or otherwise acquiring human capital would have high returns for society. This hypothesis is certainly hard to reject with available evidence. I believe Carneiro and Heckman introduce more complexity than is necessary by insisting that skill begets skill, and even worse, I believe this complexity is not necessarily supported by the available evidence in economics or neuroscience.[1] I would not want to neglect the potential of entire generations of youth because it is assumed that it is too late to remediate the skills of children from disadvantaged families after they have completed preschool.

Note

1. I suspect their taste for complexity also leads them to prefer separate estimates of the effect of the JTPA youth program by sex, which obscures possibly large long-run effects.

References

Bangser, Michael. 1985. *Lessons on Transitional Employment: The STETS Demonstration for Mentally Retarded Workers*. New York: Manpower Demonstration Research Corporation.

Card, David, and Alan Krueger. 1992. "Does School Quality Matter? Returns to Education and the Characteristics of Public Schools in the United States." *Journal of Political Economy* 100, no. 1 (February): 1–40.

Clark, Melissa, and David Jaeger. 2002. "Natives, the Foreign-Born and High School Equivalents: New Evidence on the Returns to the GED." IZA working paper no. 477.

Couch, K. (1992). "New Evidence on the Long-Term Effects of Employment Training Programs." *Journal of Labor Economics* 10, no. 4: 380–388.

Decker, Paul, and Craig V. Thornton. 1995. "The Long-Term Effects of Transitional Employment Services." *Social Security Bulletin* 58, no. 4 (winter): 71–81.

Heckman, James. 2000. "Comment." In *Economic Events, Ideas, and Policies: The 1960s and After*, George Perry and James Tobin, eds. Washington, D.C.: Brookings Institution Press.

Heckman, James, Neil Hohmann, and Jeffrey Smith. 2000. "Substitution and Dropout Bias in Social Experiments: A Study of an Influential Social Experiment." *Quarterly Journal of Economics* 116, no. 2 (May): 651–694.

Tyler, John H., Richard J. Murnane, and John B. Willett. 2000. "Estimating the Labor Market Signaling Value of the GED." *Quarterly Journal of Economics* 115, no. 2 (May): 431–468.

PEDRO CARNEIRO AND JAMES J. HECKMAN

The contrast in style and content between our chapter and Krueger's is sharp. He presents the reader with a set of "facts" and "treatment effects" in an attempt to prove that educational interventions for people of all ages and all ability and background levels are equally effective and earn a 10 percent rate of return. In parts of his chapter, Krueger goes beyond this and seeks to establish that the returns to human capital interventions are *greater* for the more disadvantaged. Our chapter uses economic theory buttressed by empirical evidence to develop the empirical and policy implications of the life cycle of learning. There are many problems in the economics of skill formation (and in economics in general) where a purely empirical approach is uninformative. To forecast the likely effects of proposed policies that have never been tried, facts need theory for their interpretation and extrapolation. For example, in his rejoinder, Krueger correctly states that the evidence on the effects of school choice from random experiments in several cities is not conclusive. However, his implicit argument that we should not implement new policies like competition and choice in schools until there is much further empirical evidence is a conservative approach that neglects a huge body of work in economics that shows that competition and incentives improve performance. Effective policy analysis requires use of all available data and theory. A purely empirical approach to assessing policy proposals is never effective, because the data almost never dovetail with the proposed policies. Our chapter integrates theory and evidence to evaluate policies in light of what is known about the problems the policies are intended to address. We organize our response to Krueger's rejoinder by topic, starting with complementarity and diminishing returns.

Complementarity and Diminishing Returns

Our chapter rests on a theory of human capital augmented to account for synergies or complementarities between different types of skills and ability. The complementary nature of human capital investments was first established by Mincer (1974), who shows the synergy between schooling and postschool investments. Skill begets skill. We add to Mincer's work by showing that skills and abilities manifested or acquired during a child's early years positively affect subsequent learning and achievement. We establish that these abilities and skills emerge early and are positively associated with parental income, ability, and socioeconomic status, and that differentials according to family status open early and widen over the life cycle. Both cognitive and noncognitive abilities matter, and both are produced and nourished by better families.

A huge body of empirical evidence supports the hypothesis of complementarity. Murnane, Willett, and Levy (1995), Blackburn and Neumark (1993), Cawley et al. (2000), Taber (2001), Heckman and Vytlacil (2001), Carneiro, Heckman, and Vytlacil (2003), Carneiro (2002), and Meghir and Palme (1999) all show that the return to education is greatest for the most able. As we show in our chapter, ability is formed early and, if anything, ability differentials between the advantaged and disadvantaged widen over the life cycle. Heckman, LaLonde, and Smith (1999) summarize a vast empirical literature on job training that shows that returns to such training are highest for the most advantaged within the participant pool, which is disadvantaged relative to the general population. Heckman et al. (1997), Heckman and Smith (1998), and Heckman (2001a) show that the greatest return to JTPA training came to those at the top end of the distribution. Evidence on British training programs by Blundell, Dearden, and Meghir (1996) shows that the most able among those targeted by a training program benefit most from the training program. Altonji and Dunn (1996) present supporting evidence on universal complementarity: Those from better family backgrounds have higher returns to schooling.[1] A huge body of empirical evidence supports this conclusion (see, e.g., Bowles and Gintis 2001, which presents a novel interpretation of the association between parental background and economic returns). There is a fractal nature to this evidence that suggests universal complementarity however far one goes down the scale of advantage. The only plausible exception to this complementarity is investment in the disadvantaged when they are very young.[2]

Krueger has three responses to this evidence. First, he appeals to diminishing returns. Second, he reports evidence from a few anomalous studies that purport to show the opposite. Third, he tries to discredit our argument by linking us to an extreme view of "brain science" that he characterizes as claiming that the only profitable skill investments are made when a child is between the ages of zero and three.

Krueger's repeated appeal to diminishing returns ignores the dynamic complementarity in the accumulation of human capital. Diminishing returns is essentially a static concept, whereas the process of skill accumulation is essentially dynamic. Suppose we have a simple Ben-Porath (1967) model in which output Y (earnings) is a function of ability A and human capital H:

$$Y = AH^{\alpha},$$

where $0<\alpha<1$. There are diminishing returns to H, but individuals with a higher A have higher return to each unit of H. In this function A and H are complementary inputs in the production of Y. A can be interpreted as ability formed early in the life cycle and influenced primarily by family factors. There is a second equation in Ben-Porath's model that concerns the production function of H. Let $\dot{H}$ be the time rate of change of the human capital stock with change in the life cycle. Ben-Porath models the skill acquisition process as

$$\dot{H} = B(HI)^{\beta} - \delta H,$$

where $0<\beta<1$. $\dot{H}$ is a function of a productivity parameter B that can vary across individuals (for example, ability) and can be influenced by the family, the accumulated stock of H, the fraction of time spent learning I, and the depreciation rate δ. There is ample evidence that this function explains the earnings of men and women (see Browning, Hansen, and Heckman 1999). Once again there are diminishing returns to current H in the production of additional H, but individuals with higher accumulated levels of H have a higher productivity of time spent learning than those with a low level of H. This dynamic complementarity plays a crucial role in the process of human capital accumulation. Krueger ignores complementarity and focuses solely on a static notion of diminishing returns. He fails to recognize the production of the complementary A and B inputs by families or the role of accumulated human capital in boosting productivity in learning.

Second, Krueger selectively appeals to a few studies that claim to show that returns to schooling are greatest for the disadvantaged, ignoring a huge body of empirical evidence that supports the evidence reported in table 2.4 of the text. His own work with Dale (Dale and Krueger 2002) is based on a highly selective sample and looks fragile. The Ashenfelter and Rouse (1998) twins study begs the central question of why twins get different amounts of schooling. Schooling is assumed to be randomly assigned once family effects are accounted for. A large literature challenges this assumption (see, e.g., Bound and Solon 1999). The Ashenfelter and Rouse study is a weak reed to lean on.[3] Even taken at face value, it does not present very strong evidence that the disadvantaged benefit more from schooling than other groups.[4]

Third, Krueger tries to portray us as fanatics who believe that all essential skills are determined at ages zero to three and that investments beyond that age are too costly to incur. We never say that. Indeed, we establish that mentoring programs directed toward teenagers improve noncognitive skills and that returns to schooling undertaken in the high school and college years are high, especially for the more able. We also show high estimates of returns to some types of job training, especially for the most able.

Krueger appeals for support to a policy polemic, *The Myth of the First Three Years* by John Bruer (1999), whom he mistakenly identifies as a neuroscientist. Bruer is a philosopher by training who heads a small foundation. He has no training in neuroscience or child development and does not contribute to the refereed scholarly literature on those topics. His work is directed toward attacking extreme applications of brain science like the "Mozart effect," which was promoted by the governor of Georgia to raise the IQ of infants by exposing them to Mozart's music. He shares with Krueger the view that humans are highly plastic and that at all stages of the life cycle, investments in skills are profitable. Bruer's study is poorly documented and is based on a selective appeal to evidence.[5] Nowhere do we endorse the extreme straw man view that Bruer attacks and Krueger attributes to us.

There is a larger issue that is central to this debate: How plastic are people? How long in the life cycle can we wait before it becomes very difficult to influence development of skills and motivation? Krueger paints the optimistic picture that the timing of investment in education and skills over the life cycle is irrelevant. Returns to education and skill interventions, he asserts, are as high at ages 20, 40, or 60 as they are at ages 1, 2, or 3. This optimism is not justified by any solid body of evidence. The payoffs to GED certification and public job training for low-skilled young adults are very low (see Cameron and Heckman 1993, Heckman and Rubinstein 2001; and Heckman, LaLonde, and Smith 1999, respectively; also see Martin and Grubb 2001). Delay in education and skill interventions is costly. Krueger wants to deny this. We regret that delay is costly, but it is a central feature of the learning process.

In the same vein, Krueger's claim that all investments at all ages earn the same rate of return is flawed. First, for reasons we develop in appendix 2A, and elaborate on below, the rate of return is not an accurate guide for evaluating many human capital programs, especially early-childhood programs. Second, Krueger ignores a huge body of evidence showing very low rates of return to public job training around the world. (See Heckman, LaLonde, and Smith 1999 and Martin and Grubb 2001.) No job training program aimed at the disadvantaged, however successful in terms of a rate-of-return criterion, has ever been shown to elevate the vast majority of its trainees out of poverty.

Job Training

In his rejoinder, Krueger repeatedly asserts that the Job Corps shows a high rate of return. He does not adequately characterize the official report issued by Mathematica that we cite in our chapter. That document shows that Job Corps participants earn $3 per week (or $624 overall) more over the whole four-year period of the study than they would have earned if they had not enrolled in Job Corps.

Except for classroom training and job search assistance, public job training has a sorry record. Returns are much closer to 0 than 10 percent and are sometimes negative. Heckman, LaLonde, and Smith (1999) present a comprehensive survey of numerous training programs from countries around the world. No serious scholar claims that public training (except classroom instruction or job search assistance) is effective even when these programs "work" in a rate-of-return sense. These programs have modest absolute benefits (e.g., $50 per year in job search assistance) and, as previously noted, rarely raise trainees above the poverty level.

Krueger selectively reports on two programs out of hundreds that have been studied: JTPA and Job Corps. His description of Job Corps job training as a success is at odds with the official report. Rates of return of 10.5 percent or 18 percent are based on unjustified extrapolations of one-year effects over long horizons.

The within-sample evidence supporting Job Corps is flimsy. The only substantial effects are measured final-year effects for certain demographic groups, and these effects are not found for the other groups. What one thinks about the program's success depends critically on what one assumes about depreciation and future effects not yet measured. The controversial feature of the Job Corps study is what is assumed about depreciation rates. The official report assumes no depreciation. Krueger is correct in saying that Ashenfelter (1978) does not find a 25 percent annual depreciation rate for males for the impact of training. Instead, he finds a 13 percent rate for adult men and a 0 percent rate for adult women. The evidence on depreciation rates for training ranges all over the map, and Ashenfelter's study has been faulted since it is based on an inconsistent estimator (see Heckman, LaLonde, and Smith 1999).

The estimates in Couch 1992 bounce around. Figures 5.1 and 5.2 present his estimated treatment effects for the on-the-job training program he studies. For adult women, the annual effect in dollar terms becomes statistically significant only in 1982, four years after treatment ended in 1978. The effect persists for four years and then falls off (see figure 5.1). There is apparent appreciation followed by depreciation and the final-year treatment is not statistically significantly

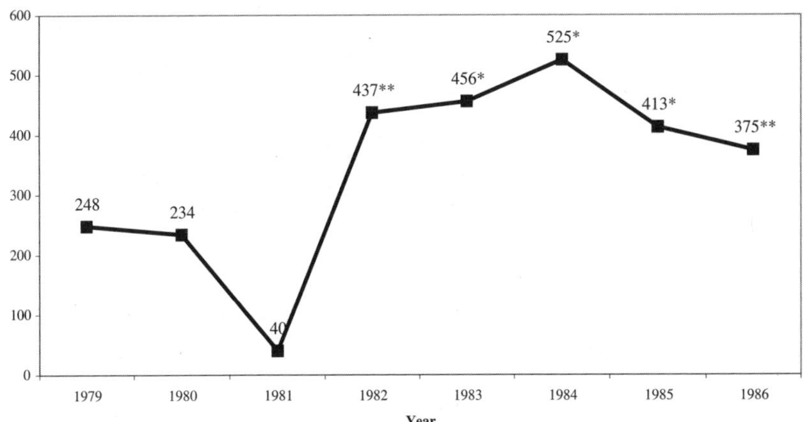

Figure 5.1
Annual difference in earnings between AFDC women and the control group after treatment.
Source: Couch 1992. *significant at 5% level; **significant at 10% level

different from zero. Figure 5.2, for youth, is more relevant for an evaluation of the Job Corps study. It shows the familiar pattern in the literature: no effects from the training program. The implicit rate of decay for the youth is over 35 percent per annum from the peak (157) to the last positive number (17). Krueger's claim that depreciation rates are zero is without foundation.

The Job Corps is a GED factory, as we document in our chapter. In an attempt to defend Job Corps, Krueger now endorses the GED program, citing two "careful" studies of the GED program by Tyler, Murnane, and Willett (2000) and Clark and Jaeger (2002) and ignoring an entire literature that shows no effect of the GED on earnings or employment for most demographic groups. (See Cameron and Heckman 1993; Heckman, Hsee, and Rubinstein 2001; and the comprehensive survey in Boesel, Alsalam, and Smith 1998.) The

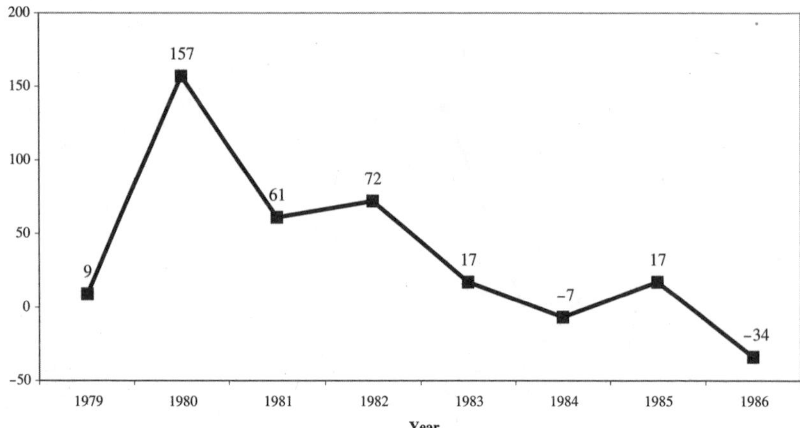

Figure 5.2
Annual difference in earnings between youths and the control group after treatment*
Source: Couch 1992. *None of the numbers are statistically significant at 10% level

Clark and Jaeger paper is seriously flawed. It does not control for cognitive-ability differences that the preceding literature has found to be important. Clark and Jaeger's estimated GED effects are just spurious ability effects. It is based on faulty data (see Heckman 2003). The Murnane et al. paper shows GED effects for some groups and not for others. It is criticized in Rubinstein (2003) and in Heckman et al. (2003), which show serious flaws in the methodology of Murnane et al. and Clark and Jaeger. Krueger makes a selective appeal to two flawed papers and fails to report the consensus view of an entire literature.[6]

Krueger's reanalysis of the JTPA data is also misleading. Heckman, Ichimura, and Todd (1997) have extensively analyzed these data. In their background studies, they test and reject equality of outcomes across the youth groups that Krueger pools. Krueger suggests that the strategy used by the U.S. General Accounting Office (1996) and us is to "divide and conquer," making it less likely to find an effect by splitting the full sample by gender and age. This suggestion is unwarranted, given the large size of each youth-gender sample. There are 1,736 young men (1,177 treatments and 559 controls) and 2,300 young women (1,593 treatments and 707 controls). In fact, pooling the disparate samples in the fashion Krueger does runs the risk of encountering the Lindley paradox (see Leamer 1978). Keeping significance levels fixed and increasing sample size virtually guarantees that the null hypothesis is rejected. The smallest misspecification of the model will lead to rejection of the null of no effect. A better practice is to adjust the size of the test to balance size and power as sample size is increased.

There is no basis for pooling the data in the way Krueger does. The hypothesis-testing sequence used by Krueger is invalid. $H_0: A=0$ and $B=0$ are not rejected, where A and B are means of treatment for the two groups. In this analysis $H_0: A=B$ is not rejected. But $H_0: A=B=0$ is rejected in tests that keep size fixed and implicitly raise power in the pooled sample over the separate samples.

More important, however, is the fact that the GAO numbers for the fifth year that Krueger uses in his pooled sample and that show such improvement over the previous years do not include all of the experimental sites. This point is discussed in the Department of Labor letter that is appended to the GAO report. High-impact sites are more likely to be included in the fifth year of the study. These are the sites in which random assignment ended earlier, which is why more follow-up data are available for them. This accounts for some of the apparent increase in youth treatment effects with the passage of time (see table 4.1). Even with this bias, however, one cannot reject the null of no effect of treatment for each demographic group using samples of roughly 2,000 each.

The big issue in this debate is whether second-chance programs for young adults that are currently in place are effective. Most of the evidence says they are not. The conclusion from the literature on remediation programs is that they are ineffective. The empirical basis of figures 2.6a and 2.6b for the young-adult years is solid, especially for disadvantaged youth.

Credit Constraints

Krueger mischaracterizes our discussion of credit constraints. In our chapter we distinguish between short-term credit constraints operative on families during a child's adolescent and college-going years and long-term constraints operative over the children's entire life cycle. We present some evidence in support of short-term credit constraints and discuss why targeted-subsidy policies might be cost effective. We also show that eliminating short-term credit constraints is unlikely to close much of the gap in college attendance between the advantaged and the disadvantaged.

We agree with Krueger that one reason why instrumental-variables estimates of the effect of schooling exceed ordinary-least-squares estimates may be the higher discount rates and distaste for schooling of disadvantaged children. These and other preference parameters are formed early. (See our evidence on antisocial behavior.) This interpretation supports our argument that early interventions that shape motivation and ability are important.[7] It does not support the tuition-adolescent family income policies advocated by Kane (2001) and others as policies that will substantially eliminate college attendance gaps between the advantaged and the disadvantaged in college attendance.

Schooling Quality and STAR

As documented by Hanushek (1998), the overall NAEP test scores of achievement for seventeen-year-olds have barely changed over the past thirty years. Claims of dramatic improvements or declines in test scores are without foundation. One cannot look to the NAEP test score data to support the claim that traditional schooling-expenditure policies substantially change test scores (see Grissmer et al. 2000).

The Tennessee STAR experiment was far from perfect (see Hanushek 1998, 1999), and the estimated effects from it are not strong. We miswrote when we said in our chapter that the effects of the early intervention did not persist. Krueger and Whitmore (2001) show a rather dramatic decline, however, in the gap in achievement between the treated and the control group after the experiment ends (see figures 2 and 3 of their paper). A five-to six-percentage-point difference between the treatment and control group declines to a one-to one-and-a-half-point postexperiment difference (albeit on a different test). Krueger and Whitmore's cost-benefit analysis is whimsical. They use the estimated impact of one test on earnings, taken from the literature, to estimate the effect of another test on earnings. Their estimated rate of return of 5.5 percent is far below the universal 10 percent that Krueger claims describes most human capital investments.

Discounting and Rates of Return

Krueger's discussion of discounting and rates of return is confusing. It is well established that in situations of limited funding availability, proposed projects with the highest present value should be selected for funding even if they have substantially postponed payoffs (see, e.g., Hirschleifer 1970). The discount rate used in evaluations represents a social opportunity cost of funds. When quick-payoff versus slow-payoff projects are compared, slow-payoff funds are not "placed in a mattress" but are implicitly reinvested at the social-opportunity cost or discount rate. Our example, presented in appendix 2A, is valid and shows how misleading the rate of return can be as a rule for choosing investment projects like early-childhood programs. Krueger does not appear to recognize that if there is a binary choice between investing in three-year-olds or investing in eighteen-year-olds, and if the present value of investments in three-year-olds exceeds that for eighteen-year-olds, and if this choice is to be made each period, as new three-year- and eighteen-year-olds become eligible, social wealth is maximized by investing in the three-year-olds: the project with the highest present value. In our appendix 2A, the present-value-maximizing project is investment in three-year-olds, period by period, even though its rate of return is lower than the job training option. It is better to invest in three-year-olds each period than to delay this investment by fifteen years and invest in eighteen-year-olds each period. This is true even though the rate of return to job training for eighteen-year-olds is higher than the rate of return to investing in three-year-olds.

Of course, the world is not so discrete. With diminishing returns to each investment activity, one would likely find it profitable to invest in both projects. But the volume of investment would follow figure 2.6b: less investment at older ages and more investment at younger ages. The exact quantitative magnitude of the trade-offs among investment projects remains to be determined, but the indicated qualitative direction is clear.[8] Moreover, even if the rate of return was a valid measure, it would only inform us about where the marginal dollar should go. It does not inform us about optimal quantities of investment. Thus the $50 annual return to job search training has a high rate of return. There are steeply diminishing returns to this activity, so that doubling job search assistance would likely not be cost effective. One has to move beyond rates of return and "treatment effects" to determine optimal investment levels.

Summary

The issues discussed in this debate are not minor. Krueger offers the sweeping claim that 10 percent is a good guide as a return to all human capital investments at all ages. We present substantial evidence against that claim. He also asserts, contrary to a vast literature, that returns to investment are greatest for the most disadvantaged or the least able. We present evidence that shows that returns are greatest for the most able. His paper shows no recognition of the need to prioritize or the need to account for the full costs of human capital programs, including the social-opportunity cost of funds. He advocates the same shotgun approach to human capital policy that has been followed for decades by the U.S. government.

Our approach builds on what is known from a vast body of scholarship about learning over the life cycle. Skill begets skill. Learning begets further learning. Abilities are multiple in character and are formed early in life. The well-established empirical relationship between family income and schooling has much more to do with the formation of motivations and abilities than it has to do with short-term credit constraints. Interventions that foster these abilities are very effective. We know this from the studies we summarize that are targeted toward disadvantaged children, which show high returns to interventions in disadvantaged families. These studies are arguably lower-bound estimates of the importance of good families in fostering motivation and ability, since the experimental subjects come from initially deprived environments, with stunted learning opportunities, and weak scope for the interplay of complementary inputs, which we find to be important. Second-chance programs like public job training and GED programs are ineffective and do not remedy a lifetime of neglect of a child.

These are not clever debating points but rather are serious issues that shape policy. A serious reformulation of human capital policy is needed. A serious reformulation of the approach to analyzing public policy is also required. The traditional focus on evaluations of existing programs ignores possible approaches that might be used that have never been empirically implemented. The traditional "treatment effect" approach to these problems can be effective in eliminating bad programs but is ineffective in designing new programs and policies.

A better approach, and the one advocated and implemented in our chapter, is to understand the sources of the problems that give rise to public-policy programs. When the basic behavioral processes are understood and measured, a discussion of alternative policies, many not yet tried, becomes possible. The contrast between a "treatment effect" approach to public-policy analysis and a structural approach is profound (Heckman 2001b). That is the contrast between our approach and Krueger's.

Notes

We thank Robert LaLonde, Dimitriy V. Masterov, Peter Schochet, Jeffrey Smith, and Gary Solon for helpful comments on this rebuttal.

1. We use Altonji and Dunn's evidence for separate demographic groups from their fixed-effect specification, which is more likely to be robust to spurious causality and which they call their "preferred" estimator. Their pooled estimator produces ambiguous evidence, and they present reasons why it should not be used. They claim the fixed-effect estimators are biased upward, but that argument rests on a crucial, untested assumption about covariance among unobservables.

2. Thus in a Cobb-Douglas model with $Y = AH_1^{\alpha}H_2^{\beta}$ (where Y is a test score or some acheivment or outcome measure) where H_1 is early human capital and H_2 is later human capital. When $H_1 = 0$, the marginal product of $H_2 = 0$. Thus human capital interventions at very early ages may have high productivity for those from disadvantaged environments (see Duncan and Magnuson 2002).

3. Ashenfelter and Rouse's entire paper is based on arbitrary functional-form assumptions connecting schooling to ability, and ability to the rate of return.

4. In all of Ashenfelter and Rouse's specifications except one based on arbitrary functional forms connecting ability to the rate of return, family background has no effect on the return to schooling.

5. For example, Bruer appeals to the analysis of Sticht et al. (1987) on how low-ability soldiers fared in the military. He claims that they achieved parity with more-able soldiers, contrary to a more scholarly study by Janice Laurence and Peter Ramsberger (1991). See Frost 2000 for a review of Bruer's book. Huttenlocher (2002) presents a more measured account of the evidence on plasticity.

6. Given the long time Job Corps participants spend in the classroom (approximately a year of academic and vocational education), the effect of Job Corps training may be genuine. As previously noted, the literature finds substantial effects of classroom training on earnings and employment. (See Heckman, Khoo, and Smith 2000.) We eagerly await the five- and six-year follow-up for the Job Corps study.

7. Krueger claims that the instrumental variables (IV) literature is more transparent than the structural econometric literature. We find this claim puzzling. The IV literature never defines the effect it is trying to identify, nor does it defend the instruments it uses. The structural literature does both and presents explicit and transparent discussions of identification. (See Carneiro, Heckman, and Vytlacil 2003, Carneiro 2002, and Carneiro, Hansen, and Heckman 2003, and contrast with Card 1999 and Card 2001.)

8. We do not understand Krueger's claim that the theories of brain development that he attributes to us justify the use of the internal rate of return. We agree that the choice of the appropriate discount rate is controversial (see the studies in Portney and Weyant 1999). Moreover, just because the IRR can be computed does not justify its application in place of a theoretically correct present-value calculation.

References

Altonji, Joseph, and Thomas Dunn. 1996. "The Effects of Family Characteristics on the Return to Education." *Review of Economics and Statistics* 78, no. 4: 692–704.

Ashenfelter, Orley. 1978. "Estimating the Effect of Training Programs on Earnings." *Review of Economics and Statistics* 6, no. 1: 47–57.

Ashenfelter, Orley, and Cecilia Rouse. 1998. "Income, Schooling, and Ability: Evidence from a New Sample of Identical Twins." *Quarterly Journal of Economics* 113, no. 1: 253–284.

Ben-Porath, Yoram. 1967. "The Production of Human Capital and Life Cycle Earnings." *Journal of Political Economy* 75, no. 4 (part 1): 352–365.

Blackburn, McKinley L., and David Neumark. 1993. "Omitted-Ability Bias and the Increase in the Return to Schooling." *Journal of Labor Economics* 11, no. 3: 521–544.

Blundell, Richard, Lorraine Dearden, and Costas Meghir. 1996. "The Determinants and Effects of Work Related Training in Britain." IFS working paper no. R50.

Boesel, David, Nabeel Alsalam, and Thomas M. Smith. 1998. *Educational and Labor Market Performance of GED Recipients*. Washington, D.C.: U.S. Department of Education.

Bound, John, and Gary Solon. 1999. "Double Trouble: On the Value of Twins-Based Estimation of the Return to Schooling." *Economics of Education Review* 18, no. 2: 69–182.

Bowles, Samuel, and Herbert Gintis. 2001. "The Inheritance of Inequality." *Journal of Economic Perspectives* 16, no. 3: 3–30.

Browning, Martin, Lars Hansen, and James Heckman. 1999. "Micro Data and General Equilibrium Models." In *Handbook of Macroeconomics*, J. Taylor and M. Woodford, eds. Amsterdam: Elsevier.

Bruer, John. 1999. *The Myth of the First Three Years: A New Understanding of Early Brain Development and Lifelong Learning*. New York: Free Press.

Cameron, Stephen, and J. Heckman. 1993. "The Nonequivalence of High School Equivalents." *Journal of Labor Economics* 11, no. 1, part 1: 1–47.

Card, David. 1999. "The Causal Effect of Education on Earnings." In *Handbook of Labor Economics*, vol. 3A, O. Ashenfelter and D. Card, eds. Amsterdam: Elsevier Science/North-Holland.

Card, David. 2001. "Estimating the Return to Schooling: Progress on Some Persistent Econometric Problems." *Econometrica* 69, no. 5: 1127–1160.

Carneiro, Pedro. 2002. "Heterogeneity in the Returns to Schooling: Implications for Policy Evaluation." Ph.D. diss., University of Chicago.

Carneiro, Pedro, Karsten Hansen, and James J. Heckman. 2003. "Estimating Distributions of Treatment Effects with an Application to the Returns to Schooling." *International Economic Review*, 44, no. 2: 361–422.

Carneiro, Pedro, James J. Heckman, and Edward Vytlacil. 2001. "Estimating the Return to Schooling When it Various across Individual." Working paper, University of Chicago.

Cawley, John, James J. Heckman, Lance Lochner, and Edward Vytlacil. 2000. "Understanding the Role of Cognitive Ability in Accounting for the Recent Rise in the Return to Education." In *Meritocracy and Economic Inequality*, K. Arrow, S. Bowles, and S. Durlauf, eds. Princeton: Princeton University Press.

Clark, Melissa, and David Jaeger. 2002. "Natives, the Foreign-Born and High School Equivalents: New Evidence on the Returns to the GED." IZA discussion paper no. 477.

Couch, Kenneth. 1992. "New Evidence on the Long-Term Effects of Employment Training Programs." *Journal of Labor Economics* 10, no. 4: 380–388.

Dale, Stacy Berg, and Alan B. Krueger. 2002. "Estimating the Payoff to Attending a More Selective College: An Application of Selection on

Observables and Unobservables." *Quarterly Journal of Economics*, 117, no. 4: 1491–1527.

Duncan, Greg, and Katherine Magnuson. 2002. "Individual and Parent-Based Intervention Strategies for Promoting Human Capital and Positive Behavior." Northwestern University working paper.

Frost, Barrie. 2000. "A Review of *The Myth of the First Three Years*." *Canadian Journal of Policy Research* 1, no. 2: 131–132.

Grissmer, David, Ann Flanagan, Jennifer Kawata, and Stephanie Williamson. 2000. *Improving Student Achievement: What NAEP Test Scores Tell Us*. MR-924-EDU. Santa Monica, Calif.: RAND.

Hanushek, Eric. 1998. "The Evidence on Class Size." In *Earning and Learning: How Schools Matter*, Susan E. Mayer and Paul Peterson, eds. Washington, D.C.: Brookings Institution.

Hanushek, Eric. 1999. "Some Findings from an Independent Investigation of the Tennessee STAR Experiment and from Other Investigations of Class Size Effects." *Educational Evaluation and Policy Analysis* 21, no. 2: 143–163.

Heckman, James J. 2001a. "Accounting for Heterogeneity, Diversity and General Equilibrium in Evaluating Social Programmes." *Economic Journal* 111, no. 475: F654–F699.

Heckman, James J. 2001b. "Micro Data, Heterogeneity, and the Evaluation of Public Policy: Nobel Lecture." *Journal of Political Economy* 109, no. 4: 673–748.

Heckman, James J., Neil Hohmann, Michael Khoo, and Jeffrey Smith. 2000. "Substitution and Dropout Bias in Social Experiments: A Study of an Influential Social Experiment." *Quarterly Journal of Economics* 115, no. 2: 651–694.

Heckman, James J., Jingjing Hsee, and Yona Rubinstein. 2001. "The GED is a 'Mixed Signal': The Effect of Cognitive and Noncognitive Skills on Human Capital and Labor Market Outcomes." University of Chicago working paper.

Heckman, James J., Hidehiko Ichimura, and Petra Todd. 1997. "Matching as an Econometric Evaluation Estimator: Evidence from Evaluating a Job Training Programme." *Review of Economic Studies* 64, no. 4: 605–654.

Heckman, James J., Lisa Kahn, Jacob Katz, and Paul LaFontaine. 2003. "Imputation Biases and the Impact of the GED on Immigrants" In *The GED*, James J. Heckman, ed. Unpublished manuscript, University of Chicago.

Heckman, James J., Robert LaLonde, and Jeffrey Smith. 1999. "The Economics and Econometrics of Active Labor Market Programs." In *Handbook of Labor Economics*, vol. 3A, O. Ashenfelter and D. Card, eds. Amsterdam: Elsevier.

Heckman, James J., and Yona Rubinstein. 2001. "The Importance of Noncognitive Skills: Lessons from the GED Testing Program." *American Economic Review* 91, no. 2: 145–149.

Heckman, James J., and Jeffrey Smith. 1998. "Evaluating the Welfare State." In *Econometrics and Economic Theory in the 20th Century: The Ragnar Frisch Centennial Symposium*, S. Strøm, ed. Cambridge: Cambridge University Press.

Heckman, James J., and Edward Vytlacil. 2001. "Identifying the Role of Cognitive Ability in Explaining the level of and Change in the Return to Schooling." *Review of Economics and Statistics* 83, no. 1: 1–12.

Hirshleifer, Jack. 1970. *Investment, Interest and Capital*. Englewood Cliffs, N.J.: Prentice Hall.

Huttenlocher, Peter R. 2002. *Neural Plasticity: The Effects of Environment on the Development of the Cerebral Cortex*. Cambridge: Harvard University Press.

Kane, Thomas J. 2001. "College Going and Inequality: A Literature Review." Russell Sage Foundation working paper.

Krueger, Alan, and Diane Whitmore. 2001. "The Effect of Attending a Small Class in the Early Grades on College-Test Taking and Middle School Test Results: Evidence from Project STAR." *Economic Journal* 111, no. 1: 1–28.

Laurence, Janice, and Peter Ramsberger. 1991. *Low-Aptitude Men in the Military: Who Profits, Who Pays?* New York: Praeger.

Leamer, Edward. 1978. *Specification Searches: Ad Hoc Inferences with Nonexperimental Data*. New York: Wiley.

Martin, John P., and David Grubb. 2001. "What Works and for Whom: A Review of OECD Countries' Experience with Active Labour Market Policies." *Swedish Economic Policy Review* 8, no. 2: 9–56.

Meghir, Costas, and Marten Palme. 1999. "Assessing the Effect of Schooling on Earnings Using a Social Experiment." IFS working paper no. W99/10.

Mincer, Jacob. 1974. *Schooling, Experience, and Earnings*. Cambridge, MA: NBER, distributed by Columbia University Press, New York.

Murnane, Richard J., John B. Willett, and Frank Levy. 1995. "The Growing Importance of Cognitive Skills in Wage Determination." *Review of Economics and Statistics* 77, no. 2: 251–266.

Murnane, Richard J., John B. Willett, and J. Tyler. 2000. "Estimating the Labor Market Signaling Value of the GED." *Quarterly Journal of Economics* 115, no. 2: 431–468.

Portney, Paul, and John Weyant. 1999. *Discounting and Intergenerational Equity*. Washington, D.C.: Resources for the Future.

Rubinstein, Yona. 2003. "The Use of Interstate Variation in GED Passing Rates for Estimating the Effect of the GED on Labor Market Outcomes: A Critique." Unpublished manuscript. University of Tel Aviv.

Sticht, Thomas G., William B. Armstrong, Daniel T. Hickey, and John S. Caylor. 1987. *Cast-Off Youth: Policy and Training Methods from the Military Experience*. New York: Praeger.

United States General Accounting Office. 1996. *Job Training Partnership Act: Long-Term Earnings and Employment Outcomes*. Report HEHS-96-40. Washington, D.C.: U.S. Government Accounting Office.

Contributors

George J. Borjas
Pforzheimer Professor of Public Policy
Kennedy School of Government
Harvard University

Pedro Carneiro
University of Chicago

Benjamin M. Friedman
William Joseph Maier Professor of Political Economy
Harvard University

Eric A. Hanushek
Paul and Jean Hanna Senior Fellow
Hoover Institution
Stanford University

James J. Heckman
Henry Schultz Distinguished Service Professor of Economics
University of Chicago

Alan B. Krueger
Bendheim Professor of Economics and Public Affairs
Princeton University

Lawrence F. Katz
Professor of Economics
Harvard University

Lisa M. Lynch
Academic Dean and William L. Clayton Professor of International Economic Affairs
Fletcher School of Law and Diplomacy
Tufts University

Lawrence H. Summers
President and Professor of Economics
Harvard University

Index